Ultimate Next.js for Modern Web Applications

Master Modern Web Development and Build High-Performance Scalable, SEO-Optimized Applications with Next.js, Typescript and Tailwind CSS

Shubham Jain

www.orangeava.com

First Published: January 2026

Published By: Orange Education Pvt Ltd, AVA®

Address: 9, Daryaganj, Delhi, 110002, India

275 New North Road Islington Suite 1314 London,
N1 7AA, United Kingdom

ISBN (PBK): 978-93-49887-19-0
ISBN (E-BOOK): 978-93-49887-64-0

Scan the QR code to explore our entire catalogue

www.orangeava.com

Dedicated To

All Those Who Inspire, Support, and Believe in the Pursuit of Knowledge and Progress, and to the Readers Whose Curiosity and Passion Give Purpose to this Work.

About the Author

Shubham Jain is a seasoned senior software engineer with expertise in full-stack web development, specializing in Next.js and modern front-end technologies. With an M.Sc. in IT and a deep passion for building high-performance web applications, he has worked on diverse projects across industries such as travel, banking, finance, and manufacturing, delivering solutions that impact millions globally.

Shubham has extensive experience leveraging Next.js to create dynamic, fast, and scalable web applications. His work includes developing innovative features, optimizing performance, and ensuring seamless user experiences. He is a committed advocate of web standards and best practices, always aiming to stay at the forefront of the latest advancements in web development.

A passionate educator and mentor, Shubham enjoys sharing his expertise through articles and tutorials focused on Next.js, React, and other cutting-edge technologies. He actively contributes to the developer community through platforms such as GitHub and Medium, fostering collaboration and innovation among tech enthusiasts.

When not coding, Shubham can be found exploring new tools, mentoring aspiring developers, or tackling real-world challenges in web development. His dedication to continuous learning and growth drives his ability to create impactful and efficient digital solutions.

About the Technical Reviewer

Nabendu Biswas is a seasoned Full Stack JavaScript Developer and Senior Software Engineer with over 21 years of experience spanning global investment banks, product companies, and fast-growing startups. Over the past decade, he has built deep expertise in the React ecosystem, delivering scalable, high-performance web applications across finance, retail, AI, and education technology domains.

Throughout his career, Nabendu has held key technical leadership roles—including Architect, Team Lead, and Associate Architect—where he guided UI teams, led micro-frontend initiatives, and steered complex enterprise applications from concept to production. As a Senior Full Stack Developer at IrisIdea, he modernized large React and Node.js codebases, improved performance, strengthened security, and contributed to mission-critical digital transformation efforts.

Nabendu is also the **author of eight books on JavaScript**, **React, and full-stack development,** including the widely acclaimed *Full-Stack Web Development with* MERN. His books have helped thousands of developers advance their careers, and master modern web technologies.

As a passionate educator, he has trained more than **1000 students** and **50+ corporate teams,** sharing his expertise in JavaScript, React, and the MERN stack. His teaching extends to his YouTube channel and tech blog, where he regularly publishes content on React, web development trends, and software career growth.

A lifelong learner and innovator, Nabendu has explored Generative AI by building chatbots and 3D avatars with lip-sync using React Fiber and LLaMA. When he is not involved in his profession, Nabendu enjoys his precious time with his family, his two dogs, and reading about AI/ML, space, and future tech. **You can c**onnect with him anytime at ***linkedin.com/in/nabendu-biswas.***

Acknowledgments

This book is a testament to the unwavering support, guidance, and inspiration I have received from many individuals and organizations.

First and foremost, I express my deepest gratitude to my beloved parents whose unconditional love, encouragement, and belief in my abilities have been the cornerstone of all my endeavors. Their wisdom and values continue to guide me at every step of my journey.

I am profoundly thankful to my mentors and colleagues who have been a constant source of motivation, pushing me to explore uncharted territories, and strive for excellence. Their insights and constructive feedback have been pivotal in shaping the content and direction of this book.

I also extend my heartfelt appreciation to the organizations that provided the resources, platforms, and opportunities to delve deeper into the fascinating domains of blockchain, decentralized finance, and emerging technologies.

Finally, I owe a special note of gratitude to my readers. Their enthusiasm, curiosity, and thirst for knowledge inspire me to contribute meaningfully to the ever-evolving landscape of technology and innovation.

To each of you who played a role in this incredible journey, thank you for believing in me, and making this endeavor possible.

Preface

The web development world changes fast, and mastering the right tools is key to staying ahead. **Next.js**, built on React, has become a top choice for creating fast, modern web applications. This book, ***Ultimate Next.js for Modern Web Applications***, is your step-by-step guide to learning and applying Next.js effectively.

Hence, whether you are new to development or looking to expand your skills, this book covers everything you need, from the basics to advanced techniques, with real-world examples to help you along the way.

A quick look at what you will learn in each chapter:

Chapter 1: Getting Started with Next.js

Learn what Next.js is, and why it is different from React, as well as how to set up your first project.

Chapter 2: Next.js File-Based Routing

Understand how Next.js organizes routes, and work with dynamic and nested routes.

Chapter 3: Rendering Strategies in Next.js

Explore server-side, static, and client-side rendering, and choose the right approach for your project.

Chapter 4: API Routes in Next.js

Build APIs directly in your Next.js app, and connect to the backend.

Chapter 5: Authentication and Authorization

Secure your app with user login, and access controls.

Chapter 6: Next.js Data Fetching

Master how to fetch data using Next.js methods such as getStaticProps and getServerSideProps.

Chapter 7: Styling in Next.js

Learn different ways to style your app, including CSS Modules, Tailwind CSS, and styled-components.

Chapter 8: State Management in Next.js

Manage app state using tools such as Context API, Redux, and other libraries.

Chapter 9: Performance Optimization in Next.js

Speed up your app with techniques such as image optimization and code splitting.

Chapter 10: Unit Testing and Integration Testing

Write unit and integration tests using Jest and React Testing Library.

Chapter 11: Deploying Next.js Applications

Deploy your app on platforms such as Vercel, AWS, or Netlify.

Chapter 12: Advanced Features in Next.js

Dive into advanced topics such as internationalization and incremental static regeneration.

Chapter 13: Real-World Projects with Next.js

Build practical projects such as e-commerce sites and dashboards.

Chapter 14: Preparing for Front-End Development Jobs

Get tips for building your portfolio, preparing for interviews, and landing a front-end developer job.

Thus, this book simplifies complex topics, and helps you gain confidence in building modern web apps. So, let us begin your Next.js journey!

Get a Free eBook

We hope you are enjoying your recently purchased book! Your feedback is incredibly valuable to us, and to all other readers looking for great books.

If you found this book helpful or enjoyable, we would truly appreciate it, if you could take a moment to leave a short review with a 5 star rating on Amazon. It helps us grow, and lets other readers discover our books.

As a thank you, we would love to send you a free digital copy of this book, and a **30%** discount code on your next cart value on our official websites:

www.orangeava.com

www.orangeava.in (For Indian Subcontinent)

☑ **Here's how:**

Leave a review for the book on Amazon.

Take a screenshot of your review, and send an email to **info@orangeava.com** (it can be just the confirmation screen).

Once, we receive your screenshot, we will send you the digital file, within 24 hours.

Thank you so much for your support – it means a lot to us!

Downloading the code bundles and colored images

Please follow the links or scan the QR codes to download the
Code Bundles and Images of the book:

https://github.com/ava-orange-education/Ultimate-Next.js-for-Modern-Web-Applications

The code bundles and images of the book are also hosted on
https://rebrand.ly/f9b954

In case there's an update to the code, it will be updated on the existing GitHub repository.

Errata

We take immense pride in our work at **Orange Education Pvt Ltd,** and follow best practices to ensure the accuracy of our content to provide an indulging reading experience to our subscribers. Our readers are our mirrors, and we use their inputs to reflect and improve upon human errors, if any, that may have occurred during the publishing processes involved. To let us maintain the quality and help us reach out to any readers who might be having difficulties due to any unforeseen errors, please write to us at :

errata@orangeava.com

Your support, suggestions, and feedback are highly appreciated.

DID YOU KNOW

Did you know that Orange Education Pvt Ltd offers eBook versions of every book published, with PDF and ePub files available? You can upgrade to the eBook version at **www.orangeava.com** and as a print book customer, you are entitled to a discount on the eBook copy. Get in touch with us at: **info@orangeava.com** for more details.

At **www.orangeava.com**, you can also read a collection of free technical articles, sign up for a range of free newsletters, and receive exclusive discounts and offers on Print Books and eBooks.

PIRACY

If you come across any illegal copies of our works in any form on the internet, we would be grateful if you would provide us with the location address or website name. Please contact us at **info@orangeava.com** with a link to the material.

ARE YOU INTERESTED IN AUTHORING WITH US?

If there is a topic that you have expertise in, and you are interested in either writing or contributing to a book, please write to us at **business@orangeava.com**. We are on a journey to help developers and tech professionals to gain insights on the present technological advancements and innovations happening across the globe and build a community that believes Knowledge is best acquired by sharing and learning with others. Please reach out to us to learn what our audience demands and how you can be part of this educational reform. We also welcome ideas from tech experts and help them build learning and development content for their domains.

REVIEWS

Please leave a review. Once you have read and used this book, why not leave a review on the site that you purchased it from? Potential readers can then see and use your unbiased opinion to make purchase decisions. We at Orange Education would love to know what you think about our products, and our authors can learn from your feedback. Thank you!

For more information about Orange Education, please visit **www.orangeava.com**.

Table of Contents

CHAPTER 1
Getting Started with Next.js

Introduction

Welcome to the first chapter of our journey into Next.js, a cutting-edge framework built on top of React. Designed to create fast, scalable, and dynamic web applications, Next.js simplifies many of the challenges developers face when building modern websites. This chapter will lay the groundwork for your Next.js expertise, equipping you with the essential knowledge to get started.

We will begin by exploring what Next.js is, and how it builds upon React's foundation to make development easier and more efficient. We will then dive into the key differences between React and Next.js, highlighting why and when you might choose Next.js for your projects.

After understanding the basics, we will guide you through the installation of Next.js, and setting up your first project step by step. This practical approach ensures that you are ready to hit the ground running with Next.js. Along the way, we will also explore some of the powerful features that make Next.js a favorite among developers, such as its built-in routing, server-side rendering, and performance optimization.

By the end of this chapter, you will have a strong understanding of Next.js fundamentals and a working project environment ready for further development.

Structure

In this chapter, the following topics will be covered:

- Understanding Next.js
- Key differences between React and Next.js
- Installing Next.js 15 and setting up the project
- Overview of new features in Next.js

Prerequisites

Before we begin, make sure that you meet the following prerequisites:

- Basic understanding of JavaScript and TypeScript.
- Familiarity with React concepts such as components, props, and state.
- Knowledge of Node.js, and how to use package managers such as npm, npx or yarn.
- We will be using VS Code as our preferred editor, so make sure that it is installed and ready.

Understanding Next.js

Next.js is an open-source framework built on top of React, created by Vercel in 2016. It simplifies building fast, scalable, and SEO-friendly web applications by integrating tools such as Server-Side Rendering (SSR), Static Site Generation (SSG), and API routes. With minimal setup, developers can create high-performance applications for modern web development needs.

Next.js stands out for its ability to improve performance, streamline development, and enhance user and developer experiences. Here are its key benefits:

Performance and SEO

- **Server-Side Rendering (SSR):** Renders pages on the server for faster load times and better SEO.
- **Static Site Generation (SSG):** Pre-builds pages at build time, ensuring ultra-fast delivery.
- **Automatic Code Splitting:** Loads only the required JavaScript for each page, optimizing performance.

Built-in Features

- **File-Based Routing:** Define routes simply by organizing files in your project.
- **API Routes:** Build backend functionality without needing a separate server.
- **Image Optimization:** Automatically resize and optimize images for improved performance.
- **Hybrid Rendering:** Combine SSR, SSG, and client-side rendering for maximum flexibility.

Developer-Friendly

- **Easy to Learn:** Simple for developers familiar with React.

- **Built-in TypeScript Support:** Ideal for large projects requiring type safety.
- **Active Community:** Backed by Vercel, frequent updates, and strong community support.

Scalability

- Suitable for projects of any size, from small websites to enterprise applications.

Modern Tools

- **Turbopack**: Ensures faster builds for better productivity.
- **Edge Runtime:** Enables global scalability for modern web applications.

Next.js is a powerful, flexible, and developer-friendly framework for building modern web applications. It combines performance, SEO, scalability, and ease of use into one package, making it an excellent choice for projects of any scale. With its continuous innovations and strong community, Next.js remains a leader in web development, trusted by developers and businesses, worldwide.

Key Differences between React and Next.js

Before diving into the comparison, it is important to understand the core focus of each. **React** is a JavaScript library primarily used for building user interfaces, focusing on the frontend. In contrast, **Next.js** is a framework built on top of React, designed to provide additional tools and features for building full-stack web applications, making it more suited for production-level projects.

Aspect	React	Next.js
Type	JavaScript library for building UI components.	Framework built on top of React for full-stack web development.
Rendering	Client-Side Rendering (CSR) by default.	Supports Server-Side Rendering (SSR), Static Site Generation (SSG), and Incremental Static Regeneration (ISR).
Routing	Requires third-party libraries like React Router.	Built-in file-based routing system.
SEO	Limited SEO support with CSR.	Excellent SEO with SSR and SSG capabilities.
Development Scope	Focuses only on the frontend and UI.	Full-stack development with built-in API routes for backend functionality.
Configuration	Requires manual setup for advanced features such as SSR or SSG.	Provides these features out of the box.

Learning Curve	Easier for beginners.	Slightly more complex due to additional features.
Image Optimization	No built-in support; requires third-party libraries.	Built-in image optimization feature.
Performance	Relies on client-side for rendering which can impact load times.	Better performance with pre-rendering and code-splitting.
Community Support	Large community with extensive resources.	Growing community with strong support from Vercel.
Use Case	Ideal for single-page applications (SPAs).	Best for SEO-driven, dynamic, or large-scale applications.

Table 1.1: *Differences between React and Next.js*

React is a flexible library suited for building user interfaces and SPAs, while Next.js offers a complete framework for creating dynamic, high-performance, and SEO-optimized applications. Choose React for simplicity and flexibility, and Next.js for advanced features and production-level requirements.

Installing Next.js and Setting up a Project (Mac, Linux, and Windows)

Setting up Next.js is straightforward, and works seamlessly across Mac, Linux, and Windows. Here is a step-by-step guide for each platform:

Prerequisites:

Before starting, ensure that you have the following installed on your system:

- **Node.js (version 14 or higher):** Download it from [nodejs.org] (https://nodejs.org/).
- **Package Manager:** npm (comes with Node.js) or yarn.
- **Text Editor:** Visual Studio Code is recommended.

Steps for Installation and Project Setup (Mac, Linux, and Windows)

1. **Open Terminal/Command Prompt**
   a. On Mac/Linux: Use the Terminal.
   b. On Windows: Open Command Prompt, PowerShell, or Windows Terminal.

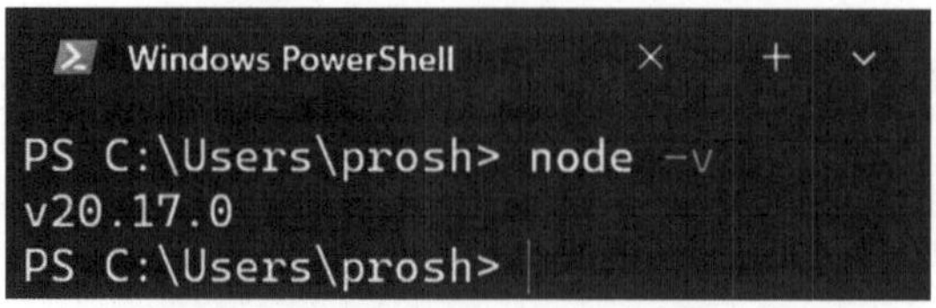

Figure 1.1: *Validate Node Version*

2. **Create a New Next.js Application**

   Use the following command to set up a new Next.js project:

   `npx create-next-app@latest my-next-app`

   a. Replace `` `my-next-app` `` with your desired project name.

   b. The `` `npx` `` command ensures you always use the latest version of `` `create-next-app` ``.

   Alternatively, you can use yarn:

   c. `yarn create next-app my-next-app`

3. **Navigate to the Project Director: `cd my-next-app`**

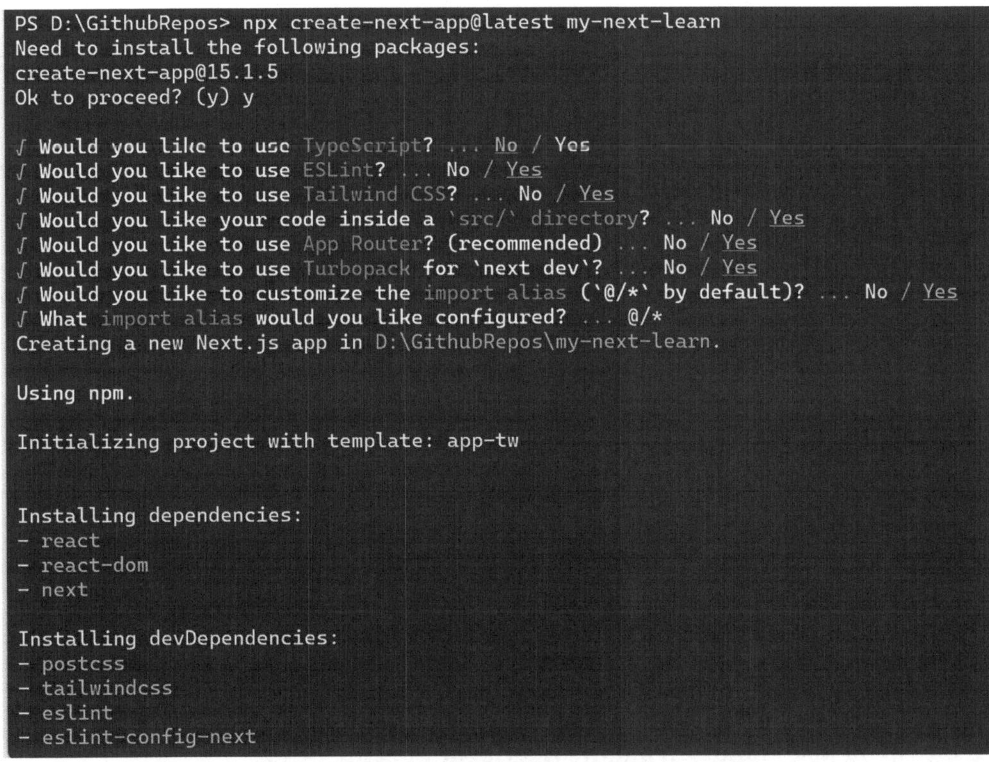

Figure 1.2: *Configuring a Basic Next.js Project in Command Prompt*

4. **Run the Development Server**

   Start the local development server to test your Next.js application:

   `npm run dev`

Or with yarn:

   `yarn dev`

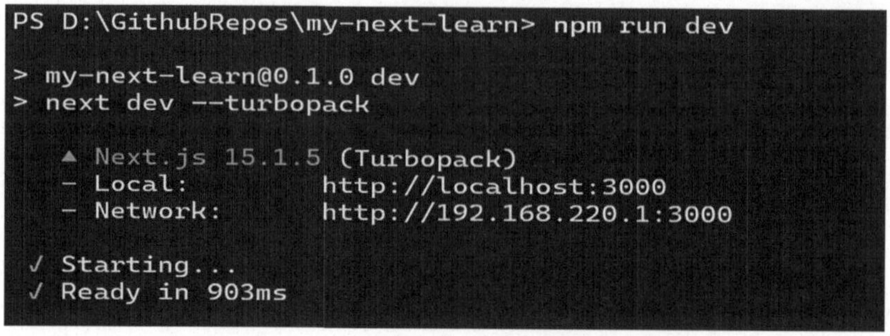

Figure 1.3: *Run the Project in Development Mode*

5. **Open the Application in Your Browser**
   a. Open your browser and go to: [http://localhost:3000].
   b. You should see the default Next.js welcome page.

Figure 1.4: *Application on Browser*

Setting Up on Mac/Linux/Windows (Platform-Specific Notes):

- Mac and Linux:
  - Use the Terminal for all commands.
  - Ensure proper permissions for global npm installs, if needed:
    `sudo npm install -g create-next-app`
- Windows:
  - Use PowerShell or Command Prompt with Administrator privileges for smoother setup.

- o If using Windows Subsystem for Linux (WSL), follow the Mac/Linux instructions.

Optional Configuration and Tools:

Use a Custom Editor Configuration

- Install extensions such as ESLint, Prettier, Bracket Pair Color DLW and Next.js snippets for better coding experience in Visual Studio Code.

Through VS Code Settings UI:

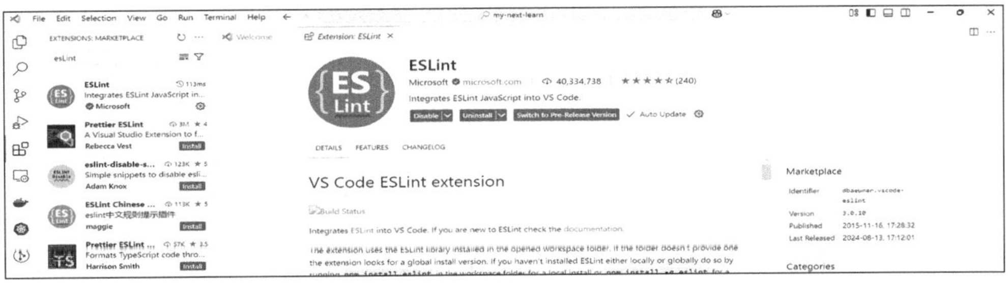

Figure 1.5: *Extensions Page VS Code*

1. Go to **`File > Preferences > Settings`** (Ctrl+, on Windows/Linux or Cmd+, on macOS).
2. In the top-right corner of the Settings UI, click **`Open Settings`** (JSON) icon: This will open the **`settings.json`** file.

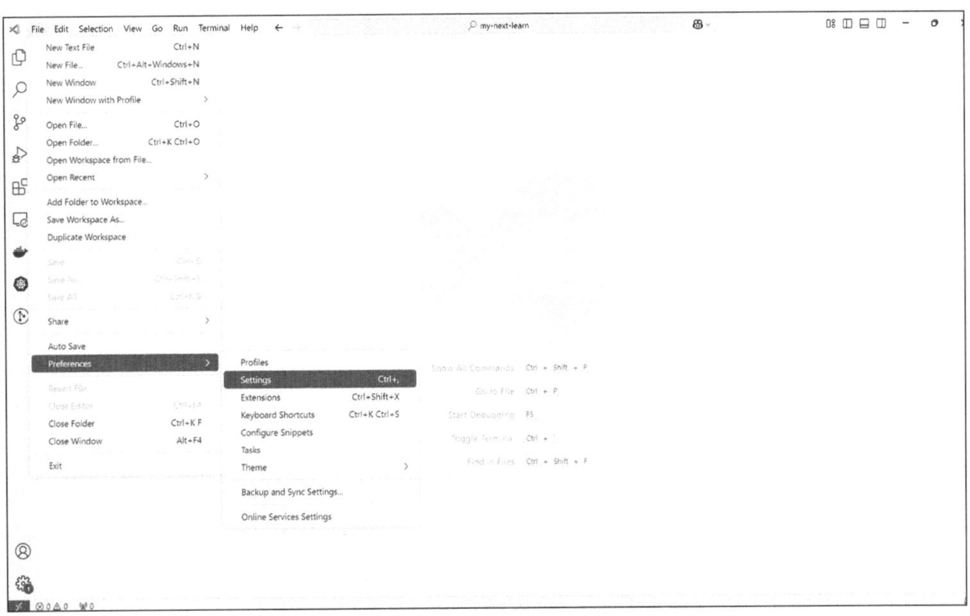

Figure 1.6: *Navigation Settings JSON File*

Figure 1.7: *Navigation Settings*

3. To configure VS Code to autoformat with Prettier on save and enable easy navigation between components, you can update the settings.json file in your workspace or globally.

```
{
  // Enable format on save
  "editor.formatOnSave": true,
  // Default formatter set to Prettier
  "[javascript]": {
    "editor.defaultFormatter": "esbenp.prettier-vscode"
  },
  "[javascriptreact]": {
    "editor.defaultFormatter": "esbenp.prettier-vscode"
  },
  // Enable Prettier as the default formatter
  "prettier.requireConfig": true,
  // Automatically organize imports on save
  "editor.codeActionsOnSave": {
    "source.organizeImports": true
  },
  // Enable JSX syntax highlighting
  "files.associations": {
    "*.js": "javascriptreact",
    "*.jsx": "javascriptreact"
  },
  // Auto-close and auto-rename tags for JSX
  "auto-close-tag.activationOnLanguage": [
    "javascript",
    "javascriptreact"
  ],
  "auto-rename-tag.activationOnLanguage": [
    "javascript",
    "javascriptreact"
  ],
  // Enable breadcrumb navigation for easier file navigation
  "breadcrumbs.enabled": true,
  // Enable IntelliSense and go-to-definition for easier naviga-
tion
  "javascript.suggest.autoImports": true,
  "javascript.preferences.importModuleSpecifier": "relative",
```

```
    // Path alias navigation for imports
    "javascript.preferences.includePackageJsonAutoImports": "on"
}
```

Understanding the Structure of a Next.js Project

In Next.js, the app directory (`/src/app`) introduces an updated project structure and a more streamlined way to build applications with enhanced routing, layouts, and CSS management. Let us dive into the structure and explain how it works:

Understanding the New 'src/app' Structure

The app directory simplifies the management of routes, layouts, and styling. Here is how it is structured:

- '**/src/app/page.js**'
    - Represents the root route (`/`) of your application.
    - Each file named `**page.js**` in a subdirectory of `**app**` corresponds to a route.
    - Example:
        - `/src/app/page.js` -> `/`
        - `/src/app/about/page.js` -> `/about`
- '**/src/app/layout.js**'
    - Used to define layouts that persist across multiple pages.
    - Layouts wrap the child routes, and can include components such as headers, footers, or sidebars.
    - Layouts are shared by default and nested, allowing for better code reuse.

    Example:

    ```
    // src/app/layout.js
    export default function RootLayout({ children }) {
      return (
        <html lang="en">
          <body>
            <header>Global Header</header>
            <main>{children}</main>
            <footer>Global Footer</footer>
          </body>
        </html>
      );
    }
    ```

- `/src/app/global.css`
  - Contains global CSS styles applied across the entire application.
  - Imported directly into `layout.js` to apply them globally.

    Example:

    ```
    /* src/app/global.css */
    body {
      margin: 0;
      font-family: Arial, sans-serif;
    }

    // src/app/layout.js
    import './global.css';

    export default function RootLayout({ children }) {
      return (
        <html lang="en">
          <body>{children}</body>
        </html>
      );
    }
    ```

Key Features of the `/app` Directory Structure

- Routing with `page.js`
  - Each folder in `/src/app` is a route segment.
  - A `page.js` file inside the folder represents the content of that route.

    Example:

    ```
    src/app/
      ├── page.js         // Route: /
      ├── about/
      │   └── page.js     // Route: /about
      ├── blog/
      │   └── [slug]/     // Dynamic route: /blog/[slug]
      │       └── page.js
      └── contact/
          └── page.js     // Route: /contact
    ```
- Dynamic Routes
  - Dynamic route segments are defined using square brackets.

    Example:

    - `/src/app/blog/[slug]/page.js` corresponds to `/blog/:slug`.

Dynamic Route Example:

```
// src/app/blog/[slug]/page.js
export default function BlogPost({ params }) {
  const { slug } = params;
  return <h1>Blog Post: {slug}</h1>;
}
```

- Nested Layouts
  - Layouts can be nested for different sections of the application.

    Example:

```
src/app/
├── layout.js        // Global layout
├── dashboard/
│   ├── layout.js    // Layout specific to /dashboard
│   └── page.js      // Route: /dashboard
└── settings/
    └── page.js      // Route: /settings
```

Code Example:

```
// src/app/dashboard/layout.js
export default function DashboardLayout({ children }) {
  return (
    <section>
      <nav>Dashboard Navigation</nav>
      <div>{children}</div>
    </section>
  );
}
```

- Static Assets in `**public**`
  - Static files like images, fonts, and other resources go in the `**public**` directory.
  - Accessible at the root level (`**/**`).
  - Example: `**/public/logo.png**` **->** `**/logo.png**`.

Folder Structure Example of how the project structure looks in a Next.js app:

```
src/
├── app/
│   ├── layout.js           // Root layout
│   ├── global.css          // Global styles
│   ├── page.js             // Root route
│   ├── about/
│   │   └── page.js         // About page
│   ├── blog/
│   │   ├── layout.js       // Blog-specific layout
│   │   └── [slug]/         // Dynamic route for blog posts
│   │
```

```
│    │       └── page.js
│    ├── dashboard/
│    │    ├── layout.js       // Dashboard layout
│    │    └── page.js         // Dashboard route
│    └── settings/
│         └── page.js         // Settings route
├── public/                   // Static assets (images, fonts,
etc.)
│    └── logo.png
├── package.json              // Project configuration
└── next.config.js           // Next.js configuration
```

Benefits of the New Structure

- File-Based Routing:
  - No need for `next/link` or `react-router` configurations–routes are inferred from the folder structure.
- Nested Layouts:
  - Layouts allow for code reuse and consistent design across sections.
- Improved Performance:
  - Automatically optimized loading, server rendering, and static generation.
- Centralized Styling:
  - Global CSS and CSS modules for better organization.
- Dynamic Routes and API:
  - Easier handling of dynamic paths with `[param]`.

This updated structure promotes modularity, scalability, and ease of use, making it a great fit for modern web applications.

Overview of New Features in Next.js

Since its launch in 2016 by Vercel, Next.js has evolved into one of the most advanced frameworks for modern web development. Each version introduced groundbreaking features, enhancing performance, scalability, and developer experience. Here is an overview of its journey:

2016: The Beginning

- **Server-Side Rendering (SSR):** Next.js was launched to simplify SSR in React applications, enabling faster page loads and improved SEO.
- **Initial File-Based Routing:** Introduced an intuitive, file-based routing system, reducing the complexity of setting up routes.

2019: Static Site Generation (SSG)

- **SSG Introduction:** Enabled pre-rendering of pages at build time, improving speed and scalability.
- **Improved Developer Experience:** Streamlined workflows for creating both static and dynamic content.

2020-2021: Dynamic Content and Optimization

- **Incremental Static Regeneration (ISR):** Allowed updates to static pages without a full rebuild, enabling dynamic content in static sites.
- **API Routes:** Introduced serverless functions directly within the Next.js ecosystem.
- **Image Optimization:** Automated resizing, compression, and lazy loading for better performance.
- **Rust-Based Compiler:** Enhanced build speeds and minimized bundles using a Rust-based compiler.

2021-2024: Advanced Tooling and Features

- **Turbopack (Beta):** A Rust-based bundler, up to 700x faster than Webpack during development.
- **Edge Runtime:** Introduced edge rendering for ultra-low latency.
- **React Server Components:** Supported streaming server-rendered React components for faster interactivity.
- **App Router (Stable in 2023):** Revolutionized routing with layouts, nested routes, and streaming.

2024: Next.js 15

- **React 19 Support:** Fully integrated React 19 features, allowing access to the latest advancements in React.
- **Turbo pack (Stable):** Turbo pack became stable, delivering even faster development builds.
- **Async Request APIs:** Updated APIs such as cookies, headers, and draft Mode to asynchronous, streamlining rendering and caching.
- **Caching Semantics Update:** Provided developers more explicit control over caching strategies with no default caching for fetch requests.
- **Static Indicator:** Visual indicators during development to identify static routes for better optimization.
- **Enhanced Forms (next/form):** New <Form> component introduced, improving client-side navigation and progressive enhancement for forms.

- **TypeScript Support in Config Files:** Allowed writing `next.config.ts` with type checking and auto completion.
- **Improved Debugging Tools:** Enhanced error messages and debugging for faster issue resolution.

From its introduction of server-side rendering in 2016 to the cutting-edge features of 2024, Next.js has consistently redefined modern web development. Each update prioritizes performance, developer experience, and scalability, making Next.js the framework of choice for building robust and future-ready applications.

Conclusion

In this chapter, we covered the essentials of **Next.js**, including its basics, standout features, history, and structure. We started by understanding how Next.js, built on React, simplifies web development with tools such as **Server-Side Rendering (SSR)**, **Static Site Generation (SSG)**, and **API routes**, making it a preferred choice for modern, scalable, and SEO-friendly applications. We explored its evolution from its inception in 2016 to the latest features in 2024, including innovations such as **Turbopack**, **React Server Components**, and **Enhanced Forms**.

Additionally, we discussed its flexible structure, and how it integrates advanced tools to improve performance and developer productivity. These foundational concepts provide a solid starting point to leverage Next.js for robust and efficient web applications.

In the next chapter, we will focus on **File-Based Routing**, a core feature of Next.js that simplifies navigation by automatically generating routes based on your project's file structure. You will also learn how to implement static, dynamic, and nested routes, along with the best practices to streamline your application's routing system. So, stay tuned as we dive deeper into this powerful feature!

Multiple Choice Questions

1. What is the primary purpose of Next.js?
    a. Build mobile applications
    b. Create dynamic and SEO-friendly web applications
    c. Develop desktop software
    d. Manage databases

2. Which rendering methods are supported by Next.js?
    a. Client-side rendering only
    b. Server-Side Rendering (SSR) and Static Site Generation (SSG)
    c. Static rendering only
    d. None of the above
3. Which tool does Next.js use for faster builds in the latest version?
    a. Webpack
    b. Turbopack
    c. Babel
    d. Gulp
4. Which feature in Next.js improves image performance?
    a. Lazy routing
    b. Image Optimization
    c. Static generation
    d. Incremental builds
5. Which company created and maintains Next.js?
    a. Google
    b. Facebook
    c. Vercel
    d. Microsoft

Answers

1. b
2. b
3. b
4. b
5. c

CHAPTER 2
Next.js File-Based Routing

Introduction

Next.js simplifies web development, and one of its standout features is file-based routing. With this system, routing in your app is as easy as creating files and folders. No need for extra configurations – your app structure automatically defines how users navigate through it.

In this chapter, we will introduce you to how file-based routing works and why it is so effective. You will also learn how to create the basic routes just by adding files to your pages folder. From there, we will explore the dynamic routes, which allow you to handle changing URLs and nested routes, perfect for creating more complex navigation structures.

We shall also cover catch-all routes and optional catch-all routes, which let you handle a wide variety of URLs without extra effort. On top of that, you will see how to use the next/link component to connect pages in your app with smooth navigation.

Finally, we will dive into layouts and nested layouts, showing you how to design consistent and reusable page structures. These tools help you to create a polished and organized user experience without repetitive codes.

By the end of this chapter, you will have all the skills you need to build a clean, efficient routing system in any Next.js project.

Structure

In this chapter, the following topics will be covered:

- Introduction to File-Based Routing
- Dynamic and Nested Routes
- Catch-all and Optional Catch-all Routes

- Linking between Pages Using Next/Link
- Layouts and Nested Layouts

Introduction to File-Based Routing

File-based routing is one of the unique features of Next.js, simplifying how developers define and manage routes in their applications. Instead of manually configuring routes in a separate file (like a routes.js), Next.js automatically generates them based on your file and folder structure. This makes building applications faster, more intuitive, and less error-prone.

At its core, file-based routing means that the structure of your application's files defines your app's URL structure. Each file represents a route, and folders are used for grouping or nesting those routes.

Benefits of File-Based Routing

File-based routing in Next.js streamlines route management by leveraging the file system, offering several advantages for developers such as:

- **No Manual Configuration:** Routes are created automatically based on file structure, saving time and reducing complexity.
- **Easy to Understand:** The directory structure visually reflects your app's URL structure.
- **Scalability:** Nesting routes and adding dynamic routes make it easy to scale for larger applications.
- **Integrated Features:** File-based routing integrates seamlessly with Next.js features such as server-side rendering, static site generation, and API routes.

File-Based Routing: Two Approaches

File-based routing in Next.js can be implemented in two ways, depending on whether you are using the pages directory or the newer **`src/app`** directory. Each has a slightly different structure and features. The following is a detailed explanation of both approaches, with text-based diagrams for clarity:

File-Based Routing without `src/app` (Using Pages)

In the pages' directory, every file corresponds to a route, and the folder structure mirrors your URL paths. This approach is simple, and works out of the box without enabling any special features.

File Structure Example:

```
├── pages/
│   ├── index.js          // Home route (/)
│   ├── about.js          // About route (/about)
│   ├── contact.js        // Contact route (/contact)
│   ├── blog/
│   │   ├── index.js      // Blog index route (/blog)
│   │   ├── [slug].js     // Dynamic route for blog posts (/
blog/:slug)
│   ├── api/
│   │   ├── hello.js      // API route (/api/hello)
```

Routing Behavior:

- **Static Routes:** Each **`.js`** file becomes a static route.
  - Example: **`about.js`** maps to **`/about`**.
- **Dynamic Routes:** Use square brackets **`[param]`** to define parameters in routes.
  - Example: **`[slug].js`** maps to **`/blog/:slug`**.
- **Catch-All Routes:** Use **`[...param]`** for flexible, multi-segment matching.
  - Example: **`[...slug].js`** handles **`/docs/*`** (For example, **`/docs/intro, /docs/setup`**).
- **API Routes:** Defined in the api folder for server-side functions.
  - Example: **`api/hello.js`** maps to **`/api/hello`**.

URL Path	**→ File Path**
/	→ src/pages/index.js
/about	→ src/pages/about.js
/blog	→src/pages/blog/index.js
/blog/:slug	→ src/pages/blog/[slug].js
/api/hello	→ src/pages/api/hello.js

Table 2.1: *File-Based Routing with Pages Folder*

File-Based Routing with `src/app`

The `src/app` directory is a more modern and flexible way to define routes, introduced in Next.js 13. It supports layouts, nested routing, React Server Components, and data fetching at the route level.

File Structure Example:

```
src/
├── app/
│   ├── layout.js          // Root layout (shared across all routes)
│   ├── page.js             // Home route (/)
│   ├── about/
│   │   ├── page.js         // About route (/about)
│   │   ├── layout.js       // Nested layout for /about
│   ├── blog/
│   │   ├── page.js         // Blog index route (/blog)
│   │   ├── [slug]/
│   │   │   ├── page.js     // Dynamic route for blog posts (/
blog/:slug)
│   ├── api/
│   │   ├── hello/
│   │   │   ├── route.js    // API route (/api/hello)
```

Routing Behavior:

- **page.js:** Defines the content for each route.
  - Example: **`about/page.js`** maps to **`/about`**.
- **Dynamic Routes:** Use **`[param]`** to define parameters in URLs, just like in pages.
  - Example: **`blog/[slug]/page.js`** maps to **`/blog/:slug`**.
- **Nested Layouts:** Add layout.js to wrap routes with shared elements (such as headers or footers).
  - Example: **`about/layout.js`** wraps all **`/about`** routes with a custom layout.
- **Server and Client Components:** Supports server-rendered components by default, with the ability to opt into client-side rendering using "**`use client`**".
- **API Routes:** Defined in folders inside **`app/api`**.

URL Path	→ File Path
/	→ `src/app/page.js`
`/about`	→ src/app/about/page.js
/blog	→ src/app/blog/page.js
/blog/:slug	→ src/app/blog/[slug]/page.js
/api/hello	→ src/app/api/hello/route.js

Table 2.2: *File-Based Routing with App Folder*

Key Differences between Pages and `src/app`

Both approaches are valid, but the app directory provides modern tools and better scalability for larger projects. Choose the method that best fits your project's requirements.

Feature	Pages Directory	src/app Directory
File for Route	`index.js` or `[param].js`	`page.js`
Dynamic Routes	`[param].js`	`[param]/page.js`
Layouts	Manual implementation	`layout.js` (built-in support)
Data Fetching	`getStaticProps/getServerSideProps`	Built-in async/await for components
Server Components	Not supported	Default behavior
Nested Routes	Limited without custom workarounds	Fully supported with nested layouts

Table 2.3: *Differences between Pages and* `src/app`

Dynamic and Nested Routes in Next.js

Dynamic and nested routes are powerful features in Next.js that allow you to handle more complex URL structures, and build scalable applications. These features are available in both the pages' directory and the modern app directory, but their implementation and behavior differ slightly.

Dynamic Routes

Dynamic routes allow you to create pages that handle variable or dynamic URL segments. These are useful when the URL contains parameters such as a user ID, product ID, or blog post slug.

In the Pages Directory

Dynamic routes are created using square brackets (`[ ]`) in the file or folder name.

Example File Structure:

```
├── pages/
│   ├── product/
│   │   ├── [id].js      // Dynamic route for product pages
```

URL Example:

```
/product/123 → Renders the content of product/[id].js.
```

Code Example:

```
// src/pages/product/[id].js
import { useRouter } from 'next/router';
export default function ProductPage() {
const router = useRouter();
const { id } = router.query; // Access the dynamic ID from the URL

return <h1>Product ID: {id}</h1>;
}
```

In the App Directory

Dynamic routes are created using the same **[ ]** naming convention but within the app folder.

Example File Structure:

```
src/
├── app/
│   ├── product/
│   │   ├── [id]/
│   │   │   ├── page.js    // Dynamic route for product pages
```

URL Example:

```
/product/123 → Renders the content of product/[id]/page.js.
```

Code Example:

```
// src/app/product/[id]/page.js
export default function ProductPage({ params }) {
const { id } = params; // Access the dynamic ID from the URL
return <h1>Product ID: {id}</h1>;
}
// Optional: Add metadata for the dynamic route
export async function generateMetadata({ params }) {
return { title: `Product ${params.id}` };
}
```

Nested Routes

Nested routes allow you to organize related routes hierarchically, grouping them together under a shared parent route.

In the Pages Directory

Nested routes are created using folders within the pages' directory. Each folder represents a URL segment.

Example File Structure:

```
├── pages/
│   ├── blog/
│   │   ├── index.js          // Blog homepage (/blog)
│   │   ├── [slug].js         // Dynamic blog post (/blog/:slug)
│   │   ├── category/
│   │   │   ├── [name].js    // Blog category page (/blog/category/
:name)
```

URL Examples:

/blog → Displays content from **blog/index.js**.
/blog/my-first-post → Displays content from **blog/[slug].js**.
/blog/category/technology → Displays content from **blog/category/[name].js**.

Code Example for Nested Category Route:

```
// src/pages/blog/category/[name].js
import { useRouter } from 'next/router';
export default function CategoryPage() {
const router = useRouter();
const { name } = router.query;
return <h1>Category: {name}</h1>;
}
```

In the App Directory

Nested routes in the app directory are created by nesting folders, with each folder containing a page.js file for the corresponding route.

Example File Structure:

```
src/
├── app/
│   ├── blog/
│   │   ├── page.js              // Blog homepage (/blog)
│   │   ├── [slug]/
│   │   │   ├── page.js          // Dynamic blog post (/blog/:slug)
│   │   ├── category/
│   │   │   ├── [name]/
│   │   │   │   ├── page.js      // Blog category page (/blog/
category/:name)
```

URL Examples:

/blog → Renders **blog/page.js**.
/blog/my-first-post → Renders **blog/[slug]/page.js**.
/blog/category/technology → Renders **blog/category/[name]/page.js**.

Code Example for Nested Category Route:

```
// src/app/blog/category/[name]/page.js
export default function CategoryPage({ params }) {
const { name } = params;
return <h1>Category: {name}</h1>;
 }
}

// Optional metadata for SEO
export async function generateMetadata({ params }) {
return { title: `Category: ${params.name}` };
}
```

Feature	pages Directory	app Directory
Dynamic Routes	`[param].js`	`[param]/page.js`
Nested Routes	Folders with files for subroutes	Nested folders with page.js
Layouts	Manually implemented	Use **`layout.js`** for nested layouts
Data Access	**`useRouter().query`**	Access **`params`** directly
SEO Metadata	Use Head from **`next/head`**	Use **`generateMetadata`**

Table 2.4: *Differences between Pages and App Directories for Dynamic and Nested Routes*

Benefits of Dynamic and Nested Routes

Dynamic and nested routes in Next.js enhance flexibility and organization, making it easier to manage complex URL structures efficiently.

- **Dynamic Routes:**
  - Perfect for handling unique IDs, slugs, or variable data in the URL.
  - Example: **`/product/:id`**, **`/blog/:slug`**.
- **Nested Routes:**
  - Great for organizing related routes logically under a shared parent.
  - Example: **`/blog/category/:name`**, **`/dashboard/settings`**.
- **Improved Scalability:**
  - Both approaches allow you to scale your application as the number of routes grows without creating messy configurations.

Next/Router Library in Next.js

The **`next/router`** library is an essential part of Next.js that allows you to programmatically navigate between routes, access the current route's details, and handle dynamic or client-side routing. It provides powerful tools for interacting with the routing system, particularly in the pages' directory or for specific client-side needs in the app directory.

Key Features of `Next/Router`

The **`next/router`** module provides powerful client-side navigation and route management features, enabling dynamic and efficient handling of application routing.

- **Programmatic Navigation**: Navigate to different pages without using **`<Link>`** components.
- **Access Route Parameters:** Retrieve dynamic route parameters, query strings, and the current route path.
- **Client-Side Routing:** Navigate between pages without a full page reload for a seamless user experience.
- **Route Events:** Listen to route change events and trigger actions based on navigation.
- **Push and Replace History:** Modify the browser's history using push or replace methods.

Use `Next/Router`

Importing the Library to use **`next/router`**, import the **`useRouter`** hook from the library:

```
import { useRouter } from 'next/router';
```

Accessing the Router Object: The **`useRouter`** hook provides access to the router object with various properties and methods.

Key Properties and Methods

- **`router.query`:** This contains the dynamic route parameters and query strings as an object.

Example:

```
// For a route like /product/[id]?ref=123
import { useRouter } from 'next/router';
export default function ProductPage() {
const router = useRouter();
const { id, ref } = router.query;
return (
<div>
```

```
<h1>Product ID: {id}</h1>
<p>Referral Code: {ref}</p>
</div>
 );
}
```

- **router.push()**: Navigates to a new page and adds a new entry to the browser's history.

Example:

```
import { useRouter } from 'next/router';
export default function HomePage() {
const router = useRouter();
const goToAbout = () => {
router.push('/about');
 };
 return <button onClick={goToAbout}>Go to About Page</button>;
}
```

- **router.replace()**: Navigates to a new page but replaces the current entry in the browser's history (no back button).

Example:

```
router.replace('/dashboard');
```

- **router.pathname**: Gets the current route path.

Example:

```
import { useRouter } from 'next/router';
export default function CurrentPath() {
const router = useRouter();
 return <p>Current Path: {router.pathname}</p>;
}
```

- **router.events**: Listen to route change events to perform custom actions.

Example:

```
import { useRouter } from 'next/router';
import { useEffect } from 'react';
export default function RouteListener() {
  const router = useRouter();
  useEffect(() => {
    const handleRouteChange = (url) => {
      console.log('App is changing to:', url);
    };
    router.events.on('routeChangeStart', handleRouteChange);
    return () => {
```

```
        router.events.off('routeChangeStart', handleRouteChange);
      };
    }, [router]);
    return <div>Check the console for route changes!</div>;
  }
```

- **`router.back()`**: Navigates back to the previous page in the browser history.

Example:

```
router.back();
```

- **`router.prefetch()`**: Prefetches data for a given page to improve performance and make navigation faster.

Example:

```
router.prefetch('/about');
```

Common Use Cases for `Next/Router`

`Next/Router` is essential for handling client-side navigation, dynamic routing, and programmatic redirections in Next.js applications.

- **Dynamic Routing:** Access and handle route parameters for dynamic pages.
  - `const { id } = router.query; // For a route like /product/[id]`
- **Client-Side Navigation:** Navigate programmatically without using <Link>.
  `router.push('/profile');`

  Query String Handling: Retrieve and manipulate query parameters.

  `const { ref } = router.query; // Access ?ref=123` in the URL
- **Custom Analytics:** Use **`router.events`** to track route changes for analytics or custom logic.
- **Conditional Redirects:** Redirect users to a specific page based on conditions.

  ```
  useEffect(() => {
  if (!user.isLoggedIn) {
  router.replace('/login');
  }
  }, []);
  ```
- **Lazy Loading and Prefetching:** Improve navigation performance by prefetching routes.

  ```
  router.prefetch('/dashboard');
  ```

Limitations of `Next/Router`

While **`next/router`** offers powerful client-side navigation, it also comes with certain limitations that developers should be aware of such as:

- **Server Components:** The app directory uses React Server Components by default, so **`next/router`** is not directly available for server-rendered pages.
- Instead, use **`params`** and server-side routing utilities in the app directory.
- **Deeply Nested Routes:** For deeply nested and complex routes, relying on **`next/router`** may make your code more difficult to manage compared to leveraging the built-in layouts in the app directory.

`Next/Router` in the App Directory

While **`next/router`** is still supported for client components in the app directory, the app routing system introduces a more declarative approach using **`params`** and server-side navigation. For most usc cascs in thc app dircctory, you will intcract dircctly with route parameters and metadata, instead of relying heavily on **`next/router`**.

Lazy Loading in Next.js

Lazy loading is a performance optimization technique where components, images, or scripts are loaded **only when needed,** rather than all at once. This reduces the initial page load time, and improves the user experience.

Next.js provides **built-in support for lazy loading** with features like:

- **Dynamic Imports** (next/dynamic)
- **Lazy Loading Images** (next/image)
- **Code Splitting and React Suspense**

Lazy Loading Components Using `next/dynamic`

In Next.js, components can be **dynamically imported** only when they are required, reducing the JavaScript bundle size.

Example: Lazy Loading a Component

```
import dynamic from 'next/dynamic';
const HeavyComponent = dynamic(() => import('../components/Heavy-
Component'), {
      ssr: false, // Prevents server-side rendering if needed
      loading: () => <p>Loading...</p>, // Optional loading state
      });
      export default function HomePage() {
```

```
                return (
                        <div>
                        <h1>Home Page</h1>
                        <HeavyComponent />
                        </div>
                );
}
```

- The `dynamic` function loads **`HeavyComponent` only when the page is rendered in the browser**.
- **`ssr: false`** ensures that the component is not loaded on the server (useful for browser-only features).
- The **`loading property (loading: () => <p>Loading...</p>)`** provides a fallback while the component is being loaded.

Lazy Loading Images Using `next/image`

The **`next/image`** component **automatically lazy loads images** for better performance.

Example: Lazy Loading Images

```
import dynamic from 'next/dynamic';
import { Suspense } from 'react';

const ExpensiveComponent = dynamic(() => import('../components/
ExpensiveComponent'), {
  suspense: true,
});

export default function HomePage() {
  return (
    <div>
      <h1>Welcome to My Website</h1>
      <Suspense fallback={<p>Loading component...</p>}>
        <ExpensiveComponent />
      </Suspense>
    </div>
  );
}
```

- **Suspense waits** for **`ExpensiveComponent`** to load and **displays a fallback (Loading component...)** in the meantime.
- **Only loads the component when necessary** instead of during initial page load.

Lazy Loading External Scripts (`next/script`)

For third-party libraries like analytics, ads, or chat widgets, Next.js provides **`next/script`** for optimized lazy loading.

Example: Lazy Loading Google Analytics

```
import Script from 'next/script';
export default function Analytics() {
  return (
    <div>
      <h1>Website Analytics</h1>
      <Script
        src="https://www.googletagmanager.com/gtag/js?id=GA_
TRACKING_ID"
        strategy="lazyOnload"
      />
    </div>
  );
}
```

- The **`strategy="lazyOnload"`** ensures that the script is **only loaded after the main page content** is loaded.

`next/dynamic()`: Dynamic Import and Lazy Loading in Next.js

The **`next/dynamic()`** function in Next.js allows dynamic imports and lazy loading of components, improving performance by reducing the initial JavaScript bundle size. Instead of loading all components at once, **`next/dynamic()`** ensures that components are loaded only when they are needed, optimizing page speed and user experience.

Uses of `next/dynamic()`

`Next/dynamic()` enables dynamic imports in Next.js, allowing components to be loaded lazily for improved performance and optimization such as:

- The Dynamic Component is only imported when it is needed.
- This reduces the initial JavaScript bundle size.
- The page loads faster since unnecessary components are not loaded upfront.
- Large UI Components: Charts, Maps, Code Editors, and Data Tables.
- Client-Only Components: Components that depend on window or document.
- Modals and Popups: Components that appear only on user interaction.

- Tabs and Accordions: Sections that are not visible on page load.
- Third-Party Libraries: Heavy libraries (For example, react-quill, react-pdf, and so on)

Using `next/dynamic()` with a Loading Fallback

If a component takes time to load, you can show a loading message or spinner while waiting.

```
import dynamic from 'next/dynamic';
const DynamicComponent = dynamic(() => import('../components/
DynamicComponent'), {
  loading: () => <p>Loading component...</p>,
});

export default function HomePage() {
  return (
    <div>
      <h1>Home Page</h1>
      <DynamicComponent />
    </div>
  );
}
```

Now, users will see "**`Loading component...`**" until the component is ready.

Preventing Server-Side Rendering (`ssr: false`)

Some components (For example, modals, maps, or window-based logic) should only be loaded on the client-side. By default, Next.js renders components on both the server and client, but you can disable SSR for a component.

```
import dynamic from 'next/dynamic';

const ClientOnlyComponent = dynamic(() => import('../components/
ClientOnlyComponent'), {
  ssr: false, // Prevents server-side rendering
});

export default function HomePage() {
  return (
    <div>
      <h1>Home Page</h1>
      <ClientOnlyComponent />
    </div>
  );
}
```

Thus, it ensures compatibility with browser-only components (For example, local storage, geolocation, window or document objects).

Avoids SSR-related errors (For example, "window is not defined" error).

Use **ssr: false** for client-side features that should not run on the server.

Example: Lazy Loading a Chart Component.

Imagine you have a dashboard that contains a heavy chart library (For example, **react-chartjs**). Instead of loading the chart on the initial page load, we use **next/dynamic()** to load it only when needed.

```
import dynamic from 'next/dynamic';

const ChartComponent = dynamic(() => import('../components/Chart-
Component'), {
  ssr: false,
  loading: () => <p>Loading chart...</p>,
});

export default function Dashboard() {
  return (
    <div>
      <h1>Dashboard</h1>
      <ChartComponent />
    </div>
  );
}
```

The page loads quickly, and the chart is loaded separately.

Example: Lazy Loading a Modal Component

Models are a great use case for **next/dynamic()**, as they are not needed until the user interacts with the page.

```
import { useState } from 'react';
import dynamic from 'next/dynamic';

const Modal = dynamic(() => import('../components/Modal'), {
  ssr: false,
  loading: () => <p>Loading modal...</p>,
});

export default function HomePage() {
  const [showModal, setShowModal] = useState(false);

  return (
```

```
      <div>
        <h1>Home Page</h1>
        <button onClick={() => setShowModal(true)}>Open Modal</
button>
        {showModal && <Modal />}
      </div>
    );
}
```

The modal is only loaded when the user clicks the button, reducing unnecessary JavaScript execution.

Catch-All and Optional Catch-All Routes

In a growing web application, handling dynamic content is crucial. Imagine you are building a **blog platform** where users can browse articles by categories, subcategories, and specific topics. At the same time, you want to ensure that if a user visits just **`/blog`**, they see a list of all posts. Instead of creating multiple individual routes for each possibility, Next.js provides a flexible solution: **Catch-All and Optional Catch-All Routes**.

The Challenge of Dynamic Paths

When structuring a Next.js application, static routes are straightforward. You create a **`blog.js` file**, and it maps to **`/blog`**. But what if you want URLs such as:

- `/blog/javascript`
- `/blog/javascript/react`
- `/blog/javascript/react/hooks`

Without a flexible routing system, you would have to manually create multiple files for every possible category depth, which is not scalable. This is where **Catch-All Routes** come in.

Catch-All Routes: Handling Multiple Path Segments

A **`Catch-All Route`** is a special type of dynamic route that captures multiple URL segments, and passes them as an array. It is defined using **square brackets and three dots (`[...param]`)** inside the pages or app directory.

In our blog example, we can create a catch-all route to handle multiple levels of categories in a single file.

Defining a Catch-All Route

```
src/
├── pages/
│   ├── blog/
│   │   ├── [...slug].js  // Catch-all route for blog categories
```

Inside **blog/[...slug].js**, we capture multiple URL segments:

```
import { useRouter } from 'next/router';

export default function BlogCategoryPage() {
  const router = useRouter();
  const { slug } = router.query; // Captures all segments as an
array

  return (
    <div>
      <h1>Blog Categories</h1>
      <p>{slug ? `You are viewing: ${slug.join(" / ")}` : "Viewing
all blog posts"}</p>
    </div>
  );
}
```

Now, this **single file** can handle all these URLs:

- `/blog/javascript → slug = ["javascript"]`
- `/blog/javascript/react → slug = ["javascript", "react"]`
- `/blog/javascript/react/hooks → slug = ["javascript", "react", "hooks"]`

Catch-All Routes in the App Directory

With the app directory in Next.js, the structure is slightly different. The same catch-all logic applies, but we create a folder instead:

```
src/
├── app/
│   ├── blog/
│   │   ├── [...slug]/
│   │   │   ├── page.js
```

And inside **blog/[...slug]/page.js**:

```
export default function BlogCategoryPage({ params }) {
  const { slug } = params; // Captures all segments as an array
  return (
    <div>
```

```
      <h1>Blog Categories</h1>
      <p>{slug ? `You are viewing: ${slug.join(" / ")}` : "Viewing
all blog posts"}</p>
    </div>
  );
}
```

This achieves the same result but works with the **server component model** in the app directory.

Optional Catch-All Routes: Handling Missing Parameters

Now, there is one limitation with catch-all routes. If a user visits /blog, it will not match the catch-all route (`[...slug].js`) because at least one segment is required. To fix this, we use **`Optional Catch-All Routes`**, defined with **double square brackets (`[[...param]]`)**.

Defining an Optional Catch-All Route

```
src/
├── pages/
│   ├── blog/
│   │   ├── [[...slug]].js  // Optional Catch-All Route
```

Inside **`blog/[[...slug]].js`**:

```
import { useRouter } from 'next/router';
export default function BlogPage() {
const router = useRouter();
const { slug } = router.query; // Can be undefined or an array
return (
    <div>
      <h1>Blog</h1>
      {slug ? (
        <p>Viewing category: {slug.join(" / ")}</p>
      ) : (
        <p>Viewing all blog posts</p>
      )}
    </div>
  );
}
```

Now, this single file can handle:

- `/blog (Shows all posts)`
- `/blog/javascript (Filters by category)`
- `/blog/javascript/react (Filters by subcategory)`

Catch-All Routes in the App Directory

Similarly, in the app directory:

```
src/
├── app/
│   ├── blog/
│   │   ├── [[...slug]]/
│   │   │   ├── page.js
```

Inside **blog/[[...slug]]/page.js**:

```
export default function BlogPage({ params }) {
 const { slug } = params; // Can be undefined or an array

  return (
    <div>
      <h1>Blog</h1>
      {slug ? (
        <p>Viewing category: {slug.join(" / ")}</p>
      ) : (
        <p>Viewing all blog posts</p>
      )}
    </div>
  );
}
```

Now, **/blog** will be valid, and it gracefully handles missing parameters.

Choosing between Catch-All and Optional Catch-All Routes

Both types of routes are useful, but they serve different purposes:

Use Case	Catch-All ([...param])	Optional Catch-All ([[...param]])
Must have at least **one** segment	Yes	No
Can handle **/route and /route/subroute**	No	Yes
Best for deeply nested paths	Yes	No
Useful for homepages inside dynamic routes	No	Yes

Table 2.5: *Differences between Catch-All and Optional Catch-All Routes*

Catch-all and optional catch-all routes are essential for handling dynamic, nested paths in a scalable way. Whether you are building a documentation site, an e-commerce category system, or a flexible blog, these routes help create a clean, organized structure without duplicating files.

Linking between Pages Using `next/link`

When building a Next.js application, navigation plays a crucial role in enhancing the user experience. Instead of relying on traditional `<a>` tags, Next.js provides an optimized **`<Link>`** component for client-side navigation. Additionally, layouts and nested layouts help create consistent UI structures across different pages, reducing redundancy and improving maintainability.

Use `next/link` Instead of `<a>`

In traditional React applications, navigating between pages using **`<a href="/about">About</a>`** triggers a **full-page reload**. This disrupts the user experience by resetting the JavaScript state. Next.js provides the **`<Link>`** component to handle client-side navigation efficiently, ensuring **faster transitions** without reloading the page.

Basic Usage of next/link

```
import Link from 'next/link';
export default function HomePage() {
  return (
    <div>
      <h1>Welcome to My Website</h1>
      <Link href="/about">Go to About Page</Link>
    </div>
  );
}
```

Clicking the "**`Go to About Page`**" link navigates to **`/about` without reloading the entire page**.

Navigating with Dynamic Paths

For dynamic routes, we can pass parameters inside **`href`**.

```
import { useRouter } from 'next/router';

export default function HomePage() {
  const router = useRouter();

  return (
    <div>
      <h1>Home Page</h1>
      <button onClick={() => router.push('/dashboard')}>Go to
Dashboard</button>
```

```
    </div>
  );
}
```

Clicking the button navigates to **`/dashboard`.**

Prefetching Pages for Faster Navigation

Next.js automatically **pre-fetches** linked pages in the background, speeding up navigation.

```
<Link href="/contact" prefetch={true}>Contact Us</Link>
```

By default, Next.js prefetches links **when they appear in the viewport**.

Layouts and Nested Layouts in Next.js

When building web applications, many pages share common UI elements such as headers, footers, or sidebars. Instead of repeating these elements on every page, Next.js allows us to define layouts.

Defining a Basic Layout

A layout component wraps around pages to maintain a consistent structure.

Example Layout Component (layout.js in pages' directory)

```
export default function Layout ({children}) {
  return (
    <div>
      <header>
        <h1>My Website</h1>
      </header>
      <main>{children}</main>
      <footer>
        <p>© 2025 My Website</p>
      </footer>
    </div>
  );
}
```

Now, we apply this layout to a page:

```
import Layout from '../components/layout';

export default function About() {
  return (
    <Layout>
```

```
      <h2>About Us</h2>
      <p>This is the about page.</p>
    </Layout>
  );
}
```

The header and footer remain persistent across all pages.

Nested Layouts for Specific Sections

Sometimes, different sections of your app may require separate layouts.

Example: Nested Dashboard Layout

```
├── pages/
│   ├── dashboard/
│   │   ├── layout.js    // Dashboard-specific layout
│   │   ├── index.js     // Dashboard home page
│   │   ├── settings.js  // Dashboard settings page
```

Defining dashboard/layout.js

```
export default function DashboardLayout({ children }) {
  return (
    <div>
      <nav>
        <h2>Dashboard Navigation</h2>
      </nav>
      <main>{children}</main>
    </div>
  );
}
```

Using the Layout in **`dashboard/index.js`**

```
import DashboardLayout from './layout';
export default function Dashboard() {

  return (
    <DashboardLayout>
      <h2>Dashboard Home</h2>
    </DashboardLayout>
  );
}
```

Now, the Dashboard Navigation stays persistent across **`/dashboard`** and **`/dashboard/settings`**.

Using Layouts in the App Directory (Next.js 13+)

In the app directory, layouts are defined differently. Instead of wrapping components manually, you use a special layout.js file.

Example Structure

```
src/
├── app/
│   ├── layout.js       // Global layout (applies to all pages)
│   ├── page.js         // Home page
│   ├── dashboard/
│   │   ├── layout.js   // Dashboard-specific layout
│   │   ├── page.js     // Dashboard home
│   │   ├── settings/
│   │   │   ├── page.js // Dashboard settings page
```

Global Layout in **`app/layout.js`**

```
export default function RootLayout({ children }) {
  return (
    <html lang="en">
      <body>
        <header>
          <h1>My Website</h1>
        </header>
        {children}
        <footer>
          <p>© 2025 My Website</p>
        </footer>
      </body>
    </html>
  );
}
```

Every page inside **`app/`** will automatically include the header and footer.

Dashboard-Specific Layout in **`app/dashboard/layout.js`**

```
export default function DashboardLayout({ children }) {
  return (
    <div>
      <nav>
        <h2>Dashboard Navigation</h2>
      </nav>
      {children}
    </div>
  );
}
```

All pages inside/**dashboard** now include the dashboard navigation.

- Layouts help structure your app by providing shared components such as headers and footers.
- Nested layouts ensure that different sections (for example, dashboard) maintain unique structures.
- With Next.js 13+, layouts persist across pages, improving performance.

Conclusion

In this chapter, we explored how file-based routing in Next.js simplifies navigation by automatically mapping files and folders to URL paths. We covered dynamic and nested routes, enabling developers to create flexible URL structures. We also learned about catch-all and optional catch-all routes, which help handle multi-segment paths efficiently.

We then discussed how Next.js optimizes navigation with `<Link>`, ensuring faster client-side transitions. Finally, we explored layouts and nested layouts that help maintain a consistent UI across multiple pages.

In the next chapter, we will dive into Rendering Strategies in Next.js. We will cover:

- Static Site Generation (SSG)
- Server-Side Rendering (SSR)
- Incremental Static Regeneration (ISR)
- Client-Side Rendering (CSR)

Therefore, understanding these strategies will help you optimize performance and user experience based on your project's needs.

Multiple Choice Questions

1. What is file-based routing in Next.js?
   a. A method where routes are manually configured in a separate file.
   b. A system where routes are automatically generated based on the folder structure.
   c. A third-party library for managing routes.
   d. A feature only available in React.
2. How do you define a dynamic route in the pages' directory?
   a. By creating a file with dynamic.js extension
   b. Using curly braces **{param}.js**

   c. Using square brackets **`[param].js`**
   d. By defining the route in **`next.config.js`**

3. What is the purpose of a catch-all route (**`[...param]`**)?
   a. It allows capturing multiple segments in a dynamic route.
   b. It redirects all requests to the homepage.
   c. It prevents errors when a page is not found.
   d. It is only used for API routes.

4. How does **`<Link>`** improve navigation in Next.js?
   a. It adds animations between page transitions.
   b. It enables client-side navigation without full-page reloads.
   c. It automatically fetches data before navigating.
   d. It only works with static pages.

5. How do layouts help in Next.js applications?
   a. They allow creating reusable UI structures such as headers and footers.
   b. They increase the performance of API calls.
   c. They are required for dynamic routes to work.
   d. They automatically generate static pages.

6. What is the difference between **`catch-all ([...param])`** and **`optional catch-all ([[...param]])`** routes?
   a. Optional catch-all routes can match URLs with missing parameters.
   b. Catch-all routes only work in API routes.
   c. Both routes work the same way.
   d. Catch-all routes allow query parameters, while optional catch-all routes do not.

7. Where is the layout.js file placed in the app directory?
   a. Inside the **`components`** folder
   b. Inside the **`api`** folder
   c. Inside the **`app`** folder or any subfolder
   d. Inside the **`styles`** folder

8. How do you define a dynamic route in the app directory?
   a. Using **`[param].js inside app/`**
   b. Using **`[param]/page.js inside app/`**
   c. Using **`param.js inside app/`**
   d. By adding the route to **`next.config.js`**
9. What happens when both **`pages/`** and **`app/`** directories exist in a Next.js project?
   a. Next.js will only use **`pages/`** for routing.
   b. Next.js will prioritize **`app/`** but still support **`pages/`**.
   c. Next.js will throw an error and stop building.
   d. Next.js will merge both directories, and create a single routing system.
10. How can you navigate programmatically in Next.js?
    a. Using **`useNavigation()`** hook
    b. Using **`window.location.href = "/about"`**
    c. Using the **`useRouter().push("/about")`** method
    d. Next.js does not support programmatic navigation.

Answers

1. b
2. c
3. a
4. b
5. a
6. a
7. c
8. b
9. b
10. c

Chapter 3
Rendering Strategies in Next.js

Introduction

Rendering strategies are fundamental to optimizing performance, scalability, and user experience in Next.js applications. Each strategy serves a specific purpose, impacting how content is delivered to users, and how efficiently the application performs under various conditions.

Next.js supports multiple rendering methods, including Server-Side Rendering (SSR), Static Site Generation (SSG), Incremental Static Regeneration (ISR), and Client-Side Rendering (CSR). Understanding these approaches is crucial for building high-performance web applications, as the right choice can enhance page load speeds, improve SEO, and reduce server load.

This chapter explores these rendering strategies in detail, explaining when to use each method based on application requirements. We will also cover how to implement them using built-in Next.js functions such as getServerSideProps, getStaticProps, and getStaticPaths. Additionally, we will discuss the best practices for choosing the right rendering strategy to balance real-time data fetching, static content, and performance optimization.

By the end of this chapter, you will have a solid understanding of how to implement and optimize rendering in Next.js, allowing you to build scalable, efficient, and SEO-friendly web applications with ease.

Structure

In this chapter, the following topics will be covered:

- Understanding SSR, SSG, ISR, and CSR
- Choosing the right rendering strategy
- Implementing SSR with `getServerSideProps`

- Static generation with `getStaticProps` and `getStaticPaths`
- Incremental Static Regeneration (ISR)

Understanding SSR, SSG, ISR and CSR

Next.js provides multiple rendering strategies tailored to specific use cases. Let us explore Server-Side Rendering (SSR), Static Site Generation (SSG), Incremental Static Regeneration (ISR), and Client-Side Rendering (CSR) in detail, including their benefits, limitations, and their work.

Server-Side Rendering (SSR)

Server-Side Rendering generates the HTML of a page on the server for every request. This means when a user accesses a page, the server fetches the necessary data, renders the page, and sends the fully formed HTML to the browser.

Real-time, dynamic data (for example, dashboards, user-specific pages like profiles).

Applications requiring fresh data for every request.

Next.js runs a special function, `` `getServerSideProps` ``, on the server at request time. This function fetches the data, and the HTML is rendered and sent to the browser.

Pros:

- Fresh, dynamic content on every request.
- Improved SEO compared to CSR since the server sends fully rendered HTML.
- Custom logic can be applied on the server such as user authentication or filtering data.

Cons:

- Slower page load due to server-side processing for every request.
- Increased server load during high traffic.

Example:

```
export async function getServerSideProps(context) {
  const res = await fetch('https://api.example.com/data');
  const data = await res.json();
  return { props: { data } };
}

export default function Page({ data }) {
  return <div>{data.content}</div>;
}
```

Static Site Generation (SSG)

SSG generates HTML at build time, creating static files that can be served directly to the user. These files are pre-built and stored on CDN, making them incredibly fast to serve.

However, the content does not change frequently such as blogs, documentation, or marketing websites.

During the build process, Next.js runs the `` `getStaticProps` `` function to fetch data and generate static HTML files. For dynamic routes, `` `getStaticPaths` `` is used to define the paths for which static pages should be created.

Pros:

- Extremely fast page loads since HTML is pre-built and served from a CDN.
- Low server load since no server-side processing is required for each request.
- Excellent for SEO as fully rendered HTML is provided to search engines.

Cons:

- Content updates require a new build and deployment process.
- Not suitable for highly dynamic or user-specific content.

Example:

```
// Static props for static generation
export async function getStaticProps() {
  const res = await fetch('https://api.example.com/data');
  const data = await res.json();
  return { props: { data } };
}

// Dynamic paths for static generation
export async function getStaticPaths() {
  const res = await fetch('https://api.example.com/paths');
  const paths = res.map((item) => ({ params: { id: item.id } }));
  return { paths, fallback: false };
}

export default function Page({ data }) {
  return <div>{data.content}</div>;
}
```

Incremental Static Regeneration (ISR)

ISR is an advanced version of SSG that allows static pages to be updated at runtime without requiring a full rebuild of the site. It is useful for content that changes periodically but does not need to be updated immediately.

- E-commerce product pages or blogs were content changes occasionally.

  Static pages are built at runtime based on the `revalidate` property defined in `getStaticProps`. If a request is made after the revalidation period, Next.js regenerates the page in the background, and updates the static file.

Pros:

- Combines the speed of SSG with the flexibility of dynamic content updates.
- No need for frequent builds or deployments.
- Minimal delay for content updates.

Cons:

- Updates are not instantaneous, leading to a slight delay for users accessing new content.
- Not suitable for applications requiring real-time updates.

Example:

```
export async function getStaticProps() {
  const res = await fetch('https://api.example.com/data');
  const data = await res.json();
  return {
    props: { data },
    revalidate: 60, // Revalidate every 60 seconds
  };
}

export default function Page({ data }) {
  return <div>{data.content}</div>;
}
```

Client-Side Rendering (CSR)

CSR shifts rendering responsibility entirely to the client (browser). The server sends a minimal HTML file with a JavaScript bundle, which fetches data and renders the content in the browser dynamically.

- Highly interactive, real-time applications (for example, chat apps, social media feeds, and so on).
- User-specific content that does not need SEO optimization.

The browser fetches the JavaScript bundle, which then executes on the client side to fetch the data and render the UI.

Pros:

- Suitable for highly dynamic applications where the content depends on user interaction.
- No server-side load since rendering happens entirely in the browser.

Cons:

- Slower initial page load due to the need to download and execute JavaScript.
- Poor SEO compared to SSR and SSG since the content is not pre-rendered.

Example:

```
import { useEffect, useState } from 'react';

export default function Page() {
  const [data, setData] = useState(null);

  useEffect(() => {
    fetch('https://api.example.com/data')
      .then((res) => res.json())
      .then((data) => setData(data));
  }, []);

  return <div>{data ? data.content : 'Loading...'}</div>;
}
```

By understanding and applying these strategies, you can build scalable, high-performance applications tailored to your project's specific needs.

Choosing the Right Rendering Strategy

Selecting the appropriate rendering strategy in Next.js is a critical decision that directly impacts the performance, scalability, and user experience of your application. The decision depends on the nature of your data, how frequently it changes, your SEO requirements, and the user interaction expectations. Let us explore the factors to consider, and how to choose between **Server-Side Rendering (SSR)**, **Static Site Generation (SSG)**, **Incremental Static Regeneration (ISR)**, and **Client-Side Rendering (CSR)** in detail.

Key Factors to Consider

When choosing the right rendering strategy (SSG, SSR, ISR, or CSR) for your application, it's important to evaluate several key factors that influence performance, scalability, and user experience.

- **Data Freshness**
  - Does the data on the page need to be real-time or near-real-time?
  - Is it acceptable for the content to be slightly outdated (for example, by a few minutes or hours)?
- **Frequency of Data Changes**
  - Is the data static, semi-static, or highly dynamic?
  - Static data (for example, marketing pages) can use SSG, while the dynamic data (for example, user dashboards) may require SSR or CSR.
- **SEO Requirements**
  - Does the page need to be optimized for search engines?
  - SSR and SSG provide fully-rendered HTML, making them more SEO-friendly than CSR.
- **Performance Requirements**
  - Does the page need to load instantly, or is some delay acceptable?
  - SSG and ISR offer faster page loads since the content is pre-built and served from a CDN.
- **User-Specific Data**
  - Is the content unique for each user?
  - For personalized experiences, SSR or CSR is often required.
- **Server Load and Traffic**
  - Will your application face heavy traffic?
  - SSG and ISR reduce server load since they serve pre-generated static files, whereas SSR generates content dynamically for each request.

Guidelines for Choosing the Right Strategy

- **Start with Static Content:** Always try to serve static content whenever possible. If your data does not change often, **SSG** is usually the best option due to its performance benefits.
- **Introduce ISR for Semi-Dynamic Content:** If the data changes occasionally, but you do not want to rebuild your site frequently, go with **ISR** to ensure updates without sacrificing speed.
- **Use SSR for Real-Time Content:** If your page needs fresh data for every request, **SSR** is the way to go. This is especially relevant for user-specific pages or applications requiring live data.

- **Fallback to CSR for Fully Dynamic Content:** If the data depends entirely on user interactions and does not need pre-rendering, **CSR** is the most suitable approach. However, be mindful of the slower initial load time and potential SEO limitations.

Examples of Combining Strategies

Modern applications often use a hybrid approach, combining multiple rendering strategies based on the needs of different pages.

- **Example 1: E-commerce Application**
  - Use **SSG** for product category pages (static content).
  - Use **ISR** for product pages to allow periodic updates for inventory and pricing.
  - Use **CSR** for the shopping cart and checkout pages that rely on real-time user data.
- **Example 2: Blogging Platform**
  - Use **SSG** for blog posts and static pages.
  - Use **ISR** to update trending blogs or featured articles.
  - Use **SSR** for the user dashboard that shows personalized recommendations.

Choosing the right rendering strategy in Next.js requires evaluating the nature of your application's data, its update frequency, and the user experience you want to deliver. Often, a hybrid approach–combining SSR, SSG, ISR and CSR–will yield the best results. By carefully matching each strategy to your application's requirements, you can optimize performance, scalability, and user satisfaction effectively.

Design Patterns Based on Next.js Rendering Strategies

Design patterns help structure applications in a way that aligns with the best practices, making them maintainable, scalable, and performant. Based on **Server-Side Rendering (SSR)**, **Static Site Generation (SSG)**, **Incremental Static Regeneration (ISR)**, and **Client-Side Rendering (CSR)** in Next.js, several design patterns can be applied depending on your application's requirements.

Server-Side Rendering (SSR)

Server-Side Rendering (SSR) is ideal for delivering dynamic, personalized, and secure content by generating HTML on each request, ensuring that users always receive the most up-to-date data.

- **Dynamic Content Delivery**
  - Applications with frequently changing, real-time data (for example, dashboards and user-specific content).
  - Use the **getServerSideProps** function to fetch data at request time, and render dynamic content on the server.
  - Benefits:
    - Fresh data for each request.
    - Personalized experiences with server-side logic.
  - Example Implementation:

```
export async function getServerSideProps(context) {
  const user = await getUser(context.req.cookies.token); //
User-specific data
  const data = await fetch(`https://api.example.com/data?user
=${user.id}`);
  return { props: { data } };
}

export default function Dashboard({ data }) {
  return <div>Welcome, {data.userName}!</div>;
}
```

- **Protected SSR Pages**
  - Pages behind authentication that require server-side validation.
  - Add authentication logic in **getServerSideProps** to restrict access.
  - Benefits:
    - Ensures secure, server-side validation.
    - Avoids exposing the sensitive data in the client.
  - Example Implementation:

```
export async function getServerSideProps(context) {
  const token = context.req.cookies.token;
  if (!token) {
    return { redirect: { destination: '/login', permanent:
false } };
  }
  const data = await fetchData(token);
  return { props: { data } };
}

export default function Profile({ data }) {
  return <div>{data.name}'s Profile</div>;
}
```

Static Site Generation (SSG)

- **Pre-Built Pages**
  - Content that rarely changes such as blogs, documentation, or marketing pages.
  - Use **`getStaticProps`** to pre-fetch and build static content during build time.
  - Benefits:
    - Blazing fast performance with CDN distribution.
    - Great for SEO since pages are pre-rendered.
  - Example Implementation:

```
export async function getStaticProps() {
  const res = await fetch('https://api.example.com/posts');
  const posts = await res.json();
  return { props: { posts } };
}

export default function Blog({ posts }) {
  return posts.map(post => <div key={post.id}>{post.title}</
div>);
}
```

- **Static Dynamic Routes**
  - Dynamic routes for static content (for example, individual blog posts).
  - Combine **`getStaticProps`** with **`getStaticPaths`**.
  - Benefits:
    - Allows dynamic routes to benefit from static generation.
    - Scalable for pages with pre-determined content.
  - Example Implementation:

```
export async function getStaticPaths() {
  const res = await fetch('https://api.example.com/posts');
  const posts = await res.json();
  return {
    paths: posts.map(post => ({ params: { id: post.id.to-
String() } })),
    fallback: false,
  };
}
export async function getStaticProps({ params }) {
  const res = await fetch(`https://api.example.com/
```

```
posts/${params.id}`);
  const post = await res.json();
  return { props: { post } };
}
export default function Post({ post }) {
  return <div>{post.title}</div>;
}
```

Incremental Static Regeneration (ISR)

- **Hybrid Content Updates**
  - Semi-static content that updates periodically such as e-commerce product details.
  - Use **getStaticProps** with a revalidate property to specify the revalidation interval.
  - Benefits:
    - Combines the speed of static generation with dynamic updates.
    - Avoids frequent full site rebuilds.
  - Example Implementation:

```
export async function getStaticProps() {
  const res = await fetch('https://api.example.com/products');
  const products = await res.json();
  return { props: { products }, revalidate: 60 }; // Update
every 60 seconds
}
export default function Products({ products }) {
  return products.map(product => <div key={product.id}>
{product.name}</div>);
}
```

- **Optimized API-Driven ISR**
  - Content updates driven by external API changes (for example, CMS-driven websites).
  - Use ISR to regenerate pages only when triggered by a CMS webhook.
  - Benefits:
    - Efficient updates without unnecessary rebuilds.
    - Flexible integration with external systems.
  - Example Implementation:

```
export async function getStaticProps() {
  const res = await fetch('https://api.cms.com/data');
  const data = await res.json();
```

```
  return { props: { data }, revalidate: 10 }; // Short
interval for rapid updates
}
```

Client-Side Rendering (CSR)

- **SPA-Like User Interactivity**
  - Applications with real-time, interactive features (for example, chat apps, dashboards, and so on).
  - Fetch data on the client using React hooks such as **useEffect**.
  - Benefits:
    - User-specific, real-time interactivity.
    - Minimal server-side processing.
  - Example Implementation:

```
import { useEffect, useState } from 'react';
export default function Page() {
  const [data, setData] = useState(null);

  useEffect(() => {
    fetch('https://api.example.com/data')
      .then(res => res.json())
      .then(data => setData(data));
  }, []);
  return data ? <div>{data.content}</div> : <div>Loading...</
div>;
}
```

- **Lazy Loading for Heavy Content**
  - Pages with large data sets or components that load after user interaction.
  - Use dynamic imports or conditional rendering to optimize performance.
  - Benefits:
    - Reduces initial load time.
    - Improves perceived performance for the user.
  - Example Implementation:

```
import dynamic from 'next/dynamic';
const HeavyComponent = dynamic(() => import('../components/
HeavyComponent'));
export default function Page() {
  return (
    <div>
      <h1>Page Title</h1>
```

```
            <HeavyComponent />
        </div>
    );
}
```

- **Hybrid Patterns (Combining Strategies)**
    - Mixed Rendering for Multi-Purpose Applications
    - Applications with diverse needs (for example, e-commerce sites).
    - Combine SSR, SSG, ISR, and CSR based on page-specific requirements.
    - Benefits:
        - Tailored optimization for each type of content.
        - Maximum flexibility and performance.
    - Example Implementation for E-Commerce:
        - **SSG:** Category pages (rarely change).
        - **ISR:** Product pages (periodically updated).
        - **SSR:** Checkout or user dashboards.
        - **CSR:** Shopping cart for real-time updates.

Thus, by applying these, you can optimize your Next.js application to meet performance, scalability, and interactivity goals. Also, carefully choose and combine rendering strategies based on the nature of your application and its data requirements, ensuring that each page or component is designed for maximum efficiency.

Implementing SSR with `getServerSideProps`

Server-Side Rendering (SSR) in Next.js enables you to fetch data on every request, and generate the HTML dynamically on the server before sending it to the client. This approach ensures that users always receive fresh and up-to-date content, making it ideal for applications that require real-time data or user-specific information.

The **`getServerSideProps`** function runs on the server during the request lifecycle. It fetches data, performs computations, or runs server-side logic, and passes the resulting data as props to the React component for rendering.

Key Characteristics:

- **Runs on the server:** This function is never executed on the client side.
- **Executed on every request:** Ensures data freshness.
- **Ideal for dynamic data:** For pages requiring personalized or real-time information.

- **SEO-friendly:** Fully rendered HTML is sent to the browser, making it easier for search engines to crawl.

Syntax of `getServerSideProps`

The function must be exported from a page file. It receives a context object, and returns an object with props, redirect, or notFound.

```
export async function getServerSideProps(context) {
  // Fetch or compute data
  const data = await fetchData();

  return {
    props: { data }, // Pass data to the page component
  };
}
```

Context Object

The context parameter provides useful information to fetch or compute data for the current request. Its key properties include:

- **`params`:** Dynamic route parameters.
- **`req` and `res`:** Incoming request and response objects (useful for cookies, headers, and so on.).
- **`query`**: Query string parameters in the URL.
- **`resolvedUrl`**: The full resolved URL, including query strings.
- **`preview` and `previewData`:** For handling preview modes.

Example:

```
export async function getServerSideProps(context) {
  const { params, query, req } = context;
  console.log('Dynamic Route:', params.id);
  console.log('Query Params:', query);
  console.log('User-Agent:', req.headers['user-agent']);

  return { props: {} };
}
```

Basic Example of SSR fetch and display real-time data from an API:

```
export async function getServerSideProps() {
  const res = await fetch('https://api.example.com/data');
  const data = await res.json();

  return {
```

```
    props: { data }, // Pass data to the component
  };
}

export default function Page({ data }) {
  return (
    <div>
      <h1>Data from Server:</h1>
      <pre>{JSON.stringify(data, null, 2)}</pre>
    </div>
  );
}
```

Handling Dynamic Routes with SSR

Dynamic routes are common in SSR, especially when fetching data for individual items.

File Structure Example:

```
pages/
  post/
       [id].js
```

Dynamic Route Example:

```
export async function getServerSideProps(context) {
  const { id } = context.params; // Extract dynamic route
parameter
  const res = await fetch(`https://api.example.com/posts/${id}`);

  if (!res.ok) {
       return { notFound: true }; // Return 404 if data not found
  }

  const post = await res.json();
  return {
       props: { post },
  };
}

export default function Post({ post }) {
  return (
       <div>
         <h1>{post.title}</h1>
         <p>{post.body}</p>
       </div>
  );
}
```

Error Handling in SSR

You can handle errors gracefully by returning custom responses or redirecting users.

Returning 404:

```
export async function getServerSideProps(context) {
  const res = await fetch('https://api.example.com/data');

  if (!res.ok) {
      return { notFound: true }; // Returns a 404 page
  }

  const data = await res.json();
  return { props: { data } };
}
```

Redirecting to Another Page:

```
export async function getServerSideProps(context) {
  const res = await fetch('https://api.example.com/user');
  const user = await res.json();

  if (!user.isLoggedIn) {
      return {
        redirect: {
            destination: '/login',
            permanent: false, // Temporary redirect
        },
      };
  }

  return { props: { user } };
}
```

SSR with Authentication

SSR is commonly used to implement protected routes by validating user authentication on the server.

Handling Dynamic Routes with SSR

Dynamic routes are common in SSR, particularly when fetching data for individual items.

File Structure Example:

```
pages/
  post/
      [id].js
```

Dynamic Route Example:

```
export async function getServerSideProps(context) {
  const { id } = context.params; // Extract dynamic route
parameter
  const res = await fetch(`https://api.example.com/posts/${id}`);

  if (!res.ok) {
      return { notFound: true }; // Return 404 if data not found
  }

  const post = await res.json();
  return {
      props: { post },
  };
}

export default function Post({ post }) {
  return (
      <div>
        <h1>{post.title}</h1>
        <p>{post.body}</p>
      </div>
  );
}
```

Error Handling in SSR

You can handle errors gracefully by returning custom responses or redirecting users.

Returning 404:

```
export async function getServerSideProps(context) {
  const res = await fetch('https://api.example.com/data');

  if (!res.ok) {
      return { notFound: true }; // Returns a 404 page
  }
```

```
  const data = await res.json();
  return { props: { data } };
}
```

Redirecting to Another Page:

```
export async function getServerSideProps(context) {
  const res = await fetch('https://api.example.com/user');
  const user = await res.json();

  if (!user.isLoggedIn) {
      return {
        redirect: {
            destination: '/login',
            permanent: false, // Temporary redirect
        },
      };
  }

  return { props: { user } };
}
```

SSR with Authentication

SSR is commonly used to implement protected routes by validating user authentication on the server.

```
export async function getServerSideProps(context) {
  const token = context.req.cookies.token;

  // Check if token exists
  if (!token) {
    return {
      redirect: {
        destination: '/login',
        permanent: false,
      },
    };
  }

  const user = await fetchUserFromToken(token);
  if (!user) {
    return { notFound: true }; // User not found, return 404
  }

  return { props: { user } };
}
```

```
export default function Profile({ user }) {
  return (
    <div>
      <h1>Welcome, {user.name}</h1>
    </div>
  );
}
```

Advantages of SSR

SSR offers several strengths that make it a powerful choice for delivering dynamic, real-time, and personalized content in modern web applications.

- **Dynamic Content:** Fresh data for every request, making it suitable for applications with frequently changing data.
- **SEO Optimization:** Fully rendered HTML is served to search engines.
- **Security:** Sensitive logic and data fetching occur on the server, reducing exposure to the client.

Limitations of SSR

Despite its benefits, SSR also introduces certain challenges and trade-offs that must be considered when deciding whether it's the right rendering strategy for your use case.

- **Performance:** Each request involves server-side computation, increasing latency.
- **Scalability:** High traffic can increase the server load.
- **Complexity:** Managing the state, error handling, and server-side logic adds complexity.

Best Practices for SSR

Follow these best practices to make server-side rendering fast, secure, and maintainable while minimizing server cost and complexity.

- **Optimize Data Fetching:**
  - Avoid unnecessary API calls by batching or caching data.
  - Use services with fast response times to reduce latency.
- **Minimize Props Size:**
  - Only send the essential data to the client to reduce payload size.

- **Combine with CSR:**
  - Fetch the critical data on the server and the non-critical or interactive data on the client using useEffect.

Example:

```
export async function getServerSideProps() {
  const res = await fetch('https://api.example.com/critical-data');
  const criticalData = await res.json();

  return {
    props: { criticalData },
  };
}

export default function Page({ criticalData }) {
  const [nonCriticalData, setNonCriticalData] = useState(null);

  useEffect(() => {
    fetch('https://api.example.com/non-critical-data')
      .then((res) => res.json())
      .then((data) => setNonCriticalData(data));
  }, []);

  return (
    <div>
      <div>{criticalData}</div>
      <div>{nonCriticalData ? nonCriticalData : 'Loading...'}</
div>
    </div>
  );
}
```

By implementing **`getServerSideProps`** effectively, you can build dynamic and user-friendly applications, while ensuring SEO optimization and fresh content for every user request.

Static Generation with `getStaticProps` and `getStaticPaths`

Next.js supports **Static Generation (SSG)**, which pre-renders pages at build time to serve them as static HTML. This approach improves performance and SEO since the pages are ready to be delivered without extra computation on the server.

To implement Static Generation, Next.js provides two important functions:

- **getStaticProps:** Retrieves data during the build process, and provides it as props to the page component.
- **getStaticPaths:** Specifies which dynamic routes need to be pre-rendered during the build.

getStaticProps: Fetch Data at Build Time

getStaticProps is used in a page component to fetch data at build time. The fetched data is then passed as props to the component.

```
export async function getStaticProps() {
 // Fetch data from an API, database, or file system
  const response = await fetch('https://api.example.com/posts');
                const posts = await response.json();

                 return {
                    props: {
                       posts, // This will be passed as props to
the component
                     },
                    };
                 }
```

- **getStaticProps runs only at build time**, not at runtime.
- The data is **statically generated** into the HTML.
- It **does not run on the client-side**.
- It is used only in **page components**, not in regular React components.
- Useful for fetching **public and non-user-specific data** (for example, blog posts, products, and so on).

```
const BlogPage = ({ posts }) => {
  return (
    <div>
      <h1>Blog Posts</h1>
      <ul>
        {posts.map((post) => (
          <li key={post.id}>{post.title}</li>
        ))}
      </ul>
    </div>
  );
};

export default BlogPage;
```

```
export async function getStaticProps() {
  const response = await fetch('https://api.example.com/posts');
  const posts = await response.json();

  return {
    props: {
      posts,
    },
  };
}
```

This page will be generated once at build time, and served statically.

`getStaticPaths`: Define Dynamic Routes at Build Time

When working with dynamic routes (for example, **`/posts/[id]`**), Next.js needs to know which pages to pre-render at build time. **`getStaticPaths`** helps define these dynamic paths.

```
export async function getStaticPaths() {
  // Fetch the list of posts (or items that need pages)
  const response = await fetch('https://api.example.com/posts');
  const posts = await response.json();

  // Generate paths for each post
  const paths = posts.map((post) => ({
    params: { id: post.id.toString() }, // Must be a string
  }));

  return {
    paths, // Paths that should be generated at build time
    fallback: false, // Control behavior for non-existent pages
  };
}
```

- It is used only with dynamic routes (for example, **`[id].js`**).
- It returns an array of paths that should be pre-rendered.
- The params inside paths must be strings.
- The fallback option controls how non-predefined routes behave.

Example with a Dynamic Page:

Create a page at **`pages/posts/[id].js`** to show the individual blog posts.

```
const PostPage = ({ post }) => {
  return (
```

```
    <div>
      <h1>{post.title}</h1>
      <p>{post.body}</p>
    </div>
  );
};

export default PostPage;

export async function getStaticPaths() {
  const response = await fetch('https://api.example.com/posts');
  const posts = await response.json();

  const paths = posts.map((post) => ({
    params: { id: post.id.toString() },
  }));

  return {
    paths,
    fallback: false, // No fallback for non-existing routes
  };
}

export async function getStaticProps({ params }) {
  const response = await fetch(`https://api.example.com/
posts/${params.id}`);
  const post = await response.json();

  return {
    props: {
      post,
    },
  };
}
```

It Works: `getStaticPaths` fetches all post IDs and generates paths like:

```
/posts/1
/posts/2
/posts/3
```

`getStaticProps` fetches the data for each post and passes it to the component.

The pages are pre-built and served as static files.

Fallback in getStaticPaths

The fallback property in **getStaticPaths** controls what happens when a requested path is not pre-generated. Options:

- **false**: Only predefined pages are generated. Any other path will return a 404.
- **true**: New pages are generated dynamically at runtime (useful for large datasets).
- **'blocking'**: Similar to true, but waits until the page is generated before displaying anything.

Example with **fallback: true**

```
export async function getStaticPaths() {
  return {
    paths: [{ params: { id: '1' } }, { params: { id: '2' } }],
    fallback: true, // Other pages will be generated dynamically
  };
}
```

If a user visits **/posts/3**, Next.js will generate the page on-demand and cache it.

This is useful for large datasets where pre-generating all pages is impractical.

Revalidating Pages (getStaticProps with revalidate)

Next.js allows updating static pages without rebuilding the entire site using the revalidate option.

```
export async function getStaticProps() {
  const response = await fetch('https://api.example.com/posts');
  const posts = await response.json();

  return {
    props: { posts },
    revalidate: 10, // Re-fetch data every 10 seconds
  };
}
```

The page will be statically generated but updated every 10 seconds.

This is called Incremental Static Regeneration (ISR).

- **getStaticProps**: Fetches data at build time, and pre-renders pages.
- **getStaticPaths**: Generates dynamic routes at build time.
- fallback controls how Next.js handles non-predefined routes.
- Use revalidates to update static pages without rebuilding the whole app.

The following table explains that getStaticProps fetches data at build time for static pages, while getStaticPaths generates multiple dynamic pages. Both improve performance and SEO. Use getStaticProps for static content such as homepages and getStaticPaths for dynamic routes like blog posts or product pages. They run before deployment.

Feature	**getStaticProps**	**getStaticPaths**
Purpose	Used to fetch and provide static data at build time	Used to define dynamic routes and generate pages
Execution Time	Runs **at build time** before deployment	Runs **at build time** before deployment
Usage	Suitable for **static pages** that don't change often	Suitable for **dynamic pages** with variable paths
Page Generation	Generates **a single page** with static content	Generates **multiple pages** based on dynamic paths
Return Value	Returns `{ props: { data } }`, which contains the static page data	Returns `{ paths: [...], fallback: true/false }`, which defines generated paths
Access to Parameters	Can access params to fetch specific data for a page	Uses params to create paths for dynamic pages
Component Scope	Can **only be used inside pages/**	Can **only be used inside pages/**
Performance	Provides **faster page loads** by pre-rendering	Improves performance by **pre-generating multiple pages**
Best Use Cases	Ideal for **homepage, blog list, product listing** pages	Best for **individual blog posts, product details, documentation pages**

Table 3.1: *Use of* `getstaticPros` *and* `getStaticPaths`

Incremental Static Regeneration (ISR)

Incremental Static Regeneration (ISR) is a powerful feature in Next.js that allows static pages to be updated after deployment without requiring a full site rebuild. This feature combines the speed of static generation with the flexibility of dynamic updates, making it perfect for websites that need frequent content updates without sacrificing performance.

In traditional static site generation, all pages are pre-built at build time. However, if any content needs updating, the entire site must be rebuilt and redeployed. ISR solves this problem by allowing individual pages to regenerate in the background after a specified time interval, ensuring that content stays fresh without rebuilding the whole application.

ISR works by following a step-by-step process to update static pages incrementally:

1. **Build-Time Page Generation**
    a. When the website is first deployed, Next.js generates static pages using `getStaticProps`.
    b. These pages are served instantly to visitors from the cache, ensuring fast performance.
2. **Serving Cached Pages**
    a. When a user visits the page, they see the pre-built version that was generated at build time.
    b. This ensures that users experience a fast-loading page without any delay.
3. **Revalidation and Background Regeneration**
    a. A `revalidate` time is set in `getStaticProps`, defining how often the page should be updated.
    b. If a new request is made after the revalidation period, Next.js fetches the fresh data in the background, and updates the page.
4. **Updated Page Delivery**
    a. While the new page is being generated, users still see the old, cached version.
    b. Once the update is complete, Next.js serves the new version to the next user who visits the page.

This entire process allows pages to be updated without requiring a full website rebuild, making it an efficient way to manage frequently updated content.

Benefits of ISR

ISR provides several advantages over traditional static site generation and server-side rendering:

- **Faster Performance:** Since pages are pre-rendered, they load instantly without waiting for server responses.
- **Automatic Updates:** Content is updated dynamically without redeploying the entire site.
- **SEO Optimization:** Since pages are pre-built, search engines can easily index them.

- **Reduced Build Times:** Large sites do not need to regenerate every page during a rebuild, saving time and resources.
- **Scalability:** Handles high traffic efficiently by serving the static content, while still keeping it up-to-date.

Using ISR in Next.js

To enable ISR, modify the `` `getStaticProps` `` function by adding a `` `revalidate` `` property:

```
export async function getStaticProps() {
  const res = await fetch('https://api.example.com/posts');
  const data = await res.json();

  return {
    props: { posts: data },
    revalidate: 10, // Page regenerates every 10 seconds
  };
}
```

This Code works in the following manner:

- The page is pre-generated at build time using `` `getStaticProps` ``.
- The `` `revalidate: 10` `` means the page will be updated every 10 seconds if there is a new request.
- Users see the cached version until a new one is generated in the background.
- The next user gets the updated page without delays.

ISR is useful for websites that need frequent updates but do not require real-time data. It is ideal for:

- **Blogs and News Websites:** Articles can be updated without redeploying the site.
- **E-commerce Stores:** Product pages can reflect inventory changes dynamically.
- **Marketing Websites:** Landing pages can be refreshed periodically.
- **Documentation Pages:** Docs can be updated without affecting other pages.

Conclusion

In this chapter, we explored various data-fetching methods in Next.js, including Server-Side Rendering (SSR), Static Site Generation (SSG), Incremental Static Regeneration (ISR), and Client-Side Rendering (CSR). We learned how to choose the right rendering strategy based on performance, SEO, and data freshness requirements. We also implemented SSR with getServerSideProps, SSG with **`getStaticProps`** as well as

`getStaticPaths`, and ISR to update static pages dynamically. These techniques help in building efficient and scalable web applications.

In the next chapter, we will dive into API Routes in Next.js, and understanding how to create backend functionalities within a Next.js app.

Multiple Choice Questions

1. Which rendering method in Next.js pre-generates pages at build time, and does not update them unless the site is rebuilt?
   a. Server-Side Rendering (SSR)
   b. Static Site Generation (SSG)
   c. Incremental Static Regeneration (ISR)
   d. Client-Side Rendering (CSR)
2. Which Next.js function is used to implement Server-Side Rendering (SSR)?
   a. `getStaticProps`
   b. `getServerSideProps`
   c. `getStaticPaths`
   d. `revalidate`
3. What is the key benefit of Incremental Static Regeneration (ISR) in Next.js?
   a. It allows pages to update without rebuilding the entire site.
   b. It fetches data on every request, improving real-time updates.
   c. It only supports client-side JavaScript rendering.
   d. It requires manual re-deployment to update pages.
4. When should you use getStaticPaths in Next.js?
   a. When generating dynamic pages at build time
   b. When fetching data on every request
   c. When only using client-side rendering
   d. When handling API routes in Next.js

5. Which approach is best suited for implementing authentication in Server-Side Rendering (SSR) with Next.js?

   a. Fetch authentication data in `getStaticProps`

   b. Use `getServerSideProps` to validate user sessions on each request

   c. Store authentication tokens in local storage only

   d. Perform authentication checks exclusively on the client side

Answers

1. b
2. b
3. a
4. a
5. b

CHAPTER 4

API Routes in Next.js

Introduction

In modern web development, building full-stack applications requires seamless integration between the frontend and backend. Next.js simplifies this process by providing built-in support for API routes, allowing developers to create backend functionality without a separate server. These routes, located in the **`pages/api/`** directory, automatically map to RESTful endpoints, enabling traditional CRUD operations. For example, a file named **`pages/api/users.js`** creates an endpoint at **`/api/users`**, where you can handle user-related logic.

This chapter introduces you to creating and managing API routes in Next.js. You will learn how to build RESTful APIs to handle HTTP methods such as **`GET`**, **`POST`**, **`PUT`**, and **`DELETE`**. For instance, a **`GET`** request can fetch a list of products, while a **`POST`** request can handle form submissions. We will explore server-side execution, ensuring security for sensitive operations like authentication. You will also discover how to deploy these routes as serverless functions for better scalability and performance.

Next.js also supports GraphQL, offering a flexible approach to data fetching. By integrating Apollo Server within API routes, developers can define a single endpoint to handle queries and mutations, reducing issues such as over-fetching and under-fetching found in REST APIs. This method improves efficiency, making it ideal for modern applications requiring optimized data handling. Hence, whether using REST or GraphQL, Next.js provides a powerful backend solution for full-stack development.

Structure

In this chapter, the following topics will be covered:

- Understanding the Basics of APIs
- Creating API routes in the **`/api`** directory
- Handling query parameters in API routes
- Middleware in API routes

- Building RESTful APIs with Next.js
- Using API routes with external APIs

Understanding the Basics of APIs

Before diving into creating API routes, it is essential to understand what an API (Application Programming Interface) is. An API defines a set of rules and protocols that enable communication between different software applications. In web development, APIs play a crucial role in retrieving, sending, updating, and deleting data from a server, allowing seamless interaction between the frontend and backend of a web application.

Real-Life Analogy

Think of an API as a waiter in a restaurant:

- You (the client) tell the waiter what you want (for example, "I want pizza").
- The waiter takes your request to the kitchen (the server).
- The kitchen prepares the food (processes the request).
- The waiter brings the food back to you (the response).

In web terms

You (the frontend) ask the server for data (for example, "Give me a list of users").

The server processes your request, and sends back the data (for example, a list of users in JSON format). The key concepts for APIs work as follows:

- **Request:** When you ask the server for data (example, "Give me the weather for London").
- **Response:** The data the server sends back (example, the current temperature in London).
- **Endpoint:** The URL you use to make the request (example, https://api.weather.com/data).
- **HTTP Methods:** Actions you can perform such as:
  - `GET`: Retrieve data (for example, fetch a list of users).
  - `POST`: Send data (for example, create a new user).
  - `PUT/PATCH`: Update data (for example, update a user's details).
  - `DELETE`: Remove data (for example, delete a user).

Example of an API Request:

Let us say you want to fetch a list of users from a server. You might use an API endpoint like:

```
GET https://api.example.com/users
The server responds with:
[
  { "id": 1, "name": "John" },
  { "id": 2, "name": "Jane" }
]
```

Understanding JSON

JSON (JavaScript Object Notation) is a lightweight format for storing and transferring data. It is easy for humans to read and write, and easy for machines to parse and generate.

Example of JSON format:

```
{
  "name": "John",
  "age": 30,
  "isStudent": false,
  "courses": ["Math", "Science"]
}
```

JSON Important: Most APIs use JSON to send and receive data.

When you fetch data from an API, it is often returned in JSON format.

Creating API Routes in the /api Directory in Next.js

API routes allow you to create backend functionality–such as handling form submissions, fetching data from a database, or integrating with third-party APIs–without needing a separate backend server.

Understanding API Routes

API routes in Next.js are server-side functions that enable you to create RESTful APIs or handle server-side logic. These routes are defined as files inside the /api directory, and Next.js automatically treats them as serverless functions (or API endpoints) accessible via HTTP requests.

Creating API Routes

Creating API routes in Next.js is straightforward, and follows a clear directory structure.

- **Directory Structure:** In a Next.js project, you create a folder named `api` inside the `pages` directory. Any file added inside this folder is treated as an API route. Example structure:

```
/
api/
users.js
posts/
index.js
[id].js
```

- **Basic API Route Example:** Create a simple API route that returns a JSON response:

```
 // pages/api/hello.js
export default function handler(req, res) {
  res.status(200).json({ message: 'Hello, world!' });
}
This creates an endpoint at `/api/hello`, returning:
{ "message": "Hello, world!"}
```

- **Handling HTTP Methods:** API routes can handle HTTP methods such as `GET`, `POST`, `PUT` and `DELETE`. Use `req.method` to determine the method and write logic accordingly:

```
  // pages/api/users.js
 export default function handler(req, res) {
   if (req.method === 'GET') {
     res.status(200).json({ message: 'Fetching users' });
   } else if (req.method === 'POST') {
     res.status(201).json({ message: 'User created' });
   } else {
     res.status(405).json({ message: 'Method not allowed' });
   }
}
```

- **Dynamic API Routes:** Use square brackets (`[]`) in the file name to create dynamic routes. For example:

```
 // pages/api/posts/[id].js
  export default function handler(req, res) {
    const { id } = req.query; // Access the dynamic parameter
    res.status(200).json({ postId: id, message: 'Post details'
});
  }
```

This creates an endpoint like `/api/posts/123`, where `123` is the dynamic `id` parameter.

- **Accessing Query Parameters:** Use `req.query` to access query parameters:

```
// pages/api/search.js
export default function handler(req, res) {
  const { q } = req.query; // Access query parameter ?q=some-
thing
  res.status(200).json({ query: q });
}

Visiting `/api/search?q=nextjs` returns:
{
  "query": "nextjs"
}
```

- **Accessing Request Body:** For `POST`, `PUT`, or `PATCH` requests, access the request body using `req.body`:

```
// pages/api/submit.js
export default function handler (req, res) {
  if (req.method === 'POST') {
    const { name, email } = req.body;
    res.status(200).json({ name, email });
  } else {
    res.status(405).json({ message: 'Method not allowed' });
  }
}
```

Key Features of API Routes

API routes in Next.js come with several powerful features that make them versatile and efficient. These include:

- **Serverless Functions**: API routes are deployed as serverless functions, meaning they are stateless and scale automatically.
- **Built-in Middleware**: Next.js provides middleware for parsing incoming requests (for example, `req.body` for JSON payloads).
- **Environment Variables**: Use `.env.local` to securely store sensitive information like API keys or database credentials.
- **CORS Support**: By default, API routes are same-origin only. Use libraries such as CORS to enable Cross-Origin Resource Sharing.
- **TypeScript Support**: Define types for your API routes to ensure type safety.

Example: Building a CRUD API

Let us build a simple CRUD API to manage a list of users. This example demonstrates how to create, read, and fetch user data using API routes.

- **Create a User**

```
// pages/api/users.js
let users = [];
export default function handler(req, res) {
  if (req.method === 'POST') {
    const { name, email } = req.body;
    const newUser = { id: users.length + 1, name, email };
    users.push(newUser);
    res.status(201).json(newUser);
  } else if (req.method === 'GET') {
    res.status(200).json(users);
  } else {
    res.status(405).json({ message: 'Method not allowed' });
  }
}
```

- **Get User by ID**

```
// pages/api/users/[id].js
let users = [{ id: 1, name: 'John', email: 'john@example.com' }];
export default function handler(req, res) {
  const { id } = req.query;
  const user = users.find(u => u.id === parseInt(id));
  if (user) {
    res.status(200).json(user);
  } else {
    res.status(404).json({ message: 'User not found' });
  }
}
```

Best Practices

The following best practices ensure that your API routes are secure, scalable, and maintainable:

- **Keep API Routes Stateless:** Avoid storing state in memory; use a database or external storage.
- **Validate Input:** Always validate and sanitize user input to prevent security vulnerabilities.
- **Use Environment Variables:** Store sensitive information like API keys securely.

- **Handle Errors Gracefully:** Return appropriate HTTP status codes and error messages.
- **Use Middleware for Common Tasks:** Implement middleware for tasks such as authentication or logging.

Handling Query Parameters in API Routes

Query parameters allow users to pass the dynamic data in API requests, enabling flexible filtering, searching, and data retrieval. In Next.js, API routes handle query parameters using the **`req.query`** object which extracts values from the URL, and makes them available for processing. This feature is particularly useful for building dynamic endpoints that respond based on user input.

Accessing Query Parameters

When a request includes query parameters, they can be accessed using **`req.query`**. Consider the following example of an API route in **`pages/api/user.js`**.

```
export default function handler(req, res) {
    const { id, name } = req.query; // Extract query parameters
    res.status(200).json({ message: `User ID: ${id}, Name: ${name}` });
}
```

If a client sends a request to:

```
GET /api/user?id=123&name=Shubham
```

The API will respond with:

```
{ "message": "User ID: 123, Name: Shubham" }
```

Handling Optional and Default Values

Not all query parameters are required in every request. Therefore, to ensure smooth processing, default values can be assigned. For example:

```
export default function handler(req, res) {
  const { id = "unknown", name = "Guest" } = req.query;
  res.status(200).json({ message: `User ID: ${id}, Name: ${name}` });
}
```

In this case, if id or name is missing, the API will return the default values. For instance, a request to **`/api/user`** will respond with:

```
{"message": "User ID: unknown, Name: Guest"}
```

Handling Multiple Query Parameters

If a parameter appears multiple times in the URL, Next.js automatically converts it into an array. Consider the following request:

```
GET /api/user?id=101&id=102
```

Next.js will interpret id as an array:

```
{ "id": ["101", "102"] }
```

To process multiple values, you can modify the handler:

```
export default function handler(req, res) {
  const { id } = req.query;
  res.status(200).json({ message: `User IDs: ${Array.isArray(id)
? id.join(", ") : id}`    });
}
```

This ensures that the API correctly handles single or multiple values. For example:

A request to **`/api/user?id=101`** will return:

```
{"message": "User IDs: 101"}
```

A request to **`/api/user?id=101&id=102`** will return:

```
{"message": "User IDs: 101, 102"}
```

Best Practices for Handling Query Parameters

Handling query parameters effectively requires following the best practices to ensure security, reliability, and a seamless user experience. By implementing these guidelines, you can build robust API routes that handle dynamic input gracefully and securely.

- **Validate Input:** Always validate and sanitize query parameters to prevent security vulnerabilities.
- **Use Default Values:** Assign default values for optional parameters to ensure consistent behavior.
- **Handle Arrays Gracefully:** Check if a parameter is an array using **`Array.isArray()`** before processing.
- **Document Your API:** Clearly document the expected query parameters and their behavior for API consumers.

Middleware in API Routes

Middleware is a powerful concept in web development that allows you to process requests before they reach the main logic of your API. In Next.js, middleware functions can be used in API routes to perform tasks such as authentication, logging, request validation, and many more. Think of middleware as a gatekeeper or a pre-processor that checks or modifies incoming requests before they are handled by your API.

For example, if you want to log every request to your API or ensure that only authenticated users can access certain endpoints, middleware is the perfect tool for the job. It acts as an intermediate layer between the incoming request and the final API handler, making your code cleaner, reusable, and more secure.

Middleware Works in Next.js

In Next.js, middleware functions are typically defined separately, and reused across multiple API routes. A middleware function takes three parameters:

- **`req` (Request Object):** Contains details about the incoming request such as headers, query parameters, and the request body.
- **`res` (Response Object):** Used to send a response back to the client.
- **`next` (Function):** A callback that passes control to the next middleware or the final API handler.

By calling **`next()`**, the middleware signals that it has finished its task, and the request can move forward. If **`next()`** is not called, the request stops at the middleware, and no further processing happens.

Creating a Simple Middleware

Let us start with a basic example of middleware that logs the details of every incoming request. This is useful for debugging and monitoring your API.

```
// middleware/logRequest.js
export function logRequest(req, res, next) {
  console.log(`Incoming request: ${req.method} ${req.url}`);
  next(); // Pass control to the next handler
}
```

To use this middleware in an API route, you simply call it before the main handler:

```
// pages/api/example.js
import { logRequest } from "../../middleware/logRequest";
export default function handler(req, res) {
  logRequest(req, res, () => {
    res.status(200).json({ message: "API route accessed success-
fully" });
  });
}
```

When a request is made to **/api/example**, the middleware logs the request method and URL, and then the main handler sends a response.

Authentication Middleware

One of the most common uses of middleware is to protect API routes by verifying user authentication. For example, you might check if the request includes a valid authentication token in its headers.

An example of an authentication middleware:

```
// middleware/authenticate.js
export function authenticate(req, res, next) {
  const authToken = req.headers.authorization;
  if (!authToken || authToken !== "Bearer secret-token") {
    return res.status(401).json({ error: "Unauthorized" });
  }
  next(); // Allow access to the API handler
}
```

To apply this middleware, you call it before the main handler:

```
// pages/api/protected.js
import { authenticate } from "../../middleware/authenticate";
export default function handler(req, res) {
  authenticate(req, res, () => {
    res.status(200).json({ message: "Authenticated request" });
  });
}
```

Chaining Multiple Middleware Functions

Sometimes, you may want to perform multiple tasks before handling a request. For example, you might want to log the request, and then check authentication. In such cases, you can chain multiple middleware functions together.

An example of two middleware functions:

```
// middleware/middlewarePipeline.js
export function logRequest(req, res, next) {
  console.log("Middleware 1: Logging request");
  next();
}

export function authenticate(req, res, next) {
  console.log("Middleware 2: Checking authentication");
  const authToken = req.headers.authorization;
  if (!authToken || authToken !== "Bearer secret-token") {
```

```
    return res.status(401).json({ error: "Unauthorized" });
  }
  next();
}
```

To apply both middleware functions, you chain them together:

```
// pages/api/secure.js
import { logRequest, authenticate } from "../../middleware/mid-
dlewarePipeline";

export default function handler(req, res) {
  logRequest(req, res, () => {
    authenticate(req, res, () => {
      res.status(200).json({ message: "All middleware executed" });
    });
  });
}
```

In this example:

- The **`logRequest`** middleware logs the request.
- The **`authenticate middleware`** checks for a valid token.
- If both **`middleware`** functions pass, the main handler sends a response.

Key Benefits of Middleware

Middleware is a powerful tool for organizing your API logic.

- **Reusability:** Write middleware once, and reuse it across multiple API routes.
- **Separation of Concerns:** Keep your API handlers focused on their main logic, while middleware handles tasks such as logging, authentication, and validation.
- **Security:** Use middleware to enforce security checks such as authentication and rate limiting.
- **Scalability:** As your application grows, middleware makes it easier to add new features without cluttering your API handlers.

Best Practices for Using Middleware

Keep Middleware Focused: Each middleware function should handle a single task (for example, logging, authentication, or validation).

- **Validate Input:** Always validate and sanitize the incoming data in middleware to prevent security vulnerabilities.
- **Handle Errors Gracefully:** If middleware detects an issue (for example, invalid authentication), return a clear error response.

- **Use Environment Variables:** Store the sensitive information (for example, API keys or tokens) in environment variables.
- **Test Thoroughly:** Ensure that your middleware works as expected in all scenarios, including edge cases.

Building RESTful APIs with Next.js

RESTful APIs are a cornerstone of modern web development, enabling applications to communicate over HTTP using structured operations such as Create, Read, Update, and Delete (CRUD). Next.js simplifies the process of building RESTful APIs by providing built-in support for API routes.

Creating a RESTful API in Next.js

In Next.js, each API route corresponds to a function that handles specific HTTP methods such as **GET**, **POST**, **PUT** and **DELETE**. This allows developers to define the behavior of their API based on the type of request. For example, a simple API route to manage users can be created as follows:

```
// pages/api/users.js
export default function handler(req, res) {
  if (req.method === "GET") {
    // Fetch user data
    res.status(200).json({ message: "List of users" });
  } else if (req.method === "POST") {
    // Create a new user
    res.status(201).json({ message: "User created successfully" });
  } else {
    res.status(405).json({ error: "Method Not Allowed" });
  }
}}
```

When a **GET** request is made to this route, it fetches a list of users and returns a 200 OK response with the data. A **POST** request creates a new user and returns a 201 Created response. Any other HTTP method results in a 405 Method Not Allowed error, ensuring that the API adheres to RESTful principles.

Organizing API Routes for Scalability

To maintain a clean and scalable codebase, developers can organize API routes into separate files for each operation. For instance:

- **api/users/index.js** → Handles **GET** (fetch all users) and **POST** (create user).
- **api/users/[id].js** → Handles **GET**, **PUT**, and **DELETE** for a specific user.

Dynamic Routing for Specific Users

Dynamic routing allows developers to handle operations for specific users based on their unique identifiers. An example to implement this:

```
// api/users/[id].js
export default function handler(req, res) {
  const { id } = req.query;
  if (req.method === "GET") {
    res.status(200).json({ message: `Fetching user with ID: ${id}` });
  } else if (req.method === "PUT") {
    res.status(200).json({ message: `Updating user with ID: ${id}` });
  } else if (req.method === "DELETE") {
    res.status(200).json({ message: `Deleting user with ID: ${id}` });
  } else {
    res.status(405).json({ error: "Method Not Allowed" });
  }
}
```

A **GET** request to this route fetches details for the user with the specified id. A **PUT** request updates the user, and a **DELETE** request removes the user. Any other **HTTP** method results in a 405 Method Not Allowed error. This modular approach ensures that the API is scalable and easy to extend as the application grows.

Advantages of Using Next.js for RESTful APIs

Next.js offers several benefits for developing RESTful APIs, making it a preferred choice among developers. It simplifies API route creation, optimizes performance through serverless execution, and enables seamless integration of frontend and backend within a single project. Additionally, its flexibility supports various use cases, from basic CRUD operations to advanced business logic.

- **Minimal Configuration:** Next.js allows developers to set up API routes easily with minimal setup, reducing development complexity.
- **Serverless Scalability:** API routes in Next.js are serverless by nature, automatically scaling based on demand for optimized performance.
- **Unified Development:** Next.js provides an integrated environment where both frontend and backend coexist within a single project, streamlining development.
- **Enhanced Performance:** API routes execute only when needed, improving efficiency and reducing unnecessary server load.
- **Flexible Use Cases:** Next.js supports a wide range of functionalities, from simple CRUD operations to handling complex business logic.

Best Practices for Building RESTful APIs in Next.js

To ensure that RESTful APIs in Next.js are robust, secure, and maintainable, developers should follow these best practices. Proper route organization, input validation, error handling, and security measures contribute to a reliable API. Additionally, clear documentation enhances usability for other developers.

- **Organize Routes Clearly:** Structure API routes using a logical folder hierarchy such as `pages/api/users/` for user-related endpoints to keep the codebase clean and manageable.
- **Validate and Sanitize Input:** Prevent security vulnerabilities by thoroughly validating and sanitizing user inputs before processing requests.
- **Use Proper HTTP Status Codes:** Ensure clear client-server communication by responding with appropriate status codes such as 200 OK for success or 404 Not Found for missing resources.
- **Handle Errors Gracefully:** Improve the user experience by providing meaningful error messages that help clients understand and resolve issues.
- **Implement Authentication and Authorization:** Protect sensitive endpoints by enforcing authentication and authorization mechanisms, ensuring that only authorized users can access specific resources.
- **Document API Routes:** Provide clear documentation detailing expected inputs, outputs, and example requests to help other developers understand and integrate with the API effectively.

Example: Building a Complete CRUD API

Let us put everything together and build a complete CRUD API for managing users:

1. **Fetch All Users (`GET /api/users`)**

```
// api/users/index.js
export default function handler(req, res) {
  if (req.method === "GET") {
    res.status(200).json({ message: "List of users" });
  } else if (req.method === "POST") {
    res.status(201).json({ message: "User created successfully"
});
  } else {
    res.status(405).json({ error: "Method Not Allowed" });
  }
}
```

2. **Fetch, Update, or Delete a Specific User (`GET /api/users/[id]`)**

```
// pages/api/users/[id].js
export default function handler(req, res) {
  const { id } = req.query;

  if (req.method === "GET") {
    res.status(200).json({ message: `Fetching user with ID:
${id}` });
  } else if (req.method === "PUT") {
    res.status(200).json({ message: `Updating user with ID:
${id}` });
  } else if (req.method === "DELETE") {
    res.status(200).json({ message: `Deleting user with ID:
${id}` });
  } else {
    res.status(405).json({ error: "Method Not Allowed" });
  }
}
```

Next.js makes it incredibly easy to build RESTful APIs that are simple, scalable, and efficient. By leveraging API routes, developers can handle backend logic directly within their Next.js application, eliminating the need for a separate server. Thus, whether building a small project or a large-scale application, Next.js provides the tools and flexibility needed to create robust and maintainable APIs. With the acquired knowledge from this chapter, developers are now equipped to build RESTful APIs in Next.js, organize routes effectively, and follow the best practices to ensure that their APIs are secure and performant.

Using API Routes with External APIs

Next.js API routes are not limited to handling internal logic; they can also act as a bridge between your frontend and external APIs. This capability is particularly useful when interacting with third-party services such as weather APIs, payment gateways, or social media platforms. By using Next.js API routes as middleware, you can securely fetch data from external APIs, transform it as needed, and send it to the frontend. This approach also allows you to hide sensitive information such as API keys from the client-side code.

Fetching Data from an External API

One of the most common use cases for API routes is fetching data from external services. For example, you might want to retrieve weather data from a public API, and display it in your application. You can achieve this using a Next.js API route:

```
// pages/api/weather.js
export default async function handler(req, res) {
  const API_KEY = process.env.WEATHER_API_KEY;
  const location = req.query.location || "London"; // Default
location
  const url = `https://api.weatherapi.com/v1/current.
json?key=${API_KEY}&q=${location}`;
  try {
    const response = await fetch(url);
    const data = await response.json();
    res.status(200).json(data);
  } catch (error) {
    res.status(500).json({ error: "Failed to fetch weather data"
});
  }
}
```

- The API route receives a request from the frontend, optionally including a location query parameter.
- It constructs the URL for the external API, using an API key stored in an environment variable (**`process.env.WEATHER_API_KEY`**).
- The route fetches data from the external API using the fetch function.
- If the request is successful, the data is returned to the frontend as a JSON response.
- If an error occurs, the route returns a 500 Internal Server Error with an appropriate error message.
- This approach ensures that the API key is never exposed to the client-side code, enhancing security.

Securing API Keys with Environment Variables

When working with external APIs, it is crucial to keep sensitive information such as API keys, secure. Next.js allows you to store these keys in environment variables, which are only accessible on the server side. You can set this up by the following method:

Create **`a .env`** local file in the root of your project:

```
WEATHER_API_KEY=your_api_key_here
```

Access the environment variable in your API route using **`process.env`**:

```
const API_KEY = process.env.WEATHER_API_KEY;
```

Hence, by using environment variables, you ensure that sensitive information remains hidden from the client-side code and version control systems.

Transforming Data before Sending to the Frontend

API routes can also be used to transform data fetched from external APIs before sending it to the frontend. For example, you might want to filter, sort, or format the data to match your application's requirements. An example of transforming weather data is as follows:

```
// pages/api/weather.js
export default async function handler(req, res) {
  const API_KEY = process.env.WEATHER_API_KEY;
  const location = req.query.location || "London";
  const url = `https://api.weatherapi.com/v1/current.
json?key=${API_KEY}&q=${location}`;
  try {
    const response = await fetch(url);
    const data = await response.json();

    // Transform the data
    const transformedData = {
      location: data.location.name,
      temperature: data.current.temp_c,
      condition: data.current.condition.text,
    };

    res.status(200).json(transformedData);
  } catch (error) {
    res.status(500).json({ error: "Failed to fetch weather data"
});
  }
}
```

In this example, the API route fetches the weather data, extracts only the relevant fields (location, temperature, and condition), and sends the transformed data to the frontend. This reduces the amount of data sent over the network, and simplifies the frontend logic.

Handling POST Requests to External APIs

API routes can also be used to send data to external APIs. For example, you might want to submit a form to a third-party service such as a payment gateway or a customer support platform. You can handle a **POST** request to an external API:

```
// pages/api/submit.js
export default async function handler(req, res) {
  if (req.method !== "POST") {
```

```
    return res.status(405).json({ error: "Method Not Allowed" });
  }

  const { name, email, message } = req.body;

  try {
    const response = await fetch("https://example.com/api/submit",
{
      method: "POST",
      headers: { "Content-Type": "application/json" },
      body: JSON.stringify({ name, email, message }),
    });

    const result = await response.json();
    res.status(200).json(result);
  } catch (error) {
    res.status(500).json({ error: "Failed to submit data" });
  }
}
```

- The API route checks if the request method is **POST**. If not, it returns a 405 Method Not Allowed error.
- It extracts the form data (name, email, and message) from the request body.
- The route sends the data to the external API using a **POST** request.
- If the request is successful, the response from the external API is forwarded to the frontend.
- If an error occurs, the route returns a **500 Internal Server Error** with an appropriate error message.

This approach ensures that the sensitive data such as payment information is never exposed to the client-side code.

Caching Responses for Better Performance

To improve performance, and reduce the load on external APIs, you can implement caching in your API routes. For example, you might want to cache weather data for a specific location for a certain period. You can achieve this using the Cache-Control header:

```
//api/weather.js
export default async function handler(req, res) {
  const API_KEY = process.env.WEATHER_API_KEY;
  const location = req.query.location || "London";
  const url = `https://api.weatherapi.com/v1/current.
json?key=${API_KEY}&q=${location}`;
```

```
  try {
    const response = await fetch(url);
    const data = await response.json();

    // Cache the response for 10 minutes
    res.setHeader("Cache-Control", "s-maxage=600, stale-while-
revalidate");
    res.status(200).json(data);
  } catch (error) {
    res.status(500).json({ error: "Failed to fetch weather data"
});
  }
}
```

In this example, the Cache-Control header is set to cache the response for 10 minutes (**`s-maxage=600`**). During this period, subsequent requests for the same location will be served from the cache, reducing the load on the external API, and improving response times.

Introduction to GraphQL and Next.js

GraphQL is a query language for APIs that allows clients to request exactly the data they need. Unlike REST APIs, which have fixed endpoints, GraphQL uses a single endpoint, and lets clients specify the structure of the response. This eliminates common issues such as over-fetching (receiving too much data) and under-fetching (not receiving enough data).

Next.js is a React framework that supports Server-Side Rendering (SSR), Static Site Generation (SSG), and API routes. By integrating GraphQL, you can:

- Fetch data more efficiently.
- Simplify your backend with a single endpoint.
- Build real-time features using GraphQL subscriptions.
- Improve performance by reducing unnecessary data transfer.

Mutations and Resolvers in GraphQL

Mutations and resolvers in GraphQL work together to handle data modifications, enabling clients to create, update, or delete resources through structured and predictable operations.

Mutations

In GraphQL, mutations are used to modify data on the server. Unlike queries, which are used to fetch data, mutations are used to create, update, or delete data. Mutations are defined in the GraphQL schema, and are executed by resolvers.

Resolvers

Resolvers are functions that handle the logic for fetching or modifying data in response to a GraphQL query or mutation. Each field in a GraphQL schema has a corresponding resolver that determines how the data for that field is retrieved or manipulated.

REST vs GraphQL API

Integrating GraphQL with Next.js remains a powerful approach for data fetching, especially when compared to the traditional REST APIs.

The following is a detailed comparison of REST and GraphQL in the context of Next.js:

Feature/Aspect	REST API in Next.js	GraphQL in Next.js
Data Fetching	Multiple endpoints for different resources.	Single endpoint for all queries and mutations.
Over-fetching	Common issue; clients receive more data than needed.	Eliminated; clients request only the data they need.
Under-fetching	Common issue; clients may need multiple requests to fetch related data.	Eliminated; clients can fetch nested or related data in a single query.
Performance	Can be slower due to multiple requests and over-fetching.	Optimized; fewer requests and minimal data transfer.
Flexibility	Limited; endpoints return fixed data structures.	Highly flexible; clients define the structure of the response.
Schema	No strict schema; relies on documentation.	Strongly typed schema; self-documenting.
Real-time Data	Requires additional setup (example, WebSockets).	Built-in support for real-time updates via subscriptions.
Error Handling	HTTP status codes (example, 200, 404, 500).	Detailed error messages in the response.
Caching	Relies on HTTP caching mechanisms.	Advanced caching with Apollo Client or other GraphQL libraries.
Tooling	Limited tooling for API exploration.	Rich tooling (example, GraphQL and Apollo Explorer).
Learning Curve	Easier for beginners; widely adopted.	Steeper learning curve due to GraphQL concepts.

Integration with Next.js	Built-in support for API routes (`pages/api`).	Requires setup (example, Apollo Server in API routes).
Scalability	Can become complex with many endpoints.	Scales well; single endpoint with modular resolvers.
Community Support	Large community; extensive resources.	Growing community; strong ecosystem (example, Apollo, Relay, and so on).

Table 4.1: *Comparison of REST and GraphQL APIS*

Setting up GraphQL with Apollo in Next.js

Apollo is a popular GraphQL client and server solution that simplifies data fetching and state management. When integrating Apollo with Next.js, it can be used in two ways:

- **Apollo Server:** To create a GraphQL API inside Next.js API routes.
- **Apollo Client:** To consume the GraphQL API from React components.

Step 1: Install Dependencies

To get started, install the necessary packages:

```
npm install @apollo/server graphql
```

Step 2: Create a GraphQL API Route

Next.js allows you to create API routes in the `` `pages/api` `` directory. So, let us create a GraphQL endpoint at `` `pages/api/graphql.js` ``.

```
// pages/api/graphql.js
import { ApolloServer } from '@apollo/server';
import { startServerAndCreateNextHandler } from '@as-integrations/
next';
import { typeDefs } from '../../schema';
import { resolvers } from '../../resolvers';
const apolloServer = new ApolloServer({
  typeDefs,
  resolvers,
});
export default startServerAndCreateNextHandler(apolloServer);
```

Defining the GraphQL Schema

This schema defines the structure of your data and the operations you can perform (queries and mutations). Create a `` `schema.js` `` file:

```
// schema.js
import { gql } from 'graphql-tag';
```

```
export const typeDefs = gql`
  type User {
    id: ID!
    name: String!
    email: String!
  }
  type Query {
    users: [User!]!
    user(id: ID!): User
  }
  type Mutation {
    createUser(name: String!, email: String!): User!
    updateUser(id: ID!, name: String, email: String): User!
    deleteUser(id: ID!): User!
  }`;
```

Implementing Resolvers

Resolvers are functions that handle the logic for fetching or modifying data. Each field in your schema has a corresponding resolver. Create a `**resolvers.js**` file:

```
// resolvers.js
let users = [
  { id: '1', name: 'John Doe', email: 'john@example.com' },
  { id: '2', name: 'Jane Smith', email: 'jane@example.com' },
];
export const resolvers = {
  Query: {
    users: () => users,
    user: (_, { id }) => users.find((user) => user.id === id),
  },
  Mutation: {
    createUser: (_, { name, email }) => {
      const newUser = { id: String(users.length + 1), name, email
};
      users.push(newUser);
      return newUser;
    },
    updateUser: (_, { id, name, email }) => {
      const user = users.find((user) => user.id === id);
      if (!user) throw new Error('User not found');
      if (name) user.name = name;
      if (email) user.email = email;
      return user;
    },
    deleteUser: (_, { id }) => {
      const userIndex = users.findIndex((user) => user.id === id);
```

```
        if (userIndex === -1) throw new Error('User not found');
        const deletedUser = users.splice(userIndex, 1)[0];
        return deletedUser;
      },
    },
  };
```

Testing Your GraphQL API

You can test your GraphQL API using tools such as GraphiQL or Apollo Explorer. Then, send queries and mutations to the `/api/graphql` endpoint.

Example Query

Fetch all users:

```
query {
  users {
    id
    name
    email
  }
}
```

Example Mutation

Create a new user:

```
mutation {
  createUser(name: "Alice", email: "alice@example.com") {
    id
    name
    email
  }
}
```

Integrating GraphQL with the Next.js Frontend

Step 1: Install Apollo Client

To use GraphQL in your Next.js frontend, install Apollo Client:

```
npm install @apollo/client
```

Step 2: Set up Apollo Client

Create an `apollo-client.js` file to configure Apollo Client:

```
// apollo-client.js
import { ApolloClient, InMemoryCache } from '@apollo/client';
```

```
const client = new ApolloClient({
  uri: '/api/graphql',
  cache: new InMemoryCache(),
});
export default client;
```

Step 3: Use Apollo Client in Your App

Wrap your Next.js app with the `**ApolloProvider**` in `**_app.js**`:

```
// _app.js
import { ApolloProvider } from '@apollo/client';
import client from '../apollo-client';
function MyApp({ Component, pageProps }) {
  return (
    <ApolloProvider client={client}>
      <Component {...pageProps} />
    </ApolloProvider>
  );
}
export default MyApp;
```

Step 4: Fetch Data in Components

Use the `**useQuery**` and `**useMutation**` hooks to fetch and modify data in your components.

```
Example: Fetching Users
import { useQuery, gql } from '@apollo/client';
const GET_USERS = gql`
  query {
    users {
      id
      name
      email
    }
  }
`;

export default function Users() {
const { loading, error, data } = useQuery(GET_USERS);
  if (loading) return <p>Loading...</p>;
  if (error) return <p>Error: {error.message}</p>;
  return (
    <ul>
      {data.users.map((user) => (
        <li key={user.id}>
          {user.name} - {user.email}
        </li>
```

```
        ))}
      </ul>
    );
  }
```

Thus, by combining Next.js with GraphQL, you can build modern, high-performance web applications with flexible and efficient data fetching. So, whether you are building a small project or a large-scale application, GraphQL's ability to reduce over-fetching and under-fetching makes it a powerful tool for developers.

Conclusion

In this chapter, we explored how to effectively use API routes in Next.js to build dynamic, server-side functionalities. We learned how to handle query parameters, implement middleware, create RESTful APIs, and integrate external APIs. Next.js API routes provide a scalable, secure, and efficient way to manage backend logic without requiring a separate server.

By leveraging API routes, developers can create robust applications that handle CRUD operations, interact with databases, authenticate users, and fetch data from third-party services. With the power of serverless execution, these APIs can be deployed efficiently, ensuring high performance and security.

Therefore, mastering API routes in Next.js allows developers to build full-stack applications with a seamless backend experience, making Next.js an excellent choice for modern web development.

In the next chapter, we will explore Authentication and Authorization, understanding how to secure API routes, manage user sessions, and implement access controls in Next.js.

Multiple Choice Questions

1. Where should API routes be defined in a Next.js project?
    a. `` `pages/routes/` ``
    b. `` `api/routes/` ``
    c. `` `pages/api/` ``
    d. `` `backend/api/` ``

2. How can you access query parameters in a Next.js API route?
   a. `req.params`
   b. `req.query`
   c. `req.body`
   d. `req.url`
3. What does the `next()` function do in a middleware function?
   a. Terminates the request immediately
   b. Sends a response to the client
   c. Passes control to the next middleware or handler
   d. Restarts the server
4. Which HTTP method is used to update an existing resource in a RESTful API?
   a. `GET`
   b. `POST`
   c. `DELETE`
   d. `PUT`
5. How can you securely store API keys in a Next.js project?
   a. Hardcoding them in the API route
   b. Storing them in the `.env.local` file
   c. Saving them in a JavaScript variable
   d. Keeping them in the public folder

Answers

1. c
2. b
3. c
4. d
5. b

Chapter 5
Authentication and Authorization

Introduction

Authentication and authorization are crucial components of modern web applications, ensuring secure access to resources, while protecting the sensitive user data. In **Next.js**, authentication verifies user identity, while authorization determines access levels based on roles and permissions. Next.js provides multiple authentication strategies, including **JSON Web Tokens (JWT), OAuth, Magic Links, and NextAuth.js**, enabling seamless integration with identity providers such as Google, GitHub, and custom backends.

This chapter covers essential authentication patterns, including **server-side authentication with API routes, middleware-based session management, and token-based authentication** for scalable security. Additionally, role-based and attribute-based authorization techniques will be explored to control user access dynamically.

By leveraging Next.js's built-in features such as **Edge Functions, Middleware, and API routes**, developers can enhance security without compromising performance. Hence, whether you are building a small SaaS platform or an enterprise-grade application, mastering authentication and authorization in Next.js is necessary for ensuring a robust and user-friendly experience.

Structure

In this chapter, the following topics will be covered:

- Understanding Authentication and Authorization
- Implementing Authentication with NextAuth.js
- JWT-based Authentication
- Role-based Authorization

- Securing API Routes
- Protecting Pages with Middleware and Auth Guards

Understanding Authentication in Detail

Authentication is the process of verifying a user's identity before granting them access to a system, application, or resource. It ensures that only authorized users can log in and interact with a system, while keeping unauthorized users out.

Authentication is important due to the following reasons:

- Prevents unauthorized access
- Protects user data from hackers
- Ensures privacy and security
- Helps in regulatory compliance (GDPR, HIPAA, and so on.)

For example, when you enter your email and password to log into an account, the system checks if the details match a stored record. If correct, you are granted access–this is authentication.

Working of Authentication

Authentication follows a structured process that involves verifying the identity of a user through credentials. The following is the step-by-step process:

- **User Identification:** The user starts by providing an identifier such as an email, username, or phone number to let the system know who they are trying to log in as.
- **Credential Submission:** The user enters his/her password (or another authentication method) to prove his/her identity.
- **Credential Verification:** The system compares the provided credentials with the stored credentials in the database. If they match, authentication is successful.
- **Access Granted or Denied:** If authentication is successful, the user is granted access.

If authentication fails (wrong password, unrecognized device, and so on.), access is denied, and the system may ask for re-authentication or take security measures.

Types of Authentications

There are different ways to authenticate users based on security needs and usability.

- **Password-Based Authentication**

This is the most common form of authentication, where users enter a username and password to log in.

- Easy to implement
- Prone to hacking (password leaks, brute force attacks, and so on)

- **Multi-Factor Authentication (MFA)**

  MFA improves security by requiring two or more verification steps.

  Example:

  - Enter a password (Something You Know)
  - Enter an OTP received via SMS (Something You Have)

MFA makes it harder for attackers to gain access, even if they steal the password.

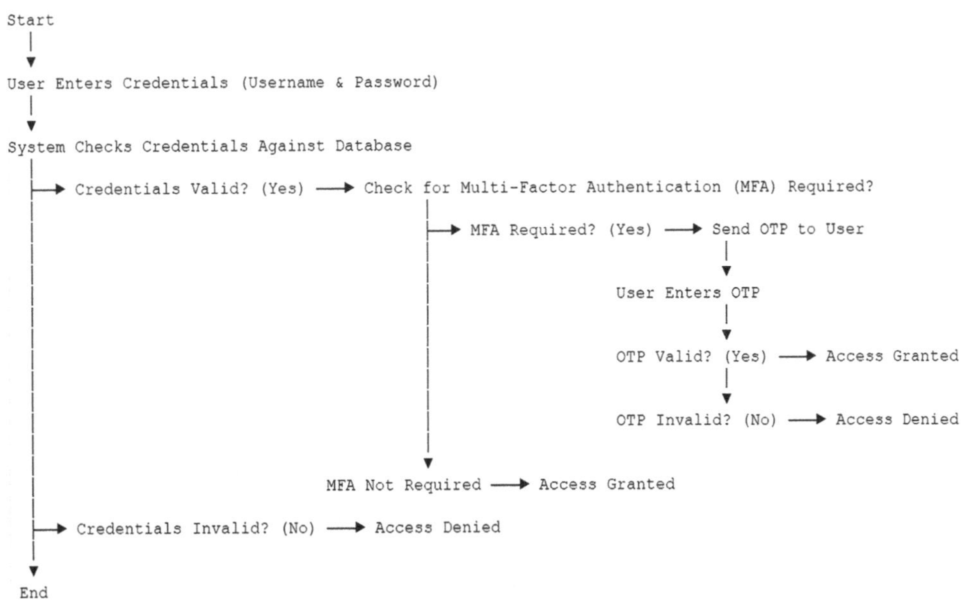

Figure 5.1: *MFA Flow*

- **Biometric Authentication**

  Uses physical characteristics to verify identity, such as:

  - Fingerprint scanners
  - Facial recognition
  - Iris scanning

It provides strong security but requires specialized hardware.

- **Token-Based Authentication**

  - Instead of asking for login details repeatedly, the system generates a token (like a digital key) after the first successful login. This is used for further authentication.
  - Commonly used in APIs and web apps (for example, JWT, Oauth, and so on).
- **Single Sign-On (SSO)**
  - SSO allows users to log in once, and gain access to multiple applications without re-entering credentials.
  - **Example:** Using Google login for different websites.

Authorization

Authorization is the process of granting or restricting access to resources based on user roles and permissions. After a user is authenticated, the system determines what actions they are allowed to perform. For example:

- **Authentication:** You log into a website with your email and password.
- **Authorization:** After logging in, you can access your profile, but you cannot access the admin dashboard, unless you have admin privileges.

Authorization Work Flow

The authorization workflow ensures that users can only access the resources and actions they are permitted to, based on their identity and assigned permissions.

- **User Authentication:** The system verifies the user's identity (login credentials).
- **Access Control Check:** The system checks what the user is allowed to do based on their role or permissions.
- **Grant or Deny Access:** If the user has the right permissions, they can access the resource. Otherwise, they see an "`Access Denied`" message.

Importance of Authorization

Authorization plays a critical role in maintaining application security by ensuring that users can only perform actions and access data that align with their assigned permissions.

- Ensures data security by restricting access.
- Prevents unauthorized actions from regular users.
- Help in compliance with data protection laws.

Types of Authorizations

Different authorization models define how access rights are assigned, managed, and enforced within an application, each offering varying levels of flexibility, security, and complexity.

- **Role-Based Access Control (RBAC)**

  Users are assigned roles, and each role has predefined permissions.

  Example:

  `Admin`: Can manage users, delete data, view reports.

  `Editor`: Can create and edit content but cannot delete users.

  `Viewer`: Can only view content but cannot make changes.

- **Attribute-Based Access Control (ABAC)**

  Access is granted based on attributes such as user location, device type, or account status.

  Example: A bank allows transactions under ₹50,000 from any device but requires MFA for transactions above ₹50,000.

- **OAuth 2.0 (Third-Party Authorization)**

  OAuth allows users to grant limited access to third-party apps without sharing passwords.

  Example: When you log in with Google to a website, Google authenticates you, and tells the website what data it can access.

- **JSON Web Token (JWT) Authorization**

  JWT is a token-based authorization method where a user receives a token after authentication, and the token is used to access the protected resources.

  Example: A user logs in and gets a JWT token. The token is then sent in every request to access the secured API routes.

Difference between Authentication and Authorization

Authentication and authorization are two fundamental concepts in cybersecurity, often used together but serving distinct purposes. **Authentication** verifies a user's identity, ensuring that they are who they claim to be, while **authorization** determines what resources and actions the authenticated user is allowed to access.

Feature	Authentication	Authorization
Definition	Verifies who the user is.	Determines what the user can access.
Purpose	Identity verification.	Access control.
Occurs when	Before authorization.	After authentication.
Implemented	Username/Password, OTP, Biometrics, Tokens, etc.	Role-based permissions, ACL (Access Control List), OAuth, and so on.
Fails	User cannot log in.	User cannot perform certain actions or access restricted areas.
Example	Logging into an email account with a password.	Checking if a logged-in user has permission to access an admin dashboard.

Table 5.1: *Authentication vs. Authorization*

Understanding to NextAuth.js

NextAuth.js is an open-source authentication library for Next.js applications. It provides an easy way to add authentication using OAuth, JWT, email/password, and social logins (Google, GitHub, and so on.).

- **Simple to set up:** No need to build authentication from scratch.
- **Supports multiple providers:** Google, GitHub, Facebook, Twitter, and so on.
- **Secure:** Uses JSON Web Tokens (JWT) and session-based authentication.
- **Customizable:** You can extend it with your own logic.

The authentication flow in NextAuth.js follows these steps:

1. User clicks "`Sign in`" on your Next.js app.
2. NextAuth.js redirects the user to the selected provider (Google, GitHub, and so on.).
3. The provider authenticates the user and redirects them back.
4. NextAuth.js creates a session, and stores user details securely.
5. Users can now access the protected pages based on their authentication status.

Setting up NextAuth.js in a Next.js App

Run the following command in your Next.js project:

```
npm install next-auth
```

OR

```
yarn add next-auth
```

All Parameters of NextAuth.js

NextAuth.js provides a flexible authentication system in Next.js. The following are the key parameters used when configuring NextAuth:

- **providers:** Defines the authentication providers (for example, Google, GitHub, Credentials, and many more.)
- **callbacks:** Allows modifying user session, JWT, or other behaviors
- **session:** Configures session behavior (for example, JWT or database sessions)
- **pages**: Customizes built-in authentication pages
- **events:** Hooks into lifecycle events such as sign-in, sign-out, and so on.
- **debug:** Enables debug mode for logging authentication flow
- **theme:** Customizes the default NextAuth.js UI theme
- **adapter:** Connects NextAuth.js to a database for persistent sessions

A complete example with different parameters:

```
import NextAuth from "next-auth";
import CredentialsProvider from "next-auth/providers/
credentials";
import GoogleProvider from "next-auth/providers/google";
export default NextAuth({
  providers: [
    GoogleProvider({
      clientId: process.env.GOOGLE_CLIENT_ID,
      clientSecret: process.env.GOOGLE_CLIENT_SECRET,
    }),
    CredentialsProvider({
      name: "Credentials",
      credentials: {
        email: { label: "Email", type: "email", placeholder:
"test@example.com" },
        password: { label: "Password", type: "password" },
      },
      async authorize(credentials) {
        const user = { id: "1", name: "John Doe", email:
credentials.email };
        if (credentials.email === "test@example.com" &&
credentials.password === "password") {
          return user;
        }
        return null;
      },
    }),
```

```
  ],
  callbacks: {
    async jwt({ token, user }) {
      if (user) {
        token.id = user.id;
        token.role = user.role || "user"; // Assign roles
dynamically
      }
      return token;
    },
    async session({ session, token }) {
      session.user.id = token.id;
      session.user.role = token.role;
      return session;
    },
  },
  session: {
    strategy: "jwt",
    maxAge: 30 * 24 * 60 * 60, // 30 days
  },
  pages: {
    signIn: "/auth/signin",
    signOut: "/auth/signout",
    error: "/auth/error",
  },
  events: {
    async signIn({ user }) {
      console.log("User signed in:", user);
    },
    async signOut({ token }) {
      console.log("User signed out:", token);
    },
  },
  debug: process.env.NODE_ENV === "development",
  theme: {
    colorScheme: "auto", // "auto", "dark", "light"
    brandColor: "#0070f3",
    logo: "/logo.png",
  },

  adapter: undefined, // Can be set to Prisma or another DB
adapter
});
```

Explanation of Parameters

These parameters define how the authentication system behaves, controlling providers, session handling, callbacks, UI customization, and event logging.

- `providers`: Defines authentication providers (Google, Credentials).
- `callbacks`:
  - `jwt`: Adds user role to the JWT.
  - `session`: Attaches role and ID to the session object.
- `session`: Uses JWT-based session with a 30-day expiration.
- `pages`: Custom routes for sign-in, sign-out, and errors.
- `events`: Logs user sign-in and sign-out actions.
- `debug`: Enables logging in development mode.
- `theme`: Customizes UI colors and branding.
- `adapter`: Can be used for database-backed authentication (for example, Prisma, MongoDB, and so on).

Authentication Methods in NextAuth.js

NextAuth.js supports multiple types of authentications, including:

- **OAuth Authentication:** Supports providers such as Google, Facebook, GitHub, Twitter, and many more.
- **Credentials Authentication:** Custom username/password-based authentication.
- **Email Authentication:** Sign in with email magic links.
- **JWT (JSON Web Token) Authentication:** Used for session handling.
- **Custom Authentication Providers:** You can integrate custom identity providers.
- **SAML / OpenID Connect / LDAP:** Indirectly supported via custom providers.

NextAuth.js supports multiple authentication methods, each with a different use case. Now, let us go step by step, and set up both frontend and backend for each authentication type.

OAuth Authentication (Google, Facebook, GitHub and Twitter)

OAuth is a protocol that allows users to log in to a website or application using their existing accounts from third-party providers such as Google, Facebook, or GitHub.

Instead of creating a new username and password, users can authenticate using these trusted platforms, making the login process more secure and convenient.

For example, when a website offers a "**`Log in with Google`**" option, it is using OAuth to authenticate the user through Google.

NextAuth.js, a popular authentication library for Next.js applications, uses OAuth by default to handle authentication. It provides built-in support for multiple OAuth providers, making it easy to integrate third-party logins like Google, GitHub, or Facebook without manually implementing OAuth from scratch.

Backend Setup (API Route)

Create an API file: `` `pages/api/auth/[...nextauth].js` ``

```
import NextAuth from "next-auth";
import GoogleProvider from "next-auth/providers/google";
export default NextAuth({
  providers: [
    GoogleProvider({
      clientId: process.env.GOOGLE_CLIENT_ID,
      clientSecret: process.env.GOOGLE_CLIENT_SECRET,
    }),
  ],
  secret: process.env.NEXTAUTH_SECRET,
});
```

Set Environment Variables (`` `.env.local` ``)

- `GOOGLE_CLIENT_ID=your-google-client-id`
- `GOOGLE_CLIENT_SECRET=your-google-client-secret`
- `NEXTAUTH_SECRET=your-random-secret`

Frontend Setup `` `pages/index.js` ``

```
import { signIn, signOut, useSession } from "next-auth/react";
export default function Home() {
  const { data: session } = useSession();
  return (
    <div>
      {session ? (
        <>
          <p>Welcome, {session.user.name}!</p>
          <button onClick={() => signOut()}>Logout</button>
        </>
      ) : (
        <button onClick={() => signIn("google")}>Login with
Google</button>
      )}
```

```
    </div>
  );
}
```

Workflow

1. User clicks "**`Login with Google`**".
2. Redirects to Google for authentication.
3. If successful, the session is stored.

SAML / OpenID Connect / LDAP Authentication

NextAuth does not support SAML/LDAP directly but can work with providers such as Auth0, Okta, or Keycloak.

Example: Using `Auth0`

```
import NextAuth from "next-auth";
import Auth0Provider from "next-auth/providers/auth0";
export default NextAuth({
  providers: [
    Auth0Provider({
      clientId: process.env.AUTH0_CLIENT_ID,
      clientSecret: process.env.AUTH0_CLIENT_SECRET,
      domain: process.env.AUTH0_DOMAIN,
    }),
  ],
});
```

Workflow

1. Redirects users to **`Auth0`**.
2. **`Auth0`** handles authentication.
3. Users are redirected back after login.

Credentials Authentication (Username and Password)

This allows users to log in with a custom email and password, instead of OAuth.

Backend Setup (API Route): `pages/api/auth/[...nextauth].js`

```
import NextAuth from "next-auth";
import CredentialsProvider from "next-auth/providers/credentials";

export default NextAuth({
  providers: [
    CredentialsProvider({
```

```
      name: "Credentials",
      credentials: {
        email: { label: "Email", type: "email", placeholder:
"user@example.com" },
        password: { label: "Password", type: "password" },
      },
      async authorize(credentials) {
        // Dummy authentication logic
        if (credentials.email === "user@example.com" &&
credentials.password === "pass123") {
          return { id: 1, name: "John Doe", email: credentials.
email };
        }
        throw new Error("Invalid email or password");
      },
    }),
  ],
  secret: process.env.NEXTAUTH_SECRET,
});
```

Frontend Setup: `pages/login.js`

```
import { signIn } from "next-auth/react";
import { useState } from "react";

export default function Login() {
  const [email, setEmail] = useState("");
  const [password, setPassword] = useState("");

  const handleSubmit = async (e) => {
    e.preventDefault();
    const res = await signIn("credentials", { email, password,
redirect: false });
    if (res?.error) alert(res.error);
  };

  return (
    <form onSubmit={handleSubmit}>
      <input type="email" value={email} onChange={(e) =>
setEmail(e.target.value)} placeholder="Email" />
      <input type="password" value={password} onChange={(e) =>
setPassword(e.target.value)} placeholder="Password" />
      <button type="submit">Login</button>
    </form>
  );
}
```

Workflow

1. User enters an email and password.
2. NextAuth calls the `authorize` function.
3. If credentials are valid, user logs in.

Email Authentication (Magic Link)

Email authentication using a magic link is a password less login method where users receive a secure, one-time-use link via email. Clicking the link automatically logs them into the application without needing a password.

Working of Magic Link Authentication

User Initiates Login: The user enters their email address in the login form, and submits it.

Server Generates a Secure Token:

- The application generates a unique, time-limited token or signed URL associated with the user's email.
- The token is securely stored in the database (for example, hashed) or signed using a cryptographic key.
- Magic Link is Sent via Email:
- The server emails the magic link to the user, containing the unique token.
- Example link: https://yourapp.com/auth/magic?token=abcd1234xyz
- This link usually expires after a short time (for example, 10–15 minutes) for security reasons.

User Clicks the Magic Link: The user clicks the link, and it directs them to the application's authentication endpoint.

Server Verifies the Token: The backend checks if the token:

- Matches the stored token (if using database storage).
- Has not expired.
- Is valid and has not been tampered with (if using JWT or HMAC-based signing).

User is Authenticated:

- If the token is valid, the user is logged in, and a session or authentication cookie is created.
- If invalid or expired, the user sees an error message, and must request a new magic link.

Advantages of Magic Link Authentication

Magic link authentication offers a secure and user-friendly alternative to traditional password-based login systems by leveraging one-time email links for verification.

- **Eliminates Passwords:** No need to remember or reset passwords.
- **Enhanced Security:** Reduces risks such as password leaks, phishing, and credential stuffing.
- **User Convenience:** Simple login process–just click a link.
- **No Need for Third-Party Providers:** Unlike OAuth (Google, GitHub, and so on.), users only need an email.

Security Considerations

To ensure magic link authentication remains secure and resistant to common attacks, several key security practices must be implemented during token generation, delivery, and validation.

- **Token Expiry:** Set a short expiration time (for example, 10–15 minutes) to prevent misuse.
- **One-Time Use:** Invalidate the token after successful login.
- **Secure Transmission:** Use HTTPS to prevent token interception.
- **Email Spoofing Protection:** Implement DMARC, DKIM, and SPF to avoid phishing attacks.

Backend Setup (API Route):`pages/api/auth/[...nextauth].js`

```
import NextAuth from "next-auth";
import EmailProvider from "next-auth/providers/email";
export default NextAuth({
  providers: [
    EmailProvider({
      server: process.env.EMAIL_SERVER,
      from: process.env.EMAIL_FROM,
    }),
  ],
  secret: process.env.NEXTAUTH_SECRET,
});
```

Environment Variables (`.env.local`)

- `EMAIL_SERVER=smtp://your-email-server`
- `EMAIL_FROM=your-email@example.com`
- `NEXTAUTH_SECRET=your-random-secret`

Frontend Setup:`pages/login.js`

```
import { signIn } from "next-auth/react";
import { useState } from "react";
export default function Login() {
  const [email, setEmail] = useState("");
  const handleSubmit = async (e) => {
    e.preventDefault();
    await signIn("email", { email });
  };
  return (
    <form onSubmit={handleSubmit}>
      <input type="email" value={email} onChange={(e) => setE-
mail(e.target.value)} placeholder="Enter Email" />
      <button type="submit">Send Magic Link</button>
    </form>
  );
}
```

Workflow

1. User enters their email.
2. A login link is sent to their email.
3. Clicking the link logs the user in.

Custom Authentication Providers

If you have a custom identity provider, you can integrate it into NextAuth.

Example: Custom API Provider

```
import NextAuth from "next-auth";
import Providers from "next-auth/providers";
export default NextAuth({
  providers: [
    Providers.Credentials({
      name: "CustomAPI",
      async authorize(credentials) {
        const res = await fetch("https://your-api.com/auth/login", {
          method: "POST",
          body: JSON.stringify(credentials),
        });
        const user = await res.json();
        if (res.ok && user) return user;
        throw new Error("Invalid credentials");
```

```
        },
      }),
    ],
  });
```

Workflow

1. Calls an external API for authentication.
2. If valid, logs in the user.

JWT (JSON Web Token) Authentication

A JSON Web Token (JWT) is a compact, URL-safe token format used for securely transmitting information between parties as a JSON object.

It is commonly used in authentication and authorization mechanisms, enabling stateless communication between a client and a server.

JWT

JWTs are signed using a secret key (HMAC algorithm) or a public/private key pair (RSA or ECDSA), ensuring that the token's integrity is verifiable, and has not been tampered with.

Structure of a JWT

A JWT consists of three parts, separated by dots (`.`): **`Header.Payload. Signature.`**

Each part is Base64Url encoded:

- **Header:** Specifies the type of token and the signing algorithm.
- **Payload:** Contains claims (data) about the user or session.
- **Signature:** Ensures token integrity and authenticity.

Example of a JWT: eyJhbGciOiJIUzI1NiIsInR5cCI6IkpXVCJ9.eyJ1c2VySWQiOjEwMCwiZXhwIjoxNjk2Mjk1MjAwfQ.4c3d6d5f4d1a56c5d0e2563cfd8ef1.

JWT Authentication Process

JWT authentication is a stateless mechanism where a client obtains a token upon successful login, and then includes it in subsequent requests to authenticate itself.

Step-by-Step Process:

1. **User Logs in:**
   a. The client (browser or mobile app) sends login credentials to the server.
   b. The server verifies the credentials.
2. **JWT is Generated:**
   a. If authentication is successful, the server creates a JWT containing the user ID, and other relevant details.
   b. The JWT is signed using a secret key.
   c. The token is sent to the client.
3. **Client stores JWT:**
   a. The client stores the JWT (for example, in the local storage, session storage, or an HTTP-only cookie).
   b. In subsequent requests, the JWT is included in the Authorization header as: `Authorization: Bearer <JWT>`
4. **Server Verifies JWT:**
   a. The server extracts the JWT from the request header.
   b. It decodes and verifies the token's signature.
   c. If the token is valid, and has not expired, the request is processed.
5. **Access is Granted:**
   a. The server allows access to the protected resources based on the token's payload.

```
+----------------------+
|    User Logs In      |
| (Sends Credentials)  |
+----------------------+
            |
+--------------------------+
| NextAuth API receies     |
| credentials ia proider   |
+--------------------------+
            |
+----------------------------+
| NextAuth erifies user      |
| (DB/API check, if needed)  |
+----------------------------+
            |
+------------------------------+
| If alid, JWT is generated    |
| (Contains user ID & claims)  |
+------------------------------+
            |
+-----------------------------------+
| JWT sent to the client            |
| (Stored in cookies/session/token) |
+-----------------------------------+
            |
+-------------------------------------+
| Client includes JWT in request      |
| (Authorization: Bearer <token>)     |
+-------------------------------------+
            |
+----------------------------------+
| NextAuth Middleware/API receies  |
| request and extracts JWT         |
+----------------------------------+
            |
+----------------------------------+
| JWT is erified using secret key  |
+----------------------------------+
            |
+-----------------------------------+
| If alid, user session is actie    |
| and request is processed          |
+-----------------------------------+
            |
+----------------------------+
| Response sent back to user |
+----------------------------+
```

Figure 5.2: *JWT Step-by-Step Process*

Stateless Authentication with JWT

- JWT authentication is stateless, meaning:
- The server does not need to store session information.
- Each request is self-contained (that is, the JWT holds user information).
- This makes authentication scalable, as no database queries are needed to verify a session.

Example:

Create pages/api/auth/[...nextauth].js

```
import NextAuth from "next-auth";
import CredentialsProvider from "next-auth/providers/credentials";

export default NextAuth({
  providers: [
    CredentialsProvider({
      name: "Credentials",
      credentials: {
        email: { label: "Email", type: "text", placeholder:
"user@example.com" },
        password: { label: "Password", type: "password" },
      },
      async authorize(credentials) {
        // Fake user verification (Replace with DB check)
        const user = { id: 1, name: "John Doe", email:
credentials.email };

        if (user) return user;
        throw new Error("Invalid credentials");
      },
    }),
  ],
  session: {
    strategy: "jwt",  // Use JWT for stateless authentication
  },
  jwt: {
    secret: process.env.JWT_SECRET, // Sign JWT securely
  },
});

Create a Login Form (components/Login.js)
import { signIn, signOut, useSession } from "next-auth/react";
export default function Login() {
  const { data: session } = useSession();
  if (session) {
    return (
      <div>
        <p>Welcome, {session.user.name}</p>
        <button onClick={() => signOut()}>Sign Out</button>
      </div>
    );
  }
```

```
  return (
    <div>
      <button onClick={() => signIn("credentials")}>Sign
In</button>
    </div>
  );
}
```

Advantages of JWT Authentication

JWT authentication provides a lightweight, scalable, and stateless way to securely transmit user identity across different parts of an application or across multiple services.

- **Stateless:** No server-side session storage required.
- **Scalable:** Ideal for microservices and distributed systems.
- **Secure:** Signed tokens prevent data tampering.
- **Cross-Platform:** Works across web, mobile, and APIs.

Security Considerations for JWT

Despite its benefits, JWT must be implemented carefully to avoid exposing sensitive data or enabling token-based attacks.

- **Token Expiry:** Always set an expiration time (`exp`) to prevent misuse.
- **Use HTTPS:** Transmit JWTs securely over HTTPS.
- **Store Securely:** Store JWTs in HTTP-only cookies to prevent XSS attacks.
- **Revoke Tokens:** Implement token revocation using refresh tokens or blacklisting.

Role-Based Authorization (RBAC)

Role-Based Authorization (RBAC) is a security mechanism that restricts user access to certain parts of an application based on their assigned roles. In Next.js, RBAC can be implemented using authentication and authorization techniques, middleware, and role-based checks at both the API and UI levels.

Key Components of RBAC

To implement RBAC, we need:

- **Authentication:** Identifies the user (for example, JWT, Next AUTH, and so on.).

- **Authorization:** Determines what actions/resources a user can access based on their role.
- **Roles and Permissions:** Define different user roles and their access levels.
- **Middleware:** Protects pages and APIs dynamically.
- **Frontend Role Checks:** Restricts UI elements based on user permissions.

Importance of RBAC

Role-Based Access Control (RBAC) plays a crucial role in securing applications by defining structured access permissions. It ensures that users can only perform actions relevant to their roles, leading to improved security, efficient management, and compliance with industry regulations. The following are the key benefits of implementing RBAC:

- **Improved Security:** RBAC prevents unauthorized access to the sensitive data, ensuring that only privileged users perform critical operations such as user management, financial transactions, or system settings modifications.
- **Simplified User Management:** Instead of assigning permissions individually to each user, RBAC groups users into roles. This makes it easy to manage access control when onboarding new employees or changing permissions.
- **Compliance and Auditability:** For businesses in healthcare (HIPAA), finance (PCI-DSS), or data privacy (GDPR, CCPA), RBAC ensures compliance by restricting unauthorized data access, and maintaining access logs.
- **Reduces Human Error:** By enforcing structured access levels, RBAC minimizes the risk of accidental modifications or deletions by users who should not have those privileges.
- **Scalability:** As applications grow, managing access for thousands of users becomes complex. RBAC simplifies this by applying permissions based on user roles, rather than handling individual permissions manually.

RBAC Implementation

Implementing Role-Based Access Control (RBAC) in Next.js requires careful planning to ensure security, scalability, and ease of management. By following these best practices, developers can create a structured access control system that protects the sensitive data, and enhances user experience.

The following are the key guidelines for implementing RBAC effectively in Next.js:

- **Define Clear Roles and Permissions:** Before implementing RBAC, define the exact roles and permissions needed in your application.

- **Store Role Information Securely:** User roles should be stored in a secure location such as:
    - **Database:** Users have a `role` field in their records.
    - **JWT Token:** Store the user's role inside authentication tokens.
    - **Session Storage:** Use NextAuth.js or session-based authentication for role management.
- **Apply Role Checks in the UI:** Restrict access to certain UI elements based on user roles:
    - Show/hide buttons, forms, or menus based on role-based permissions.
    - Use conditional rendering to prevent unauthorized actions.
- **Use Role-Based Authentication Providers:** NextAuth.js, Firebase, and OAuth providers support role-based authentication. Use them to fetch user roles dynamically from a database or external provider.
- **Ensure Role Integrity in Backend and Frontend:** RBAC should be enforced on both the backend and frontend to prevent unauthorized API requests. Never rely solely on frontend restrictions, as they can be bypassed.
- **Periodic Review and Role Updates:** Regularly audit and update roles and permissions to ensure that users have appropriate access levels, especially in large organizations where responsibilities change frequently.

RBAC in Real-World Applications

Role-Based Access Control (RBAC) is widely used across industries to ensure that users only access features and data appropriate to their responsibilities.

- **Corporate Employee Access**

    A company intranet uses RBAC to restrict access:

    - Employees see general announcements.
    - Managers can approve expense reports.
    - HR/Admin can view and modify payroll data.
- **SaaS Applications**

    A project management app implements RBAC:

    - Project Owners can create and delete projects.
    - Team Members can add/edit tasks but cannot delete them.
    - Clients can view project progress but not modify tasks.

- **E-Commerce Platforms**

  An online store enforces RBAC:

  - Customers can place orders and track deliveries.
  - Vendors can manage their products but not access order data.
  - Admins can oversee the entire platform, including payments.

Securing API Routes in Next.js

Securing API routes in Next.js is essential to prevent unauthorized access to the sensitive data and ensure that only authenticated and authorized users can interact with backend services. Thus, by implementing proper authentication and authorization mechanisms, developers can enforce strict access control on API endpoints.

Best Practices for Securing API Routes

Securing API routes is essential to protect sensitive data, prevent unauthorized access, and ensure that your application remains reliable and resilient against attacks.

- **Authenticate Users before Processing Requests**
  - Use JWT (JSON Web Tokens), NextAuth.js, Firebase Auth, or OAuth to verify users.
  - Ensure that all API requests include a valid authentication token.
- **Implement Role-Based Authorization**
  - Restrict API access based on user roles (Admin, Editor, Viewer).
  - Prevent unauthorized users from performing sensitive actions such as modifying or deleting records.
- **Use Middleware for API Protection**
  - Apply authentication checks at the middleware level before allowing access to API routes.
  - Centralized middleware makes it easier to manage security policies across multiple API routes.
- **Validate and Sanitize the Incoming Data**
  - Prevent SQL injection, XSS attacks, and CSRF vulnerabilities by validating user inputs.
  - Use libraries such as Zod or Joi to enforce data validation rules.

- **Rate Limiting and Throttling**
    - Prevent brute-force attacks by limiting the number of API requests a user can make.
    - Implement rate limiting using tools such as Express Rate Limit or Next.js middleware solutions.
- **Use HTTPS and Secure Headers**
    - Enforce HTTPS to encrypt the data in transit.
    - Set security headers such as Content Security Policy (CSP), X-Frame-Options, and CORS policies to prevent attacks.

By implementing these security measures, Next.js API routes remain protected from unauthorized access, data breaches, and malicious attacks.

Protecting Pages with Middleware and Auth Guards

Protecting pages in Next.js ensures that only authenticated and authorized users can access the specific parts of the application. This helps prevent unauthorized users from viewing sensitive content or performing restricted actions.

Best Practices for Page Protection

- **Use Middleware for Global Route Protection**
    - Next.js middleware can intercept requests and redirect unauthorized users.
    - It can be used to enforce authentication across multiple pages dynamically.
- **Protect Client-Side Routes with Auth Guards**
    - Use Higher-Order Components (HOCs) or custom hooks to check user authentication before rendering the protected pages.
    - Redirect unauthorized users to the login page or an error page.
- **Restrict Access Based on User Roles**
    - Use RBAC (Role-Based Access Control) to allow or deny access based on user permissions.
    - Hide certain UI elements or restrict navigation for users without the necessary privileges.
- **Server-Side Authentication with `getServerSideProps`**
    - Validate user sessions or tokens on the server before rendering the protected pages.

 - Redirect unauthenticated users to the login page if their session is invalid.
- **Use Session-Based Authentication**
 - Store user sessions securely using NextAuth.js, Firebase Auth, or custom authentication logic.
 - Prevent session hijacking by setting appropriate expiration times and renewal mechanisms.

Implementing **RBAC (Role-Based Access Control), Securing API Routes, and Protecting Pages with Middleware and Auth Guards** in **Next.js** requires a structured approach.

The following is a step-by-step implementation that covers authentication, role-based authorization, API protection, and route guards:

1. **Setting Up Authentication with NextAuth.js**

   To manage user authentication and roles, we use NextAuth.js with JWT-based authentication.

   a. Install Dependencies: `npm install next-auth @next-auth/prisma-adapter`

   b. Configure NextAuth in `[...nextauth].js`

      i. This file handles authentication and assigns user roles.

      ii. Roles are assigned to the session using the JWT callback.

      iii. Password hashing (for example, bcrypt) should be implemented for production.

```
import NextAuth from "next-auth";
import CredentialsProvider from "next-auth/providers/
credentials";
import { PrismaAdapter } from "@next-auth/prisma-adapter";
import { PrismaClient } from "@prisma/client";

const prisma = new PrismaClient();
export default NextAuth({
  adapter: PrismaAdapter(prisma),
  providers: [
    CredentialsProvider({
      name: "Credentials",
      credentials: {
        email: { label: "Email", type: "email", required: true
},
        password: { label: "Password", type: "password",
required: true },
```

```
        },
        async authorize(credentials) {
          const user = await prisma.user.findUnique({
            where: { email: credentials.email },
          });

          if (!user || user.password !== credentials.password) {
            throw new Error("Invalid credentials");
          }

          return { id: user.id, email: user.email, role: user.
role };
        },
      }),
    ],
    callbacks: {
      async jwt({ token, user }) {
        if (user) {
          token.role = user.role; // Attach role to the token
        }
        return token;
      },
      async session({ session, token }) {
        session.user.role = token.role; // Pass role to the
session
        return session;
      },
    },
    secret: process.env.NEXTAUTH_SECRET,
});
```

2. **Implementing RBAC (Role-Based Access Control) in Next.js**

   To enforce role-based restrictions in the UI and API, we create an RBAC utility.

   a. Restricts UI elements based on user roles.

   b. Hides pages or sections for unauthorized users.

RBAC Utility (`rbac.js`)

```
const roles = {
  admin: ["dashboard", "users", "settings"],
  editor: ["dashboard", "posts"],
  viewer: ["dashboard"],
};

export function hasAccess(role, resource) {
  return roles[role]?.includes(resource);
```

```
}
```

```
Protect UI Elements with RBAC

import { useSession } from "next-auth/react";
import { hasAccess } from "../utils/rbac";

const AdminPanel = () => {
  const { data: session } = useSession();

  if (!session || !hasAccess(session.user.role, "settings")) {
    return <p>Access Denied</p>;
  }
  return <div>Welcome to the Admin Panel</div>;
};

export default AdminPanel;
```

3. **Securing API Routes with Role-Based Authorization**

   We ensure that only authorized users can access certain API endpoints.

   Middleware for API Protection (`middleware.js`)

```
import { getSession } from "next-auth/react";
import { hasAccess } from "./rbac";

export async function requireAuth(req, res, resource) {
  const session = await getSession({ req });

  if (!session) {
    return res.status(401).json({ error: "Unauthorized" });
  }

  if (!hasAccess(session.user.role, resource)) {
    return res.status(403).json({ error: "Forbidden" });
  }
}
```

```
Secure API Route (`/api/admin.js`)

import { requireAuth } from "../../utils/middleware";

export default async function handler(req, res) {
  await requireAuth(req, res, "settings"); // Only admins can
access
```

```
  res.status(200).json({ message: "Welcome, Admin!" });
}
```

a. Validates authentication before processing requests.

b. Restricts access based on user roles.

4. **Protecting Pages with Middleware and Auth Guards**

   To secure frontend routes, we redirect unauthorized users.

   Middleware for Protecting Pages (`middleware.js`)

```
import { NextResponse } from "next/server";
import { getToken } from "next-auth/jwt";

export async function middleware(req) {
  const token = await getToken({ req, secret: process.env.NEXT-
AUTH_SECRET });
  if (!token) {
    return NextResponse.redirect(new URL("/login", req.url));
  }
  return NextResponse.next();
}

export const config = {
  matcher: ["/dashboard/:path*", "/admin/:path*"], // Protect
these pages
};
```

   a. Redirects unauthenticated users to `/login`.

5. **Role-Based Route Protection in Frontend**

   Use Higher-Order Components (HOCs) or hooks for role checks.

   Auth Guard for Pages (`useAuthGuard.js`)

```
import { useSession } from "next-auth/react";
import { useRouter } from "next/router";
import { useEffect } from "react";
export function useAuthGuard(requiredRole) {
  const { data: session, status } = useSession();
  const router = useRouter();
  useEffect(() => {
    if (status === "loading") return;
    if (!session) router.push("/login");
    if (session && requiredRole && session.user.role !== required
Role) {
      router.push("/403"); // Forbidden page
    }
```

```
  }, [session, status, router, requiredRole]);
}
```

Protecting a Page (`admin.js`)

```
import { useAuthGuard } from "../hooks/useAuthGuard";
const AdminPage = () => {
  useAuthGuard("admin"); // Only admin can access
  return <div>Admin Dashboard</div>;
};
export default AdminPage;
```

a. Automatically redirects unauthorized users.

Thus, by combining RBAC, API security, and route protection, we create a robust authentication and authorization system in Next.js. This approach ensures:

- Only authenticated users access protected routes.
- Role-based access control restricts actions based on permissions.
- API routes remain secured against unauthorized access.
- Frontend pages and UI elements are dynamically protected.

Conclusion

In this chapter, we explored the necessary authentication and authorization techniques in Next.js, focusing on securing applications effectively. We implemented authentication with NextAuth.js, enabling secure user login and session management. We also covered JWT-based authentication, ensuring token-based security for verifying user identities.

A critical aspect of this chapter was Role-Based Authorization (RBAC), where we assigned user roles and permissions to control access to various features dynamically. Additionally, we secured API routes by enforcing authentication, and restricting access based on user roles, ensuring that only authorized users can interact with the sensitive endpoints.

To further enhance security, we implemented middleware and auth guards, which protect pages dynamically by redirecting unauthorized users, enforcing access rules at the frontend level. These strategies ensure that only authenticated and authorized users can access specific parts of the application, improving overall security and usability. By applying these authentication and authorization techniques, you can build scalable, secure, and role-based Next.js applications.

In the next chapter, we will explore Styling in Next.js, covering different approaches such as CSS Modules, Tailwind CSS, Styled Components, and Global CSS to enhance UI design.

Multiple Choice Questions

1. What is the primary purpose of NextAuth.js in a Next.js application?
    a. To style Next.js components
    b. To optimize API routes for performance
    c. To manage state in a Next.js application
    d. To implement authentication and session management
2. How does JWT-based authentication work in Next.js?
    a. It uses a JSON Web Token (JWT) to verify and authenticate users securely.
    b. It does not support session management.
    c. It requires users to log in every time they refresh the page.
    d. It stores user credentials directly in local storage.
3. In Role-Based Authorization (RBAC), what determines a user's access level?
    a. Their email address.
    b. Their assigned role and associated permissions.
    c. The number of times they visit the application.
    d. The time of login.
4. How can you protect API routes in Next.js?
    a. By checking authentication and authorization inside the API route handler
    b. By only allowing GET requests
    c. By using global CSS for API security
    d. By using React state management
5. What is the purpose of middleware in Next.js for authentication?
    a. To style pages dynamically
    b. To improve API performance
    c. To fetch data from external sources
    d. To restrict access to certain pages based on user roles

Answers

1. d
2. a
3. b
4. a
5. d

CHAPTER 6
Next.js Data Fetching

Introduction

Efficient API fetching is crucial for building high-performance Next.js applications. While the built-in fetch API provides flexibility, third-party libraries such as **Axios** and **Stale-While-Revalidate (SWR)** offer additional features that optimize data retrieval and state management. Axios simplifies HTTP requests with automatic request and response transformations, built-in error handling, and support for request interceptors. On the other hand, **SWR** is a powerful React hook designed for caching, background revalidation, and real-time data synchronization, making it ideal for frequently updated content.

Using SWR improves performance by reducing unnecessary API calls, and ensuring that the data remains fresh with minimal latency. It automatically revalidates data in the background and supports optimistic UI updates, which enhance user experience. Properly handling **errors and loading states** ensure smooth application behavior, while **prefetching and revalidation strategies** help optimize responsiveness.

Next.js also allows developers to define **API routes**, enabling backend logic within the same codebase. This approach provides better control over server-side data processing, authentication, and request handling. Understanding the differences between **fetch, Axios, and SWR**, along with the best practices for error management and revalidation, helps developers make informed decisions about data fetching strategies. This chapter explores these concepts in-depth to maximize efficiency in Next.js applications.

Structure

In this chapter, we will cover the following topics:

- Understanding the Basics of API-Related Tools
- Fetching Data on the Server with SWR
- Handling Errors and Loading States
- Prefetching with SWR

- Revalidation Strategies
- Data Fetching in API Routes versus Components

Understanding the Basics of API-Related Tools

Now that you have understood APIs and JSON in *Chapter* 4, *API Routes in Next.js*, let us explore the tools used to fetch data from APIs.

Using Fetch in Next.js

Fetch is a built-in browser API that allows you to make HTTP requests. Think of it as asking a server for data (such as a list of users) or sending the data to a server (such as creating a new user). Fetch uses Promises, which makes it easy to handle asynchronous operations (tasks that take time, such as waiting for a server response).

For example, if you want to get a list of users from a server, you can use Fetch to send a request to the server's API. The server will process your request, and send back the data, usually in JSON format.

Understanding How Fetch Works

When you use `fetch()`, it performs the following steps:

1. **Initiates a request:** You provide a URL (API endpoint) to `fetch()`.
2. **Sends the request to the server:** The browser (or server) makes an HTTP request.
3. **Receives a response:** The server processes the request and returns data.
4. **Processes the response:** You handle the returned data, typically in JSON format.

Basic Fetch Workflow

- Call `fetch(url)`, where `url` is the API endpoint.
- `fetch()` returns a Promise that resolves to a Response object.
- Convert the Response object to JSON using `.json()`.
- Handle the extracted data.

Fetching Data with Fetch in Next.js

Next.js provides different ways to use **`fetch()`** for data fetching, depending on whether you need client-side or server-side data retrieval.

Fetching Data on the Client-Side

Client-side fetching happens when a page loads and runs in the user's browser. You typically use **`useEffect`** and **`useState`** in a React component to handle this.

Example: Client-side Fetch in a Next.js Component

```
import { useEffect, useState } from "react";
export default function Users() {
  const [users, setUsers] = useState([]);
  const [loading, setLoading] = useState(true);

  useEffect(() => {
    fetch("https://jsonplaceholder.typicode.com/users")
      .then((response) => response.json()) // Convert response to
JSON
      .then((data) => {
        setUsers(data); // Store data in state
        setLoading(false);
      })
      .catch((error) => {
        console.error("Error fetching data:", error);
        setLoading(false);
      });
  }, []);

  if (loading) return <p>Loading...</p>;

  return (
    <div>
      <h1>Users List</h1>
      <ul>
        {users.map((user) => (
          <li key={user.id}>{user.name}</li>
        ))}
      </ul>
    </div>
  );
}
```

Explanation:

- We use **useState** to store the fetched data and track the loading state.
- **useEffect** is used to make the fetch request when the component mounts.
- We convert the response to JSON using **.json()**.
- The data is stored in users, and the component re-renders to display the data.

Fetching Data on the Server-Side

Next.js allows server-side data fetching using **getServerSideProps()**. This approach fetches data on each request, ensuring fresh data.

Example: Server-side Fetch in Next.js

```
export async function getServerSideProps() {
  const res = await fetch("https://jsonplaceholder.typicode.com/
users");
  const users = await res.json();
  return { props: { users } };
}

export default function Users({ users }) {
  return (
    <div>
      <h1>Users List</h1>
      <ul>
        {users.map((user) => (
          <li key={user.id}>{user.name}</li>
        ))}
      </ul>
    </div>
  );
}
```

Explanation:

- **getServerSideProps** runs on the server before rendering the page.
- The **fetch** function retrieves data before sending the page to the browser.
- The data is then passed as props to the component and displayed.

Fetching Data at Build Time (Static Generation)

If the data does not change often, **getStaticProps()** allows fetching at build time, improving performance.

Example: Static Fetch in Next.js

```
export async function getStaticProps() {
  const res = await fetch("https://jsonplaceholder.typicode.com/
users");
  const users = await res.json();
  return { props: { users } };
}

export default function Users({ users }) {
  return (
    <div>
      <h1>Users List</h1>
      <ul>
        {users.map((user) => (
          <li key={user.id}>{user.name}</li>
        ))}
      </ul>
    </div>
  );
}
```

Explanation:

- **`getStaticProps`** fetches data at build time, making pages load faster.
- Suitable for data that does not change frequently.
- Data is passed as props, and the page is pre-rendered.

Understanding the key differences between fetch methods in Next.js is vital for optimizing data handling, improving performance, and choosing the right strategy for your application's needs.

Fetch Method	**Runs on**	**When It Runs**	**Best Used for**
useEffect + fetch	Client (Browser)	After Page Load	Dynamic Data, User Input
`getServerSideProps`	Server	Every Request	Live Data (for example, User Authentication)
`getStaticProps`	Server (at Build Time)	Once at Build Time	Static Data, Blogs, and Product Pages

Table 6.1: *Key Differences between Fetch Methods in Next.js*

Using Axios in Next.js

Axios is a popular JavaScript library used for making HTTP requests. It provides a more powerful and flexible alternative to the built-in **fetch()** function by offering features such as:

- Automatic JSON data transformation
- Request and response interception
- Built-in error handling
- Support for request cancellation and timeouts

In Next.js, Axios can be used for both client-side and server-side data fetching.

Installing Axios

To use Axios in your Next.js project, first install it:

```
npm install axios
```

or

```
yarn add axios
```

Client-Side Data Fetching with Axios

Client-side fetching happens in the browser after the page loads. You typically use **useEffect** and **useState** in a React component.

Example: Client-side Fetching with Axios

```
import { useEffect, useState } from "react";
import axios from "axios";
export default function Users() {
  const [users, setUsers] = useState([]);
  const [loading, setLoading] = useState(true);
  const [error, setError] = useState(null);
  useEffect(() => {
    axios.get("https://jsonplaceholder.typicode.com/users")
      .then((response) => {
        setUsers(response.data);
        setLoading(false);
      })
      .catch((error) => {
        setError(error.message);
        setLoading(false);
      });
  }, []);
  if (loading) return <p>Loading...</p>;
  if (error) return <p>Error: {error}</p>;
  return (
    <div>
      <h1>Users List</h1>
```

```
      <ul>
        {users.map((user) => (
          <li key={user.id}>{user.name}</li>
        ))}
      </ul>
    </div>
  );
}
```

Advantages of Axios over Fetch

- **Shorter syntax:** No need to manually call **`.json()`** on responses.
- **Better error handling:** Fetch does not reject HTTP errors (like 404), but Axios does.
- **Supports request cancellation:** Helps avoid unnecessary API calls.

Server-Side Data Fetching with Axios

In Next.js, **`getServerSideProps()`** fetches data on each request.

Example: Server-side Fetching with Axios

```
import axios from "axios";
export async function getServerSideProps() {
  try {
    const res = await axios.get("https://jsonplaceholder.
typicode.com/users");
    return { props: { users: res.data } };
  } catch (error) {
    return { props: { users: [] } };
  }
}

export default function Users({ users }) {
  return (
    <div>
      <h1>Users List</h1>
      <ul>
        {users.map((user) => (
          <li key={user.id}>{user.name}</li>
        ))}
      </ul>
    </div>
  );
}
```

Benefits of Server-side Fetching

- Ensures up-to-date data on every request
- Runs securely on the server, avoiding exposure of API keys

Fetching Data at Build Time with Axios

If the data does not change frequently, use **`getStaticProps()`** to fetch at build time.

Example: Static Fetching with Axios

```
import axios from "axios";
export async function getStaticProps() {
  const res = await axios.get("https://jsonplaceholder.typicode.
com/users");
  return { props: { users: res.data } };
}
export default function Users({ users }) {
  return (
    <div>
      <h1>Users List</h1>
      <ul>
        {users.map((user) => (
          <li key={user.id}>{user.name}</li>
        ))}
      </ul>
    </div>
  );
}
```

Benefits of Static Fetching

- Faster page loads since data is pre-fetched.
- Great for static content such as blogs and product pages.

Making POST Requests with Axios

Axios also makes it easy to send data to APIs using POST requests.

Example: Sending Data with Axios

```
import { useState } from "react";
import axios from "axios";
export default function AddUser() {
  const [name, setName] = useState("");
  const [message, setMessage] = useState("");
```

```
  const handleSubmit = async (e) => {
    e.preventDefault();
    try {
      const res = await axios.post("https://jsonplaceholder.typi-
code.com/users", {
        name,
      });
      setMessage(`User ${res.data.name} added successfully!`);
    } catch (error) {
      setMessage("Error adding user.");
    }
  };

  return (
    <div>
      <h1>Add User</h1>
      <form onSubmit={handleSubmit}>
        <input
          type="text"
          placeholder="Enter name"
          value={name}
          onChange={(e) => setName(e.target.value)}
        />
        <button type="submit">Submit</button>
      </form>
      {message && <p>{message}</p>}
    </div>
  );
}
```

Using **axios.post()**, we send the name input as JSON to the API, and display the response message upon submission.

- We use **axios.post()** to send data to the API.
- The name input is sent as JSON.
- The response message is displayed after submission.

Global Axios Configuration in Next.js

To avoid repetitive codes, configure Axios globally in Next.js.

Example: Setting up Axios Defaults

```
Create a new file: utils/axiosInstance.js
import axios from "axios";
const api = axios.create({
  baseURL: "https://jsonplaceholder.typicode.com",
```

```
  headers: { "Content-Type": "application/json" },
});
export default api;
Now, import and use it in components:

import api from "../utils/axiosInstance";
export async function getServerSideProps() {
  const res = await api.get("/users");
  return { props: { users: res.data } };
}
```

Creating a custom Axios instance reduces repetition by eliminating the need to rewrite full API URLs, and allows setting default headers, which is especially useful for authentication.

- **Reduces repetition:** No need to write full API URLs every time.
- **Adds default headers:** Useful for authentication.

Using SWR in Next.js

Stale-While-Revalidate (SWR) is a data-fetching library for React, designed by the team at Vercel (creators of Next.js). It improves performance by fetching data in the background, and updating the UI automatically when the new data is available.

Key Benefits of SWR

SWR offers powerful, modern data-fetching capabilities that improve performance, user experience, and developer productivity by handling caching, revalidation, and state management automatically.

- Automatic caching and revalidation
- Background data fetching
- Focus-based revalidation (fetches fresh data when the user returns to the page)
- Supports error handling, pagination, and optimistic UI updates

Installing SWR

To use SWR in a Next.js project, install it using:

```
npm install swr
```

or

```
yarn add swr
```

Basic Example: Fetching Data with SWR

SWR uses a simple **useSWR** hook for fetching the data.

```
import useSWR from "swr";
const fetcher = (url) => fetch(url).then((res) => res.json());
export default function Users() {
  const { data, error, isLoading } = useSWR("https://jsonplace-
holder.typicode.com/users", fetcher);

  if (isLoading) return <p>Loading...</p>;
  if (error) return <p>Error: {error.message}</p>;

  return (
    <div>
      <h1>Users List</h1>
      <ul>
        {data.map((user) => (
          <li key={user.id}>{user.name}</li>
        ))}
      </ul>
    </div>
  );
}
```

The **useSWR** hook simplifies data fetching by caching API responses, auto-revalidating on page revisit, and managing loading and error states effortlessly.

- **useSWR(url, fetcher)**: Calls the API and caches the result.
- SWR automatically revalidates in the background when the page is revisited.
- Handles loading and error states seamlessly.

Fetching Data with Axios in SWR

While SWR works seamlessly with the native Fetch API, you can also integrate Axios as a custom fetcher to take advantage of its richer features, such as automatic JSON parsing and enhanced error handling.

```
Instead of fetch(), you can use Axios for data fetching.
import useSWR from "swr";
import axios from "axios";

const fetcher = (url) => axios.get(url).then((res) => res.data);
export default function Users() {
  const { data, error, isLoading } = useSWR("https://jsonplace-
holder.typicode.com/users", fetcher);
  if (isLoading) return <p>Loading...</p>;
```

```
  if (error) return <p>Error: {error.message}</p>;
  return (
    <div>
      <h1>Users List</h1>
      <ul>
        {data.map((user) => (
          <li key={user.id}>{user.name}</li>
        ))}
      </ul>
    </div>
  );
}
```

Using Axios with SWR

- Axios has built-in JSON transformation (no need to manually parse **`res.json()`**).
- Better error handling with automatic rejection of HTTP errors.

Mutating Data: Revalidating and Updating SWR Cache

SWR provides the **`mutate()`** function to update the cache without re-fetching the entire dataset.

Example: Adding a User and Updating SWR Cache

```
import useSWR, { mutate } from "swr";
import axios from "axios";
import { useState } from "react";
const fetcher = (url) => axios.get(url).then((res) => res.data);
export default function Users() {
  const { data, error, isLoading } = useSWR("https://jsonplace-
holder.typicode.com/users", fetcher);
  const [name, setName] = useState("");

  const addUser = async () => {
    const newUser = { id: data.length + 1, name };

    // Optimistically update UI
    mutate("https://jsonplaceholder.typicode.com/users", [...
data, newUser], false);

    // Send POST request
    await axios.post("https://jsonplaceholder.typicode.com/
users", { name });

    // Revalidate data
```

```
    mutate("https://jsonplaceholder.typicode.com/users");
  };

  if (isLoading) return <p>Loading...</p>;
  if (error) return <p>Error: {error.message}</p>;

  return (
    <div>
      <h1>Users List</h1>
      <ul>
        {data.map((user) => (
          <li key={user.id}>{user.name}</li>
        ))}
      </ul>

      <input type="text" value={name} onChange={(e) => setName(e.
target.value)} placeholder="Enter name" />
      <button onClick={addUser}>Add User</button>
    </div>
  );
}
```

With SWR, features like optimistic UI updates and the mutate function enable instant UI feedback and efficient cache management for a smoother user experience.

- **Optimistic UI Update:** Updates UI instantly before the API response arrives.
- **Mutate Function:** Updates SWR cache with new data, and refetches it.

Fetching Data on the Server with SWR

SWR is designed for client-side fetching. However, you can preload data on the server using Next.js' **`getServerSideProps()`**.

Example: Combining Server and Client Fetching

```
import useSWR from "swr";
import axios from "axios";
const fetcher = (url) => axios.get(url).then((res) => res.data);
export async function getServerSideProps() {
  const res = await axios.get("https://jsonplaceholder.typicode.
com/users");
  return { props: { fallbackData: res.data } };
}

export default function Users({ fallbackData }) {
  const { data, error } = useSWR("https://jsonplaceholder.typi-
code.com/users", fetcher, { fallbackData });
```

```
  if (error) return <p>Error loading users.</p>;
  if (!data) return <p>Loading...</p>;

  return (
    <div>
      <h1>Users List</h1>
      <ul>
        {data.map((user) => (
          <li key={user.id}>{user.name}</li>
        ))}
      </ul>
    </div>
  );
}
```

Advantages of Using This Approach

Combining server-side data fetching with SWR provides the best of both worlds—optimized initial load performance and seamless real-time updates.

- **Fast Page Load:** Server-side fetching ensures that the data is already available when the page loads.
- **Fresh Updates:** SWR refetches the data in the background for real-time updates.
- **Reduced API Calls:** The page is served with preloaded data, avoiding an extra request on mount.

Comparison of Fetch, Axios, and SWR in Next.js

The following is a detailed comparison of **Fetch API, Axios, and SWR** based on different aspects of data fetching in Next.js:

Feature	Fetch API	Axios	Stale-While-Revalidate (SWR)
Installation	No installation needed (built-in feature of JavaScript).	Requires installation using **`npm install axios`**.	Requires installation using **`npm install swr`**.
Ease of Use	Requires more code since you need to manually check the response status and convert data to JSON.	Easier than Fetch, as it automatically handles JSON conversion and response errors.	Simplifies data fetching by handling caching, revalidation, and state management.

Automatic JSON Parsing	No, you must use **`response.json()`** to parse the response.	Yes, Axios automatically converts the response into JSON format.	Yes, when using the fetcher function, it can automatically parse JSON.
Error Handling	Errors must be manually handled using **`response.ok`** or **`try-catch blocks`**.	Automatically rejects HTTP errors (such as 404 or 500), making error handling simpler.	Provides built-in error handling with **`error`** state.
Timeout Handling	No built-in timeout feature. You need to use **`AbortController`**.	Supports request timeouts using the **`timeout`** option.	Uses revalidation strategies but does not have direct timeout handling.
Request Cancelation	Can cancel requests using **`AbortController`**.	Supports request cancellation with **`cancelToken`**.	Automatically cancels stale requests when the component unmounts or when new data is available.
Global Configuration	No global configuration available. Each request must be configured separately.	Supports global configurations using **`axios.defaults`**.	Provides **`SWRConfig`** for setting global options.
Caching	No built-in caching. You need to manually store and retrieve data.	No built-in caching, but you can use an external library such as localStorage or React Query.	Automatically caches responses and updates data in the background.
Revalidation	Does not fetch fresh data automatically. You need to call the API again.	No automatic revalidation. You must manually refresh the data.	Automatically revalidates data in the background when the user revisits the page or when network status changes.
Optimistic UI Updates	Not supported.	Not supported.	Supported using the **`mutate()`** function, allowing UI updates before receiving new data.
Best Use Case	Simple, one-time API calls where performance and error handling are not a major concern.	Best for making complex API requests with better control over responses and errors.	Ideal for Next.js applications that require automatic caching, background updates, and real-time data fetching.

Table 6.2: *Differences between Fetch, Axios and SWR*

SWR Parameters and Their Meanings

To fully utilize SWR, it is important to understand its various configuration options. The following table lists the key SWR parameters, along with their descriptions and examples:

Parameter	Description	Example Usage
key	Unique identifier for the request (usually API URL).	useSWR('/api/users', fetcher)
fetcher	Function to fetch data from the API.	const fetcher = url => fetch(url).then(res => res.json())
options	Configuration object to customize SWR behavior.	useSWR('/api/users', fetcher, { refreshInterval: 5000 })
data	Holds the fetched data.	const { data } = useSWR('/api/users', fetcher)
error	Stores the error if the fetch request fails.	if (error) return <p>Error loading data</p>
isLoading	Returns true while fetching data.	if (isLoading) return <p>Loading...</p>
mutate()	Manually revalidate and update data.	mutate('/api/users')
fallbackData	Provides default data before fetching completes.	useSWR('/api/users', fetcher, { fallbackData: [] })
refreshInterval	Time in milliseconds to auto-revalidate data.	useSWR('/api/users', fetcher, { refreshInterval: 5000 })
dedupingInterval	Time interval (ms) to avoid duplicate requests.	useSWR('/api/users', fetcher, { dedupingInterval: 2000 })
revalidateOnFocus	Re-fetch data when the user focuses on the page.	useSWR('/api/users', fetcher, { revalidateOnFocus: true })
revalidateOnReconnect	Re-fetch when the user regains the internet connection.	useSWR('/api/users', fetcher, { revalidateOnReconnect: true })
shouldRetryOnError	Determines whether to retry on failure.	useSWR('/api/users', fetcher, { shouldRetryOnError: false })

`onSuccess`	Callback function after successful fetch.	`useSWR('/api/users', fetcher, { onSuccess: (data) => console.log(data) })`
`onError`	Callback function when fetch fails.	`useSWR('/api/users', fetcher, { onError: (err) => console.error(err) })`

Table 6.3: *SWR Parameters*

Handling Errors and Loading States

When fetching data in Next.js, handling errors and loading states is crucial to ensuring a seamless user experience. Let us explore how to effectively manage these states using Fetch API, Axios, and SWR.

Handling Errors and Loading States with Fetch API

The Fetch API is a built-in JavaScript function used for making HTTP requests. However, it does not automatically handle HTTP errors, meaning you must manually check the response status, and handle errors accordingly.

Steps to Handle Errors and Loading States in Fetch API

1. Set a loading state before making the request.
2. Use `**try-catch**` to handle errors.
3. Check `**response.ok**` to determine success.
4. Update state based on success or failure.

Example: Fetch API with Error and Loading Handling

```
import { useEffect, useState } from 'react';
export default function Users() {
  const [data, setData] = useState(null);
  const [loading, setLoading] = useState(true);
  const [error, setError] = useState(null);

  useEffect(() => {
    const fetchData = async () => {
      setLoading(true);
      try {
        const response = await fetch('/api/users');
```

```
        if (!response.ok) {
          throw new Error(`HTTP error! Status: ${response.
status}`);
        }

        const result = await response.json();
        setData(result);
      } catch (err) {
        setError(err.message);
      } finally {
        setLoading(false);
      }
    };

    fetchData();
  }, []);

  if (loading) return <p>Loading...</p>;
  if (error) return <p>Error: {error}</p>;

  return (
    <ul>
      {data.map((user) => (
        <li key={user.id}>{user.name}</li>
      ))}
    </ul>
  );
}
```

Handling Breakdown:

- Before fetching, `**loading**` is set to `**true**`.
- A `**try-catch**` block handles errors.
- If an error occurs, it is stored in the `**error**` state.
- After the request completes, `**loading**` is set to `**false**`.

Handling Errors and Loading States with Axios

Axios is a promise-based HTTP client that simplifies API requests. Unlike Fetch, Axios automatically rejects HTTP errors, making error handling easier.

Steps to Handle Errors and Loading States in Axios

1. Set a loading state before making the request.
2. Use `**try-catch**` to handle errors.

3. Axios automatically throws errors for failed responses.
4. Update state accordingly.

Example: Axios with Error and Loading Handling

```
import { useEffect, useState } from 'react';
import axios from 'axios';
export default function Users() {
  const [data, setData] = useState(null);
  const [loading, setLoading] = useState(true);
  const [error, setError] = useState(null);
  useEffect(() => {
    const fetchData = async () => {
      setLoading(true);
      try {
        const response = await axios.get('/api/users');
        setData(response.data);
      } catch (err) {
        setError(err.response?.data?.message || 'Something went
wrong');
      } finally {
        setLoading(false);
      }
    };
    fetchData();
  }, []);

  if (loading) return <p>Loading...</p>;
  if (error) return <p>Error: {error}</p>;
  return (
    <ul>
      {data.map((user) => (
        <li key={user.id}>{user.name}</li>
      ))}
    </ul>
  );
}
```

Handling Breakdown:

- Axios automatically rejects HTTP errors, and so no need to check `**response.ok**`.
- Error messages are extracted from `**error.response.data.message**`.
- The `**loading**` state is set before fetching, and reset afterward.

Handling Errors and Loading States with SWR

SWR is a data-fetching library optimized for React and Next.js. It automatically caches, revalidates, and handles errors, eliminating the need for `**useState**` and `**useEffect**`.

Steps to Handle Errors and Loading States in SWR

- Use `**useSWR()**` for automatic fetching.
- Check `**isLoading**` for the loading state.
- Check `**error**` for error handling.

Example: SWR with Error and Loading Handling

```
import useSWR from 'swr';
const fetcher = async (url) => {
  const response = await fetch(url);
  if (!response.ok) throw new Error('Failed to fetch data');
  return response.json();
};
export default function Users() {
  const { data, error, isLoading } = useSWR('/api/users', fetcher);
  if (isLoading) return <p>Loading...</p>;
  if (error) return <p>Error: {error.message}</p>;
  return (
    <ul>
      {data.map((user) => (
        <li key={user.id}>{user.name}</li>
      ))}
    </ul>
  );
}
```

Handling Breakdown:

- SWR manages the request lifecycle automatically.
- `**isLoading**` replaces manual loading state handling.
- Errors are automatically caught and stored in `**error**`.

Prefetching with SWR

SWR automatically prefetches the data, and updates it in the background. You can prefetch the data on hover, or focus to improve UX.

Example: Prefetching on Hover

```
import useSWR, { preload } from 'swr';
const fetcher = (url) => fetch(url).then((res) => res.json());
export default function UserList() {
  preload('/api/users', fetcher); // Prefetch data when the
component loads
  const { data, error } = useSWR('/api/users', fetcher);
  if (!data) return <p>Loading...</p>;
  if (error) return <p>Error loading users</p>;
  return (
    <ul>
      {data.map((user) => (
        <li key={user.id}>{user.name}</li>
      ))}
    </ul>
  );
}
```

SWR prefetches the data before the request is needed. Thus, the data updates automatically in the background.

Revalidation Strategies

Revalidation refers to updating the stale data after a certain time interval, or under specific conditions (for example, when the user focuses on the page).

Revalidation in Next.js (ISR - Incremental Static Regeneration)

Next.js allows revalidation at an interval to keep the **static pages fresh**.

Example: Revalidate Every 10 Seconds

```
export async function getStaticProps() {
  const res = await fetch('https://api.example.com/news');
  const news = await res.json();
  return {
    props: { news },
    revalidate: 10 // Revalidate every 10 seconds
  };
}
```

- Data **stays cached** but **updates every 10 seconds**.
- Improves performance, while keeping the data fresh.

Revalidation with SWR

SWR automatically revalidates the data under multiple conditions.

Automatic Revalidation Triggers in SWR

- `revalidateOnFocus`: Re-fetches when the user switches back to the page (*default: true*).
- `revalidateOnReconnect`: Re-fetches when the user regains an internet connection (*default: true*).
- `refresh Interval`: Re-fetches the data at a fixed time interval.
- `mutate ()`: Manually revalidates the data on demand.

Example Auto Revalidating Every 5 Seconds

```
import useSWR from 'swr';
const fetcher = (url) => fetch(url).then((res) => res.json());
export default function StockPrices() {
  const { data, error } = useSWR('/api/stocks', fetcher,
{ refreshInterval: 5000 });
  if (!data) return <p>Loading...</p>;
  if (error) return <p>Error loading stock prices</p>;
  return (
    <ul>
      {data.map((stock) => (
        <li key={stock.id}>{stock.name}: ${stock.price}</li>
      ))}
    </ul>
  );
}
```

SWR supports automatic data refreshing and efficient caching, enabling real-time updates every few seconds, while minimizing unnecessary network requests.

- Data refreshes every 5 seconds without user interaction.
- Efficient caching reduces unnecessary network requests.

Example: Manual Revalidation with `mutate()`

Sometimes, you want to refresh the data manually when an action happens (for example, after a form submission).

```
import useSWR, { mutate } from 'swr';
const fetcher = (url) => fetch(url).then((res) => res.json());
export default function Users() {
  const { data, error } = useSWR('/api/users', fetcher);
  const refreshData = () => mutate('/api/users'); // Manually
refresh data
```

```
  if (!data) return <p>Loading...</p>;
  if (error) return <p>Error loading users</p>;
  return (
    <div>
      <button onClick={refreshData}>Refresh Users</button>
      <ul>
        {data.map((user) => (
          <li key={user.id}>{user.name}</li>
        ))}
      </ul>
    </div>
  );
}
```

In SWR, clicking the 'Refresh Users' button triggers **`mutate()`** to revalidate and update data, while its smart caching ensures that the new data is fetched only when the cache is stale. SWR only fetches the new data if the previous cache is stale, making it highly efficient.

Data Fetching in API Routes versus Components

Next.js provides two primary ways to fetch the data:

- **Using API Routes (`/pages/api/`):** Fetching data on the server side.
- **Fetching Data in Components:** Fetching data directly in React components (Client-side).

Each method has its own use cases, advantages, and limitations. Let us explore them in detail.

Fetching Data Using API Routes in Next.js

API Routes in Next.js allow developers to create backend-like endpoints inside the **`/pages/api/`** directory. These routes execute only on the server, making them useful for handling data securely without exposing the sensitive details to the front end.

Use API Routes When You:

- Want to hide API keys and sensitive credentials from the client.
- Need to process the data on the server before sending it to the client.
- Want to fetch the data from a database directly without exposing queries to the front end.
- Need custom business logic such as authentication, authorization, or request validation.

Example: Creating an API Route in Next.js

```
File: /pages/api/users.js
export default async function handler(req, res) {
  if (req.method === 'GET') {
    try {
      const response = await fetch('https://jsonplaceholder.typi-
code.com/users');
      if (!response.ok) {
        throw new Error('Failed to fetch users');
      }
      const users = await response.json();
      res.status(200).json(users);
    } catch (error) {
      res.status(500).json({ message: error.message });
    }
  } else {
    res.status(405).json({ message: 'Method Not Allowed' });
  }
}
```

Using This API Route in a React Component

Once the API route is set up, you can fetch the data from your React components:

```
import { useEffect, useState } from 'react';
export default function Users() {
  const [users, setUsers] = useState([]);
  const [loading, setLoading] = useState(true);
  const [error, setError] = useState(null);

  useEffect(() => {
    fetch('/api/users')
      .then((res) => {
        if (!res.ok) {
          throw new Error('Error fetching users');
        }
        return res.json();
      })
      .then((data) => {
        setUsers(data);
        setLoading(false);
      })
      .catch((err) => {
        setError(err.message);
        setLoading(false);
      });
```

```
    }, []);

    if (loading) return <p>Loading users...</p>;
    if (error) return <p>Error: {error}</p>;

    return (
      <div>
        <h2>Users List</h2>
        <ul>
          {users.map(user => <li key={user.id}>{user.name}</li>)}
        </ul>
      </div>
    );
  }
```

Advantages of Using API Routes

API routes provide a secure and flexible way to handle server-side logic, offering several benefits when interacting with external services or managing backend operations.

- **Security:** API routes run on the server, hiding the sensitive details such as API keys and database credentials.
- **Data Processing:** You can modify or filter the data before sending it to the front end.
- **Centralized API Handling:** Instead of making multiple API calls from the front end, the API route can manage all the requests.

Limitations of API Routes

Despite their advantages, API routes also come with certain trade-offs that may affect performance and design choices depending on your use case.

- **Additional Latency:** API routes introduce an extra layer between the client and the actual API.
- **Not Needed for Public APIs:** If the data is already public, fetching directly from the front end might be more efficient.

Fetching Data Directly in React Components

Fetching data directly in a component means making an API request from the front end using the fetch API, axios, or a data-fetching library such as SWR or React Query.

Use Client-side Fetching When:

- SEO is not important (for example, user dashboards, profile pages, and so on).
- Data updates frequently, and should be refreshed dynamically.
- Fetching from public APIs that do not require authentication.
- Fetching user-specific data that depends on interactions (for example, searching, filtering, and so on).

Example: Fetching Data in a React Component

```
import { useState, useEffect } from 'react';
export default function Users() {
  const [users, setUsers] = useState([]);
  const [loading, setLoading] = useState(true);
  const [error, setError] = useState(null);
  useEffect(() => {
    fetch('https://jsonplaceholder.typicode.com/users')
      .then((res) => {
        if (!res.ok) {
          throw new Error('Failed to fetch users');
        }
        return res.json();
      })
      .then((data) => {
        setUsers(data);
        setLoading(false);
      })
      .catch((err) => {
        setError(err.message);
        setLoading(false);
      });
  }, []);

  if (loading) return <p>Loading...</p>;
  if (error) return <p>Error: {error}</p>;

  return (
    <div>
      <h2>Users List</h2>
      <ul>
        {users.map(user => <li key={user.id}>{user.name}</li>)}
      </ul>
    </div>
  );
}
```

Advantages of Fetching Components

Fetching data directly inside components offers a simple and flexible approach for handling dynamic, client-side updates without additional backend complexity.

- Simple to implement without creating an extra API route.
- Ideal for dynamic or real-time data updates.
- Reduces server-side processing load by shifting work to the client.

Limitations of Client-side Fetching

Despite its convenience, client-side fetching also introduces limitations that can affect performance, security, and SEO.

- **Slower First Load:** The data is fetched after the page renders which may cause flashing content.
- **Exposes API Calls:** Public APIs are visible in the browser's network tab, making them less secure.
- **Not SEO-Friendly:** Data fetching happens on the client that search engines might not index properly.

Choosing between API routes and fetching directly in components depends on your app's architecture, with API routes offering better abstraction and reuse, while in-component fetching provides simplicity for client-side data needs.

The following table provides a clear comparison between using API routes and fetching data directly within components, helping you determine which approach best fits your application's requirements:

Use Case	API Routes (Server-side Fetching)	Fetching in Components (Client-side Fetching)
Security	Hides API keys and database queries.	Exposes API calls in the browser (less secure).
Authentication	Suitable for authenticated requests.	Not ideal for handling secure authentication.
Data Processing	Allows pre-processing, filtering, or modifying data before sending.	Fetches raw data directly from the API.
API Management	Acts as a centralized entry point for managing all API requests.	Each component handles its own data fetching individually.
Performance	Reduces client-side load by handling requests on the server.	Increases client-side processing and load.

SEO Optimization	Ideal for pages requiring SEO as data is pre-fetched before rendering.	Not SEO-friendly since data is fetched after the page loads.
Real-Time Updates	Requires manual revalidation or WebSockets for real-time updates.	Better suited for dynamic, frequently changing data.
Use Case Examples	Fetching from a database, hiding API keys, processing API data.	Fetching open APIs, real-time stock prices, and weather updates.

***Table 6.4:** Use API Routes versus Fetching in Components*

Conclusion

In this chapter, we explored different data-fetching methods in Next.js, including fetch, axios, and SWR. Each approach has its advantages: Fetch API is built-in but requires manual handling of errors and response transformation; Axios simplifies requests with built-in features, and SWR provides automatic caching and revalidation for real-time updates.

We also covered error handling, loading states, prefetching, revalidation strategies, and the differences between API routes and client-side fetching. Choosing the right data-fetching approach is essential for optimizing performance, security, and scalability. API routes are best for handling sensitive data and authentication, while client-side fetching is suitable for public APIs and real-time updates. Understanding these techniques allows developers to build efficient and maintainable applications.

In the next chapter, we will explore Styling in Next.js, covering CSS Modules, Styled Components, Tailwind CSS, and the best practices for styling modern applications effectively.

Multiple Choice Questions

1. Which data fetching method in Next.js provides automatic caching and revalidation?

    a. Fetch API

    b. Axios

    c. SWR

    d. GraphQL

2. What is a key advantage of using API routes in Next.js?
    a. Faster execution on the client side
    b. Hides API keys and database queries
    c. Increases SEO ranking directly
    d. Eliminates the need for authentication
3. Which parameter in SWR ensures that the data is revalidated when the user focuses on the page?
    a. `refreshInterval`
    b. `mutate`
    c. `revalidateOnFocus`
    d. `dedupingInterval`
4. When should you prefer client-side data fetching over API routes?
    a. When working with sensitive data that requires authentication.
    b. When the API response is fast, and does not require modification.
    c. When the SEO is critical for the page.
    d. When API calls need to be hidden from the user.
5. Which of the following is NOT a benefit of using Axios over Fetch API?
    a. Automatic request and response transformation
    b. Built-in timeout support
    c. Automatic caching and revalidation
    d. Ability to cancel requests

Answers

1. c
2. b
3. c
4. b
5. c

CHAPTER 7
Styling in Next.js

Introduction

Styling in Next.js is highly flexible, offering various methods to manage styles effectively, while maintaining performance and scalability. Whether using traditional CSS, modern CSS frameworks, or CSS-in-JS solutions, Next.js provides seamless integration with multiple styling approaches.

Global and scoped CSS can be implemented using standard CSS files or CSS Modules. CSS Modules help avoid style conflicts by automatically scoping styles to specific components. For enhanced maintainability, SCSS modules extend this functionality with features such as variables, mixins, and nested selectors, making styling more structured and reusable.

Tailwind CSS, a utility-first framework, integrates well with Next.js, enabling rapid UI development with predefined classes that eliminate the need for writing custom styles. Additionally, CSS-in-JS solutions such as styled-components and Emotion allow dynamic styling within JavaScript files, offering benefits like theming and component-level styling.

To maintain performance and scalability, best practices include minimizing render-blocking styles, structuring styles efficiently, and leveraging static extraction for optimized loading. By using these styling techniques effectively, developers can build modern, maintainable, and visually appealing Next.js applications that deliver an excellent user experience.

Structure

In this chapter, the following topics will be covered:

- Global and Scoped CSS in Next.js
- Using SCSS Modules
- Tailwind CSS Integration
- CSS-in-JS with Styled Components and Emotion
- Best Practices for Styling in Next.js Projects

Global and Scoped CSS in Next.js

Styling is a fundamental part of any web application, and Next.js provides multiple ways to handle styles efficiently. Two primary methods of styling in Next.js are global CSS and scoped CSS (CSS Modules). Understanding these approaches helps in maintaining a clean and structured application without style conflicts.

Understanding CSS

CSS (Cascading Style Sheets) is used to design and structure web pages by defining how elements appear on the screen. Next.js, being a React-based framework, allows developers to use different styling techniques, including:

- **Global CSS:** Styles that apply to the entire application.
- **Scoped CSS (CSS Modules):** Styles that are limited to a specific component.

Next.js has built-in support for CSS, enabling developers to use styles effectively without additional configurations.

Global CSS

Global CSS refers to styles that apply universally across the application. This means that once a style is defined in a global CSS file, it affects all the components and pages, unless overridden.

Use Global CSS

To use global CSS in a Next.js project, the styles must be imported inside the `_app.js` or `_app.tsx` file. This ensures that the styles are available across all pages.

Steps to Implement Global CSS

To apply consistent styling across your entire Next.js application, you can configure global CSS so that shared styles load automatically on every page.

1. **Create a Global CSS File**

   Inside the `styles` directory, create a file called `globals.css`:

   ```
   /* styles/globals.css */
   body {
     margin: 0;
     padding: 0;
     font-family: Arial, sans-serif;
     background-color: f5f5f5;
   ```

```
}

h1 {
  color: 333;
}
```

2. **Import the Global CSS File in `_app.js`**

   Open `_app.js` inside the `pages` directory, and import the CSS file:

```
import '@/styles/globals.css';
function MyApp({ Component, pageProps }) {
  return <Component {...pageProps} />;
}
export default MyApp;
```

This ensures that `globals.css` is loaded and applied across all components and pages, such as:

- Base styles such as typography, default colors, and spacing.
- Styles that apply to multiple pages.
- CSS resets and global layout styling.

Note: *In Next.js, global CSS can only be imported inside `_app.js`. Importing it elsewhere will cause an error, as Next.js enforces modular styling for better maintainability.*

Scoped CSS (CSS Modules)

Scoped CSS ensures that styles are applied only to a specific component, preventing unintended style conflicts. Next.js provides built-in support for CSS Modules which automatically scope styles locally to the component that imports them.

A CSS Module file uses the `.module.css` extension which makes it different from regular CSS files. When imported into a component, its class names are dynamically generated, preventing conflicts with other styles.

Use Scoped CSS (CSS Modules)

Scoped CSS using CSS Modules allows you to style components without worrying about class name conflicts, ensuring styles apply only to the specific component where they are imported.

- Create a CSS Module file

  Inside the `styles` folder, create a file named `Home.module.css`:

```
/* styles/Home.module.css */
.container {
  padding: 20px;
```

```
  background-color: white;
  border-radius: 8px;
  box-shadow: 0 4px 6px rgba(0, 0, 0, 0.1);
}
.heading {
  color: 0070f3;
  text-align: center;
}
```

Import and Apply Styles in a Component

Inside the `pages/index.js` file, import the CSS Module, and use the class names as JavaScript properties:

```
import styles from '@/styles/Home.module.css';
export default function Home() {
  return (
    <div className={styles.container}>
      <h1 className={styles.heading}>Welcome to Next.js</h1>
    </div>
  );
}
```

In this example, `styles.container` and `styles.heading` apply styles only to the `Home` component. Other components cannot access these styles, making CSS Modules an excellent choice for modular and maintainable styling. CSS Modules are particularly useful:

- When styling specific components without affecting other components.
- To prevent style conflicts in large applications.
- For better maintainability in component-based architecture.

Feature	**Global CSS**	**Scoped CSS (CSS Modules)**
Scope	Entire application	Only the component where it's used
File Extension	`.css`	`.module.css`
Import Location	Only in `_app.js`	In any component
Best for	Base styles, resets	Component-specific styles

Table 7.1: *Key Differences: Global CSS vs. Scoped CSS (CSS Modules)*

Best Practices for Using CSS in Next.js

Following CSS best practices in Next.js helps keep your styles maintainable, scalable, and predictable as your application grows:

- **Use Global CSS Sparingly:** Only for base styles and resets to avoid unexpected style overrides.

- **Prefer CSS Modules for Component Styling:** Ensures encapsulation, and prevents conflicts.
- **Organize Styles Properly:** Keep styles inside a `` `styles` `` directory, and separate them based on usage (for example, `` `globals.css` `` for global styles, `` `Component.module.css` `` for component styles).
- **Minimize Unused Styles:** Optimize performance by avoiding large global stylesheets.

Using a combination of global CSS and scoped CSS (CSS Modules) helps in maintaining a well-organized, scalable, and efficient Next.js project.

Using SCSS Modules

SCSS, or Sassy CSS, is a powerful extension of standard CSS. It allows developers to write cleaner, more efficient, and more organized stylesheets by introducing features such as variables, nesting, mixins, and functions. SCSS is one of the syntaxes of SASS (Syntactically Awesome Style Sheets) and is fully compatible with traditional CSS, meaning you can gradually introduce SCSS into your project without breaking anything.

In comparison to plain CSS, SCSS significantly improves productivity and maintainability—especially in large projects. For example, with SCSS you can define a $primary-color variable, and use it throughout your styles. If you ever need to update that color, you only change it in one place. Similarly, nested rules in SCSS allow styles to follow the structure of your HTML more naturally, making them easier to read and maintain.

In a Next.js project, SCSS becomes even more powerful when used with **SCSS Modules**. These are `.module.scss` files that scope styles to a specific component, preventing styles from leaking into other parts of your app. This avoids common bugs that occur with global CSS, like unintended style overrides.

The following steps walk you through how to set up SCSS and use SCSS Modules in a Next.js project, ensuring clean, maintainable, and component-scoped styling:

1. **Installing SASS**

   Before using SCSS in a Next.js project, you need to install the SASS package, which is required to compile SCSS files.

   Open your terminal in your project directory and run:

   ```
   npm install sass
   ```

   or, if you are using Yarn:

   ```
   yarn add sass
   ```

This enables Next.js to understand **`.scss`** and **`.module.scss`** files.

2. **Creating an SCSS Module File**

   SCSS Modules are written using the **`.module.scss`** extension. This tells Next.js to treat the file as a CSS Module which scopes all class names locally to the file that imports them.

   Example Directory Structure

```
components/
  ├── Button.tsx
  └── Button.module.scss
```

   Example SCSS Module: `Button.module.scss`

```
.button {
  background-color: #0070f3;
  color: white;
  padding: 10px 16px;
  border: none;
  border-radius: 5px;
  cursor: pointer;
  font-size: 16px;
  transition: background-color 0.3s ease;
}

.button:hover {
  background-color: #0051a2;
}
```

   This file defines a **`.button`** class that will be scoped only to the component that imports it.

3. **Importing SCSS Module in a Component**

   Once your **`.module.scss`** file is ready, import it in the related component file using ES6 import syntax.

   Example Component: `Button.tsx`

```
import React from 'react';
import styles from './Button.module.scss';
const Button = () => {
  return <button className={styles.button}>Click Me</button>;
};
export default Button;
```

   Styles is an object containing all the class names defined in the SCSS module.

   a. **`styles.button`** accesses the class named **`.button`** from **`Button.module.scss`**.

   b. This class is automatically scoped and compiled to a unique class name in the browser, preventing any global conflict.

4. **SCSS Modules Work behind the Scenes**

   When you use SCSS modules in Next.js:

   a. The class names are automatically renamed to unique identifiers.

      i. For example, button in your SCSS file might become. **`Button_button_XX`** in the generated CSS.

   b. This ensures that the styles do not clash with other components using the same class names.

   c. The mapping between the original class name and the generated one is handled automatically by Next.js.

5. **Using Global SCSS Files (Optional)**

   If you want to apply global styles (such as resets, font styles, or layout styles), use a regular **`.scss`** file, and import it in the custom **`_app.tsx`** file.

   Example:

```
styles/globals.scss
body {
  margin: 0;
  font-family: Arial, sans-serif;
  background-color: #f4f4f4;
}

Import in _app.tsx
Import '../styles/globals.scss';
function MyApp({ Component, pageProps }) {
  return <Component {...pageProps} />;
}
export default MyApp;
```

   Note: *Only import global styles in **`_app.tsx`**. Do not import global styles inside components, as this breaks component encapsulation.*

6. **Comparison between SCSS Modules and Global SCSS**

   In a Next.js project, styling can be applied either through SCSS Modules or through global SCSS files, and each approach serves a distinct purpose. SCSS Modules are intended for component-level styling, and ensure that styles are scoped locally to avoid unintended overrides. On the other hand, global SCSS is used for styles that should apply across the entire application such as resets, base typography, or layout structures.

The following table outlines the key differences between these two methods to help you choose the appropriate one based on your use case:

Feature	SCSS Modules	Global SCSS
Scope	Component-level (local)	Application-wide (global)
Naming Conflicts	Avoided due to name mangling	Possible if reused globally
File Extension	`.module.scss`	`.scss`
Where to Use	Component-specific styles	Base styles, resets, layout

Table 7.2: *SCSS Modules vs Global SCSS*

To use SCSS in a Next.js project, the first step is to install the SASS package which enables SCSS file support within the framework. When defining styles specific to a component, it is recommended to use files with the **`.module.scss`** extension. These SCSS Modules allow styles to be scoped locally to the component, preventing global conflicts. Once the SCSS module is created, it should be imported using the syntax **`import styles from './filename.module.scss'`**, and class names can then be applied within JSX, using **`className={styles.className}`**. For styles that are meant to affect the entire application–such as base resets, layout settings, or global typography, it is best to use a regular **`.scss`** file, and import it exclusively in the **`_app.tsx`** file. This structured approach to styling helps maintain modularity, promotes reusability, and ensures that style definitions remain predictable and maintainable as the application scales.

CSS vs SCSS: Understanding the Difference

When styling websites or web applications, developers often start with plain CSS (Cascading Style Sheets). While CSS works well for small projects, it becomes difficult to manage as the codebase grows. This is where SCSS, a more powerful extension of CSS, comes in. SCSS introduces features such as variables, nesting, mixins, and modularization – making stylesheets easier to write, maintain, and scale. In Next.js, using SCSS Modules helps keep styles scoped to individual components, preventing unwanted global conflicts. The following comparison outlines the key differences between CSS and SCSS to help you understand why SCSS is often the better choice in modern frontend development.

Feature	CSS	SCSS (SASS)
Syntax	Simple and standard	Extended syntax with extra features
Nesting	Not supported	Fully supported (**`.parent { .child { } }`**)

Variables	Limited (with `--var`)	Powerful and easy using `$` syntax
Mixins / Reusability	Not available	Fully supported with `@mixin`, `@include`
Functions	Not available	Custom and built-in SCSS functions available
Modularity	Requires manual scoping	SCSS Modules offer automatic local scoping
File Extension	`.css`	`.scss` or `.sass`
Imports	`@import` (deprecated in CSS)	Uses `@use` and `@forward` for better reuse
Ease of Maintenance	Becomes hard in large projects	Easier with SCSS structure and modularity
Usage in Next.js	Global styling in `_app.js`	SCSS Modules for component-level styling

Table 7.3: CSS *vs.* SCSS

Integrating Tailwind CSS

Before integrating any styling solution into a Next.js application, it is important to consider what each UI framework brings to the table—and more importantly, how well it fits into a modern, component-based architecture. Among the most used frameworks are **Bootstrap**, **Material UI**, and **Tailwind CSS**. Each has its own strengths and use cases, but they also come with trade-offs that can impact developer experience and project flexibility.

Bootstrap is a powerful and widely used CSS framework that comes with a large collection of pre-built UI components. It is great for quickly building layouts and responsive designs. However, it relies heavily on class-based components and opinionated design patterns, which can make customizations harder, and the final product feel less unique. It also tends to conflict with modern React and Next.js component encapsulation practices.

Material UI (MUI) is a popular React-based UI library that implements Google's Material Design. While it integrates well with React (and by extension Next.js), it often adds significant bundle size, has a steep learning curve, and imposes a very specific design system. Customizing it deeply to match a brand identity or specific UI guideline can be complex and time-consuming.

In contrast, **Tailwind CSS** takes a utility-first approach to styling. Instead of providing ready-made UI components, Tailwind gives you a set of low-level utility classes that let you build completely custom interfaces without leaving your HTML, TSX or JSX. This approach fits perfectly with the **component-driven mindset of Next.js**. Tailwind is lightweight, easily customizable via a configuration file, and offers excellent performance when paired with Next.js's optimization capabilities. It also avoids global

CSS conflicts, supports dark mode, animations, and responsive design out of the box, all while keeping the developer in full control of the visual design.

Tailwind's **PostCSS-based architecture** integrates naturally with the Next.js build pipeline, and it supports **Just-in-Time (JIT) compilation**, meaning only the styles you actually use are included in the final CSS bundle. This makes your project faster, smaller, and easier to maintain.

Its integration with Next.js is seamless and highly efficient, enabling fast styling without the need to write custom CSS for most cases.

The following is a step-by-step guide on properly set up and use Tailwind CSS in a Next.js application.

Step 1: Initialize Your Next.js Project (if not already done)

a. If you do not have a Next.js project yet, you can create one using the following command:

```
npx create-next-app@latest my-project
cd my-project
```

b. If your project already exists, you can skip this step.

Step 2: Install Tailwind CSS and the Required Dependencies

a. Tailwind requires a few additional packages to work correctly with Next.js. Install them using npm or yarn:

```
npm install -D tailwindcss postcss autoprefixer
```

b. Then initialize the Tailwind and PostCSS configuration files:

```
npx tailwindcss init -p
```

c. This will generate two files in the root of your project:

   i. `tailwind.config.js`

   ii. `postcss.config.js`

Step 3: Configure Tailwind to Remove Unused Styles in Production

a. Open the **`tailwind.config.js`** file, and update the content array to include all the relevant file types from your project:

```
/** @type {import('tailwindcss').Config} */
module.exports = {
  content: [
    "./pages/**/*.{js,ts,jsx,tsx}",
    "./components/**/*.{js,ts,jsx,tsx}",
    "./app/**/*.{js,ts,jsx,tsx}" // If using /app directory
  ],
```

```
    theme: {
      extend: {},
    },
    plugins: [],
  }
```

This configuration ensures that Tailwind scans all your page and component files for class names, and removes the unused styles from the production build.

Step 4: Add Tailwind Directives to Your CSS

a. Create a global CSS file, if you already do not have one. Typically, this would be `styles/globals.css`.

b. Add the Tailwind base layers to that file:

```
@tailwind base;
@tailwind components;
@tailwind utilities;
```

These directives import Tailwind's base styles, component classes, and utility classes respectively.

c. Then, import this file in `pages/_app.js` or `pages/_app.tsx`:

```
import '../styles/globals.css'
```

Step 5. Install and Use SCSS

```
npm install sass
```

a. Create an SCSS module file, for example `components/Button.module.scss`

```
.button {
  background-color: #4f46e5;
  padding: 10px 20px;
  color: white;
  border-radius: 8px;
}
```

b. Use it in a component, for example `components/Button.jsx`

```
import styles from './Button.module.scss'
export default function Button() {
  return <button className={styles.button}>Click Me</button>
}
```

Step 6. Use Tailwind and SCSS Together

a. You can also combine both in one component:

```
import styles from './Card.module.scss'
export default function Card() {
  return (
```

```
    <div className={`p-4 bg-white shadow-lg rounded-lg ${styles.
card}`}>
      <h2 className="text-xl font-bold">Card Title</h2>
      <p>This combines Tailwind and SCSS!</p>
    </div>
  )
}
```

Step 7. (Optional) Organize SCSS Modules

a. Use /components/styles/ComponentName.module.scss

b. Keep SCSS for layout or complex UI logic

c. Use Tailwind for spacing, typography, flex, grid, and so on.

Now your Next.js project is fully set up to: Use Tailwind CSS for fast, utility-first styling, Use SCSS Modules for complex, reusable component styles. This setup gives you maximum flexibility – allowing you to build quickly with Tailwind, and fall back on SCSS when you need deep styling control.

Integrating Tailwind CSS into a Next.js application provides a streamlined and scalable approach to styling user interfaces. After installing the necessary packages (**tailwindcss**, **postcss**, and **autoprefixer**), the developer initializes configuration files and links Tailwind's layers through a global CSS file. This global file is imported into the custom **_app.tsx** component to ensure styles are available throughout the application. Tailwind's utility classes can then be used directly within JSX to style elements without writing custom CSS.

The configuration also includes content paths that allow Tailwind to tree-shake unused classes from the production build, resulting in optimized output. Developers can further customize the Tailwind configuration by extending its default theme. This integration supports rapid development, component reusability, and maintainable code – especially valuable in large-scale, design-consistent applications.

CSS-in-JS with Styled Components and Emotion

CSS-in-JS is a styling technique where CSS is written directly within JavaScript or TypeScript files, enabling component-scoped styles, dynamic styling based on props, and better developer experience through JavaScript tooling. In the Next.js ecosystem, the most commonly used libraries for CSS-in-JS are `**styled-components**` and `**@emotion/react**`. Both libraries allow you to encapsulate styles with components, eliminating the need for separate style sheets, and simplifying style management in large applications.

Using Styled Components in Next.js

To integrate `**styled-components**` into a Next.js project, begin by installing the necessary packages:

```
npm install styled-components
npm install --save-dev babel-plugin-styled-components
```

After installing, you need to configure Babel to support Server-Side Rendering (SSR) with styled-components. Create or modify the `**.babelrc**` file (or `**babel.config.js**`) with the following:

```
{
  "presets": ["next/babel"],
  "plugins": [["styled-components", { "ssr": true }]]
}
```

Next.js supports styled-components without additional setup for rendering, but to ensure correct server-side rendering of styles, you should customize the `**Document**` **file. Create a custom** `**_document.tsx**` in the `**pages**` directory, and configure it as follows:

```
// pages/_document.tsx
import Document, { DocumentContext, DocumentInitialProps, Html,
Head, Main, NextScript } from 'next/document';
import { ServerStyleSheet } from 'styled-components';

export default class MyDocument extends Document {
  static async getInitialProps(ctx: DocumentContext): Prom-
ise<DocumentInitialProps> {
    const sheet = new ServerStyleSheet();
    const originalRenderPage = ctx.renderPage;

    try {
      ctx.renderPage = () =>
        originalRenderPage({
          enhanceApp: (App) => (props) =>
            sheet.collectStyles(<App {...props} />),
        });

      const initialProps = await Document.getInitialProps(ctx);
      return {
        ...initialProps,
        styles: (
          <>
            {initialProps.styles}
            {sheet.getStyleElement()}
          </>
```

```
          ),
        };
      } finally {
        sheet.seal();
      }
    }

    render() {
      return (
        <Html>
          <Head />
          <body>
            <Main />
            <NextScript />
          </body>
        </Html>
      );
    }
  }
```

Once set up, you can define styled components directly inside your TSX files:

```
import styled from 'styled-components';
const Button = styled.button`
  background-color: #0070f3;
  color: white;
  padding: 0.75rem 1.5rem;
  border: none;
  border-radius: 0.5rem;
  font-size: 1rem;

  &:hover {
    background-color: #005bb5;
  }
`;

export default function HomePage() {
  return <Button>Click Me</Button>;
}
```

Using Emotion in Next.js

Emotion is another popular CSS-in-JS library with similar goals but slightly different syntax and architecture. To use Emotion in a Next.js project, you will have to first install the core Emotion packages:

```
npm install @emotion/react @emotion/styled
```

You do not need a custom **`_document.tsx`** for Emotion by default, unless you are using SSR or theming features with caching. The basic usage is straightforward:

```
/** @jsxImportSource @emotion/react */
import styled from '@emotion/styled';

const Card = styled.div`
  background: white;
  padding: 2rem;
  border-radius: 12px;
  box-shadow: 0 4px 8px rgba(0, 0, 0, 0.1);
`;

export default function EmotionExample() {
  return <Card>This card is styled with Emotion.</Card>;
}

Emotion also supports the `css` prop for inline styles with
dynamic behavior:
/** @jsxImportSource @emotion/react */
import { css } from '@emotion/react';

const style = css`
  color: hotpink;
  font-size: 1.5rem;
`;

export default function Text() {
  return <div css={style}>Styled using Emotion's css prop.</div>;
}
```

If you are using server-side rendering and advanced theming, you may need to set up an Emotion cache provider and modify **`_document.tsx`** using Emotion's SSR utilities. This is similar to the styled-components setup but requires additional configuration from the Emotion documentation.

Integrating CSS-in-JS libraries such as **`styled-components`**, and **`Emotion`** into a Next.js project provides enhanced flexibility in managing component-level styles. With both libraries, you can co-locate your styles with your components, avoid global CSS conflicts, and apply dynamic styles based on props or application state. **`styled-components`** requires minimal setup with a custom **`_document.tsx`** for SSR, while Emotion offers additional styling patterns like the **`css`** prop and theming. These tools are particularly powerful for teams working on large, component-driven codebases that demand scalable and maintainable styling solutions aligned with modern React development practices.

Best Practices for Styling in Next.js Projects

Styling your Next.js application effectively is crucial for creating a visually appealing, maintainable, and performant project. The following best practices helps keep your styles organized and scalable:

1. **Choose a Consistent Styling Method**

   Next.js supports various ways to style your app. Pick one method, and use it consistently:

   CSS Modules (Recommended)

   Scoped automatically to avoid conflicts.

   Example:

```
import styles from './Button.module.css';
export default function Button() {
  return <button className={styles.primaryButton}>Click
Me</button>;
}
```

   Tailwind CSS (Great for rapid UI)

   Utility-first CSS framework that simplifies styling.

   Example:

```
export default function Button() {
  return <button className="bg-blue-500 hover:bg-blue-700 text-
white py-2 px-4 rounded">Click Me</button>;
}
```

   Styled Components / Emotion

   CSS-in-JS libraries allow writing CSS in JavaScript.

   Example:

```
import styled from 'styled-components';
const Button = styled.button`
  background-color: blue;
  color: white;
  padding: 8px 16px;
  border-radius: 4px;

  &:hover {
    background-color: darkblue;
```

```
  }
`;

export default function MyComponent() {
  return <Button>Click Me</Button>;
}
```

2. **Component-Based Styling**

   Keep styles close to the components they style. Create separate CSS files for each component.

   Example Project Structure:

```
components/
├── Button.jsx
└── Button.module.css
```

3. **Use Global CSS Sparingly**

   Use global CSS for resets, typography, or basic layout only. Import it once in `pages/_app.js`.

```
import '../styles/globals.css';
export default function MyApp({ Component, pageProps }) {
  return <Component {...pageProps} />;
}
```

4. **CSS Modules Naming Convention**

   Use descriptive and readable class names.

   Good Example:

```
.primary-button {
  background-color: blue;
  color: white;
}
```

   Avoid generic names such as `.button` or `.header`.

5. **Organize Styles Clearly**

   Structure your CSS logically. Group related properties, and use comments.

```
/* Primary Button */
      .primary-button {
        background-color: blue;
        color: white;
        padding: 10px 20px;
      }
```

```
/* Hover State */
.primary-button:hover {
  background-color: darkblue;
}
```

6. **Optimize for Performance**

   Avoid deep nesting and overly complex selectors.

   Better:

   ```
   css
    .nav-link {
     color: blue;
   }
   ```

   Avoid:

   ```
   .navbar .menu .links .link a {
     color: blue;
   }
   ```

7. **Use Utility Classes (Tailwind CSS)**

   Tailwind CSS allows rapid and reusable styling directly in HTML/JSX.

   Example:

   ```
   <div className="flex flex-col items-center justify-center
   space-y-4">
     <h1 className="text-xl font-bold">Welcome</h1>
     <button className="bg-green-500 text-white px-4 py-2 rounded"
   >Start</button>
   </div>
   ```

8. **Responsive Design**

   Use media queries or Tailwind responsive utilities.

   Tailwind Example:

   ```
   <div className="text-sm md:text-lg lg:text-xl">
     Responsive Text
   </div>
   ```

   CSS Modules Example:

   ```
   .container {
     width: 100%;
   }

   @media (min-width: 768px) {
     .container {
   ```

```
    max-width: 720px;
  }
}
```

9. **Avoid Inline Styling**

   Avoid using inline styles like:

   `<div style={{ color: 'red' }}>`

   They are hard to maintain and override. Use CSS Modules or Tailwind instead.

10. **Use CSS Variables**

    Use CSS custom properties for themes and reusability.

    Example:

```
css
 :root {
  --primary-color: #3498db;
}

.button {
  background-color: var(--primary-color);
  color: white;
}
```

11. **Purge Unused Styles (Tailwind CSS)**

    When using Tailwind, remove unused CSS from production builds.

    Example Config:

```
// tailwind.config.js
module.exports = {
  content: ['./pages//*.{js,jsx}', './components//*.{js,jsx}'],
  theme: {
    extend: {},
  },
  plugins: [],
}
```

12. **Accessibility-Friendly Styling**

    Ensure high contrast, focus styles, and visible interactive elements.

    Example:

```
a {
  color: blue;
  text-decoration: underline;
}
```

```
a:hover,
a:focus {
  color: darkblue;
  text-decoration: none;
}
```

Effective styling in Next.js requires balancing organization, performance, and accessibility to ensure a clean, scalable, and user-friendly design system.

- **CSS Management:** CSS Modules or Tailwind CSS
- **File-Structure:** Component-specific CSS
- **Global-CSS:** Use minimally
- **Responsiveness:** Media queries or Tailwind classes
- **Performance:** Short selectors, no deep nesting
- **Maintainability:** Use variables, clean naming
- **Accessibility:** Follow WCAG guidelines

Conclusion

Styling in Next.js offers a range of options, each catering to different project needs and team preferences. Whether using SCSS modules for component-scoped styles, global styles for application-wide consistency, CSS-in-JS libraries such as styled-components and Emotion for dynamic and scoped styling, or utility-first frameworks like Tailwind CSS, developers can craft modern and maintainable UIs effectively. Best practices such as keeping styles modular, avoiding global conflicts, and maintaining consistency across the codebase are crucial for scalable development. Choosing the right styling approach depends on factors such as project complexity, team experience, and long-term maintainability. Thus, by following structured styling patterns and adopting tools that align with the project architecture, developers can ensure a clean, efficient, and visually consistent user interface in any Next.js application.

In the next chapter, we will explore **State Management in Next.js**, where you will learn how to handle local, shared, and server-side state using both built-in React tools and popular libraries such as Flux, Redux, Zu stand, and React Query.

Multiple Choice Questions

1. What is the correct way to apply a class from an SCSS module in JSX?
   a. `class={styles.className}`
   b. `style={styles.className}`
   c. `className={styles.className}`
   d. `id={styles.className}`

2. Which file should global SCSS be imported in for a Next.js app?
    a. `_document.tsx`
    b. `index.js`
    c. `page.module.scss`
    d. `_app.tsx`
3. What is the primary benefit of using CSS Modules?
    a. Inline styles for faster rendering
    b. Avoiding server-side rendering
    c. Scoped styling to components
    d. Access to custom fonts
4. Which CSS-in-JS library requires a custom `_document.jsx` setup for SSR?
    a. Tailwind CSS
    b. Emotion
    c. Styled-components
    d. SCSS Modules
5. What is a recommended best practice for styling in large Next.js projects?
    a. Use inline styles only.
    b. Mix SCSS, Tailwind, and inline styles.
    c. Keep styles global and deep-nested.
    d. Choose one styling approach, and remain consistent.

Answers

1. c
2. d
3. c
4. c
5. d

Chapter 8
State Management in Next.js

Introduction

State management is a fundamental aspect of building scalable and interactive web applications. In Next.js, which combines the power of React with server-side rendering and static site generation, managing state efficiently becomes even more crucial. As applications grow, handling global and local states, syncing data between client and server, and maintaining performance can become challenging without a proper strategy.

This chapter introduces the concept of state management in the context of Next.js. It explores the different types of state—local, global, server, and URL state—and how each plays a unique role in a Next.js application. We will examine when to use React's built-in useState and useReducer hooks, and when to adopt more robust solutions such as Context API, Redux, Zustand, or Recoil for global state handling.

Additionally, this chapter covers the best practices for integrating client-side state with Next.js features such as Server-Side Rendering (SSR) and API routes, ensuring data consistency and optimal user experience. Hence, whether you are building a simple blog or a complex dashboard, mastering state management is the key to success.

Structure

In this chapter, we will cover the following topics:

- Managing State in Next.js: useState and useReducer
- Using Context API for State Sharing across Pages
- Integrating Third-Party State Management Libraries
- Server-Side State Management with `getServerSideProps`

Managing State in Next.js: `useState` and `useReducer`

When building interactive React components in a Next.js application, effectively managing state becomes crucial. React provides two primary hooks for state management–`useState` and `useReducer`. While both hooks manage data that impacts component behavior, each is designed for different use cases.

Understanding useState

The `useState` hook is ideal for managing simple, discrete state values in functional components. It is easy to implement, making it suitable for scenarios with minimal state complexity.

Syntax

```
const [state, setState] = useState(initialValue);
```

Example

```
import { useState } from 'react';
function Counter() {
  const [count, setCount] = useState(0);
  return (
    <div>
      <p>Current Count: {count}</p>
      <button onClick={() => setCount(count + 1)}>Increment</button>
    </div>
  );
}
```

In this example, clicking the "Increment" button increases the `count` state, causing the component to re-render and update the displayed count.

Use `useState` when:

- Managing independent, simple states (numbers, strings and booleans).
- States are updated by direct, straightforward actions.
- State logic is minimal, and not interconnected with other state variables.

Understanding useReducer

The '`useReducer`' hook is more powerful and suitable for complex state management, especially when the state involves multiple sub-values or depends on previous states. It encapsulates state updates in a reducer function, providing a clearer structure and enhanced readability.

Syntax

```
const [state, dispatch] = useReducer(reducer, initialArg, init);
```

- `'**reducer**': A pure function determining how the state changes based on actions.
- '**initialArg**': The initial state.
- '**init**': Optional function to initialize the state lazily.

Example

```
import { useReducer } from 'react';
const initialState = { count: 0 };
function reducer(state, action) {
  switch (action.type) {
    case 'increment':
      return { count: state.count + 1 };
    case 'decrement':
      return { count: state.count - 1 };
    case 'reset':
      return { count: 0 };
    default:
      throw new Error('Unknown action type');
  }
}

function CounterWithReducer() {
  const [state, dispatch] = useReducer(reducer, initialState);
  return (
    <div>
      <p>Count: {state.count}</p>
      <button onClick={() => dispatch({ type: 'increment' })}>
Increment</button>
      <button onClick={() => dispatch({ type: 'decrement'
})}>Decrement</button>
      <button onClick={() => dispatch({ type: 'reset' })}>Reset</
button>
    </div>
  );
}
```

In this example, the `**dispatch**` function triggers state updates by sending actions to the reducer, clearly outlining each possible state transition.

Use **useReducer** when:

- Managing complex states with multiple interdependent or nested state variables.

- The next state depends on the previous state.
- Seeking clearer, more maintainable code when managing multiple state transitions or actions.
- Sharing state logic across multiple components or extracting state logic into separate functions.

Choosing between `useState` and `useReducer`

- **`useState`:** Prefer straightforward, independent state variables with direct updates.
- **`useReducer`:** Choose complex, interconnected state management involving structured, predictable transitions.

In summary, effectively leveraging both `` `useState` `` and `` `useReducer` `` in Next.js helps you manage the state cleanly and predictably, optimizing your application's maintainability and scalability.

Using Context API for State Sharing across Pages

When building large-scale applications with Next.js, managing the state across different components and multiple pages becomes challenging, especially as the application grows. This complexity can often result in prop drilling, which occurs when props are passed through multiple intermediate components unnecessarily. React's Context API provides an effective solution by allowing developers to share the state globally, and efficiently manage the state without prop drilling.

Context API

The Context API is a powerful feature in React designed to simplify state management across components by providing a mechanism to pass the data deeply through the component tree without manually passing props at every level. It creates a global "context" or a storage place accessible to any component within the context provider's hierarchy. This helps components access the shared data such as user authentication status, themes, or global settings directly.

Context API Workflow

Context API works using three main parts:

- **Context Object:** Created using React's **`createContext`** function.

- **Provider Component:** A component wrapping the tree of components that need access to the context data.
- **Consumer Component:** Any component within the provider's scope accessing context data via React's **useContext** hook or Context Consumer component.

Step-by-Step Guide to Implementing Context API in Next.js:

Step 1: Creating the Context

First, define the context using React's built-in **createContext** function.

```
// context/UserContext.js
import { createContext, useState } from 'react';
// Creating context with a default value (optional)
export const UserContext = createContext(null);
// Creating a provider component
export const UserProvider = ({ children }) => {
    const [user, setUser] = useState(null);
    return (
        <UserContext.Provider value={{ user, setUser }}>
            {children}
        </UserContext.Provider>
    );
};
```

Step 2: Wrapping the Application with Context Provider

To ensure that your context is available globally, wrap your main application file (**_app.js in Next.js**) with the provider:

```
// pages/_app.js
import { UserProvider } from '../context/UserContext';
export default function App({ Component, pageProps }) {
    return (
        <UserProvider>
            <Component {...pageProps} />
        </UserProvider>
    );
}
```

Step 3: Accessing Context Data in Components

Components can access the context data using the **useContext** hook:

```
// components/UserProfile.js
import { useContext } from 'react';
import { UserContext } from '../context/UserContext';
const UserProfile = () => {
    const { user, setUser } = useContext(UserContext);
    return (
```

```
        <div>
            {user ? (
                <p>Welcome, {user.name}</p>
            ) : (
                <p>No user logged in</p>
            )}
            <button onClick={() => setUser({ name: 'John Doe'
})}>Login as John Doe</button>
        </div>
    );
};

export default UserProfile;
```

Advanced Use Cases

Context API in Next.js can also manage complex scenarios such as:

- **Authentication:** Managing global user authentication state.
- **Theming:** Dynamically changing application themes (dark mode, light mode, and so on).
- **Localization:** Handling internationalization and multi-language support.
- **Benefits** of using Context API
- **Eliminates Prop Drilling:** Reduces code complexity by eliminating the need to pass props manually at each level.
- **Global State Management:** Easily manages the global state accessible across various components and pages.
- **Enhances Maintainability:** Facilitates better-organized code and easier debugging by clearly defining the global state logic.

Best Practices for Context API in Next.js

Define Clear Boundaries: Create smaller, focused contexts for specific concerns to maintain clarity and separation of concerns.

- **Avoid Overuse:** Use Context API only for data that genuinely needs global access to prevent performance overhead.
- **Combine with Other State Management Solutions:** For very complex state management, consider integrating Context API with state libraries such as Redux or Zustand for enhanced functionality.
- By fully utilizing the Context API in your Next.js applications, developers can achieve scalable, maintainable, and highly efficient state management, significantly enhancing the developer experience and application robustness.

Integrating Third-Party State Management Libraries

In Next.js, you get powerful tools such as Server-Side Rendering (SSR), Static Site Generation (SSG), and API routes – but it does not come with built-in global state management. That is where third-party libraries come in.

When your app grows beyond a few components, you often need to share the global state, such as:

- Authenticated user info
- Shopping cart data
- Theme settings (dark/light)
- Data fetched from APIs
- UI states across pages (modals and notifications)

While React's built-in tools such as `useState` and `useContext` work fine for smaller apps, they become inefficient for large-scale applications. That is where the third-party state management libraries help you:

Feature	`useState/useContext`	Third-Party Libraries
Scope	Local/Context-wide	Global, structured
Scalability	Poor for large apps	Excellent
Dev Tools	None	Built-in tools in many
Middleware Support	Manual	Available
SSR Support	Limited	Many offer SSR integration

Table 8.1: *In-Built versus Third-Party Libraries*

Top 5 State Management Libraries for Next.js

State management plays a critical role in modern React-based frameworks such as Next.js, especially when applications grow complex and involve shared state across components or pages. Choosing the right library depends on the balance between simplicity, flexibility, performance, and integration with server-side rendering.

- **Zustand**

  Zustand is a minimalistic, fast, and flexible state management library developed by the creators of Jotai and React Spring. It follows a "store-first" approach and uses hooks internally, making it fully compatible with the React ecosystem.

- Uses a simple and intuitive API.
- Maintains performance by avoiding unnecessary re-renders.
- Great for both small apps and large, scalable architectures.

Suitability for Next.js:

- **SSR Support:** Fully supported with custom hydration logic.
- **Lightweight:** Very lightweight (~1KB).
- **TypeScript Support:** Strong support with type-safe stores.
- **Developer Tools:** Compatible with Redux DevTools.

Ideal for developers who want simplicity with scalability. It is especially good for applications that prefer a functional programming style and clean separation of state.

- **Redux Toolkit**

  Redux Toolkit is the officially recommended way to use Redux. It simplifies boilerplate code, and promotes the best practices through utilities such as createSlice, configureStore, and built-in support for async logic via thunks.

  - Provides a standardized way to organize logic.
  - Great ecosystem support, including middleware and tools.
  - Supports large-scale apps with complex state logic.

  Suitability for Next.js:

  - **SSR Support:** Supported via wrapper libraries such as next-redux-wrapper.
  - **Lightweight:** Not lightweight; introduces more boilerplate compared to Zustand or Jotai.
  - **TypeScript Support:** Excellent with inferred types from slices.
  - **Developer Tools:** Rich dev tooling, including Redux Dev Tools.

Best for enterprise-scale Next.js apps where predictable, testable, and centralized state management is required.

- **Jotai**

  Jotai is an atomic state management library. It allows defining and managing state as individual "atoms", making it intuitive and granular. It also avoids prop drilling, and offers better tree-shaking, benefiting performance.

  - Atomic architecture promotes fine-grained reactivity.
  - Simpler mental model compared to Redux.
  - Works well with Suspense and Concurrent features of React.

Suitability for Next.js:

- **SSR Support:** Fully supported with hydration.
- **Lightweight:** Extremely light (~1KB core).
- **TypeScript Support:** Full TypeScript support out of the box.
- **Developer Tools:** DevTools plugin available for atom inspection.

Suitable for developers who prefer minimal syntax and isolated reactivity over global stores. Great for apps that need modular, lazy-loaded features.

- **Recoil**

  Recoil is a state management library developed by Meta (Facebook). It is designed to offer React-like declarative data flow with atoms and selectors. Recoil works well for fine-grained updates and complex derived state.

  - Supports async state out-of-the-box via selectors.
  - Efficient dependency tracking.
  - Designed with React's future in mind (Suspense, Concurrent features, and so on).

  Suitability for Next.js:

  - **SSR Support:** Limited and experimental. Recoil was not originally designed for SSR, and may require workarounds.
  - **Lightweight:** Lightweight core (~2KB).
  - **TypeScript Support:** Supported, but some generics may require boilerplate.
  - **Developer Tools:** Good DevTools support for tracking atom changes.

Good choice for Single Page Applications (SPAs) inside Next.js or hybrid apps where SSR is not essential for all pages.

- **MobX**

  MobX provides a reactive, object-oriented approach to state management. It emphasizes automatic tracking of observable state and reactions. With its class-based model, MobX is unique compared to other function-based libraries.

  - State changes automatically propagate to observers.
  - Reduces manual subscription logic.
  - Can manage deeply nested or complex object graphs efficiently.

Suitability for Next.js:

- ○ **SSR Support:** Supported with hydration solutions such as mobx-react-lite.
- ○ **Lightweight:** Slightly heavier footprint due to observability engine.
- ○ **TypeScript Support:** Strong support with decorators and classes.
- ○ **Developer Tools:** MobX DevTools and Chrome extensions available.

Recommended for developers who prefer OOP paradigms, and want a more implicit reactivity model. Good for feature-rich apps with a lot of UI-bound state.

Redux Toolkit is the most industry-standard, scalable, and predictable state management solution among the top 5 libraries for Next.js, making it the preferred choice in enterprise environments and job-driven development.

Choosing Redux Toolkit over Other Libraries

Redux Toolkit stands out for its structured architecture, predictable data flow, and deep ecosystem support, which are critical for building and maintaining large-scale, maintainable applications. It is designed to handle complex business logic, global shared state, and team-based development efficiently.

Unlike simpler libraries such as Zustand or Jotai, which excel in minimalism and flexibility, Redux Toolkit:

- Standardizes code across teams, reducing onboarding and handover friction.
- Enforces clear separation of concerns using slices, actions, reducers, and middleware.
- Offers excellent tooling support, including time-travel debugging, DevTools integration, and Redux middleware such as redux-thunk or redux-saga.
- Handles both synchronous and asynchronous workflows with built-in utilities such as createAsyncThunk.
- Provides robust TypeScript support with auto-inferred action types and strict typing on reducers and selectors.

These capabilities make Redux Toolkit a long-term, future-proof choice for production-grade applications that demand stability, maintainability, and strong team collaboration practices.

Redux Toolkit in Next.js

Redux Toolkit (RTK) is the official, recommended way to use Redux – simplifying setup, reducing boilerplate, and promoting the best practices. It provides a powerful abstraction layer for managing global state, particularly in scalable and enterprise-grade applications.

Redux Toolkit was introduced to solve the pain points of traditional Redux:

- Too much boilerplate code.
- Difficult setup for beginners.
- No standardized approach for async logic or slices.

Redux Toolkit brings:

- A single configuration point using configureStore.
- Simplified reducers and actions via createSlice.
- Built-in support for async thunks with createAsyncThunk.

Redux Toolkit is best used when:

- You need a global state across multiple pages.
- You have complex state transformations.
- You want predictable, testable, and maintainable code.
- You work on large-scale projects or collaborate across teams.

Integration Steps: Redux Toolkit with Next.js

1. Install the Required Packages

   ```
   npm install @reduxjs/toolkit react-redux
   ```

2. Create a Redux Slice (Example: **`features/todos/todoSlice.ts`**)

   ```
   import { createSlice, PayloadAction } from '@reduxjs/toolkit'

   interface Todo {
     id: number;
     title: string;
     completed: boolean;
   }

   interface TodoState {
     todos: Todo[];
   }

   const initialState: TodoState = {
     todos: []
   }

   const todoSlice = createSlice({
     name: 'todo',
   ```

```
  initialState,
  reducers: {
    addTodo: (state, action: PayloadAction<string>) => {
      state.todos.push({
        id: Date.now(),
        title: action.payload,
        completed: false
      })
    },
    updateTodo: (state, action: PayloadAction<{ id: number;
 title: string }>) => {
      const todo = state.todos.find(t => t.id === action.payload.
id)
      if (todo) {
        todo.title = action.payload.title
      }
    },
    toggleTodo: (state, action: PayloadAction<number>) => {
      const todo = state.todos.find(t => t.id === action.payload)
      if (todo) {
        todo.completed = !todo.completed
      }
    },
    deleteTodo: (state, action: PayloadAction<number>) => {
      state.todos = state.todos.filter(t => t.id !== action.
payload)
    }
  }
})

export const { addTodo, updateTodo, toggleTodo, deleteTodo } =
todoSlice.actions
export default todoSlice.reducer
```

3. Configure Store (**store.ts**)

```
import { configureStore } from '@reduxjs/toolkit'
import todoReducer from './features/todos/todoSlice'

export const store = configureStore({
  reducer: {
    todo: todoReducer
  }
})

export type RootState = ReturnType<typeof store.getState>
export type AppDispatch = typeof store.dispatch
```

4. Set Up Provider in **_app.tsx**

```
import { Provider } from 'react-redux'
import { store } from '../store'
function MyApp({ Component, pageProps }) {
  return (
    <Provider store={store}>
      <Component {...pageProps} />
    </Provider>
  )
}
export default MyApp
```

5. Using Redux State in a Component (for example, **pages/index.tsx**)

```
import { useDispatch, useSelector } from 'react-redux'
import { RootState } from '../store'
import { addTodo, deleteTodo, toggleTodo } from '../features/
todos/todoSlice'
import { useState } from 'react'
export default function Home() {
  const todos = useSelector((state: RootState) => state.todo.
todos)
  const dispatch = useDispatch()
  const [input, setInput] = useState('')

  const handleAdd = () => {
    if (input.trim()) {
      dispatch(addTodo(input))
      setInput('')
    }
  }

  return (
    <div>
      <h1>Todo List</h1>
      <input
        value={input}
        onChange={(e) => setInput(e.target.value)}
        placeholder="Enter todo"
      />
      <button onClick={handleAdd}>Add</button>

      <ul>
        {todos.map(todo => (
          <li key={todo.id}>
            <span
              onClick={() => dispatch(toggleTodo(todo.id))}
```

```
                style={{ textDecoration: todo.completed ?
'line-through' : 'none' }}
              >
                {todo.title}
              </span>
              <button onClick={() => dispatch(deleteTodo(todo.
id))}>Delete</button>
            </li>
          ))}
        </ul>
      </div>
  )
}
```

Note: *Redux Toolkit remains the most job-relevant state management library due to its maturity, tooling, TypeScript support, and compatibility with both CSR and SSR in Next.js.*

Server-Side State Management with `getServerSideProps`

In Next.js, `getServerSideProps` is a special server-side function that runs on every request, and allows you to fetch or prepare data on the server before rendering a page. It plays a key role in server-side state management by injecting state into the component as initial props, enabling Server-Side Rendering (SSR).

Purpose of getServerSideProps

- Used to fetch data at request time (not during build).
- Ideal for personalized, dynamic, or secure data (for example, user sessions, database queries, and so on).
- Enables true server-side rendering with fresh data per request.
- Useful for hydrating Redux or other state with server-fetched values.

Workflow

The function **`getServerSideProps`** is exported from a page file (for example, **`pages/index.tsx`**).

- It runs on the server for every request to that page.
- The returned object's props key is passed into the page component.
- These props can be used to initialize client-side state (for example, Redux store or **`useState`**).

Basic Example (Without Redux)

```
// pages/index.tsx
export async function getServerSideProps(context) {
  const res = await fetch('https://api.example.com/posts')
  const posts = await res.json()

  return {
    props: {
      posts
    }
  }
}

export default function HomePage({ posts }) {
  return (
    <div>
      <h1>Server-Side Posts</h1>
      <ul>
        {posts.map(p => (
          <li key={p.id}>{p.title}</li>
        ))}
      </ul>
    </div>
  )
}
```

With Redux Toolkit: Hydrating State

To manage server-side state using Redux, you often combine **`getServerSideProps`** with Redux store hydration logic. The approach includes:

- Initializing the Redux store on the server.
- Dispatching actions during **`getServerSideProps`**.
- Passing the Redux state to the client.
- Hydrating the store on the client side.

Example with Redux Integration (Simplified)

```
// pages/index.tsx
import { wrapper } from '../store'
import { fetchPosts } from '../features/posts/postsSlice'

export const getServerSideProps = wrapper.getServerSideProps(
  (store) => async () => {
    await store.dispatch(fetchPosts())
    return { props: {} }
  }
```

```
)

function HomePage() {
  // useSelector to get posts from Redux state
  return (
    <div>
      <h1>Posts from Redux (SSR)</h1>
      {/* render posts from Redux */}
    </div>
  )
}

export default HomePage
```

When to Use `getServerSideProps` for State Management:

- **Authenticated content:** Fetch user-specific state such as profile, orders, and dashboard data.
- **Frequently updated content:** Live pricing, stock data, and latest articles.
- **SEO-critical pages:** Content should be rendered with real data for search engines.
- **Secure backend access:** Access DB or APIs that require server secrets not exposed to the client.

Pros of Using getServerSideProps for State:

- Fresh data on each request.
- Keeps sensitive logic on the server.
- Enables initial server hydration of global state (Redux or Context).
- No need for loading spinners on the client–HTML arrives pre-rendered.

Limitations:

- Slower than static generation because it runs on every request.
- Cannot be used in API routes or non-page components.
- Adds load to the server on every hit.
- Not suitable for data that does not change often – for that, use **`getStaticProps`**.

`getServerSideProps` is an essential tool in Next.js to handle server-side state management. It:

- Fetches data securely and dynamically.
- Integrates with Redux or other state libraries to provide initial server-side state.
- Helps improve SEO and performance for dynamic pages.

It is a perfect fit when your application requires user-specific data, secure state computation, or real-time rendering on each page request.

Conclusion

In this chapter, we explored the fundamentals and practical use of Redux Toolkit in Next.js, especially in the context of server-side rendering and state management. Redux remains a leading choice in large-scale applications due to its predictable data flow, DevTools support, and structured architecture. By combining Redux Toolkit with `**getServerSideProps**`, developers can manage server-fetched state efficiently, and ensure initial hydration for the client, leading to better SEO and user experience. We have also seen how CRUD operations can be cleanly handled using Redux slices, making it a scalable solution for real-world apps.

In the next chapter, we will dive into optimization techniques in Next.js, covering topics such as dynamic imports, image optimization, bundle analysis, memoization, and performance tuning strategies to build faster and leaner applications.

Multiple Choice Questions

1. Which function in Next.js fetches data on every request?
   a. `getStaticProps`
   b. `getClientProps`
   c. `getServerSideProps`
   d. `useEffect`
2. Redux Toolkit replaces which common Redux setup component?
   a. Middleware
   b. Provider
   c. Reducer
   d. Boilerplate
3. Which method is best for fetching user-specific data at runtime?
   a. getStaticProps
   b. getServerSideProps
   c. useState
   d. SWR

4. What is the purpose of `createSlice` in Redux Toolkit?
    a. Create middleware
    b. Create reducers and actions
    c. Replace dispatch
    d. Combine stores
5. Which state library is most widely used in enterprise-grade React/Next.js apps?
    a. Zustand
    b. Jotai
    c. Redux Toolkit
    d. Recoil

Answers

1. c
2. d
3. b
4. b
5. c

CHAPTER 9
Performance Optimization in Next.js

Introduction

Performance is a key factor in building fast, user-friendly web applications, and Next.js offers powerful tools to help developers achieve it. This chapter focuses on practical strategies for optimizing performance in Next.js projects—from reducing load times to improving Core Web Vitals.

We will begin by exploring Next.js's built-in features such as automatic code splitting and dynamic imports, which help minimize initial bundle size. You will also learn how to optimize images using the next/image component, ensuring faster loading and better responsiveness. We shall also cover caching strategies using Incremental Static Regeneration (ISR) and data fetching with SWR to keep the content fresh without sacrificing speed.

Additionally, this chapter guides you through analyzing the Next.js build output to identify performance bottlenecks and using tools like Lighthouse to audit and measure improvements. With these techniques, you will be well equipped to build high-performance applications that load quickly, scale well, and deliver a smooth user experience across all devices.

Structure

In this chapter, the following topics will be covered:

- Optimizing images with the next/image component
- Code splitting and dynamic imports
- Catching strategies with ISR and SWR

- Using Lighthouse to measure performance
- Analyzing the Next.js build output

Optimizing Images with `next/image` Component

Optimizing images in Next.js is straightforward and efficient, thanks to the built-in `next/image` component. This component is specifically designed to improve performance by automatically handling several important image optimization tasks, which are often manual or complex in traditional React apps.

The `next/image` component is a powerful image-rendering solution that provides:

- Automatic resizing and cropping based on device screen size.
- Lazy loading by default, so that off-screen images do not slow down the initial load.
- Modern format delivery such as WebP, when supported by the browser.
- Caching and optimization at build-time or on-demand.

These features contribute directly to faster page loads, better Core Web Vitals scores, and reduced bandwidth usage, especially on mobile.

Workflow

When you use `next/image`, you do not just load an image file—you tell Next.js where the image comes from, and how it should behave across different screen sizes. Next.js then handles all the heavy lifting behind the scenes.

Example Usage:

```
import Image from 'next/image';
export default function Profile() {
  return (
    <Image
      src="/me.jpg"          // Path to your image (public folder
or remote)
      alt="My Profile"
      width={400}            // Desired width
      height={400}           // Desired height
    />
  );
}
```

Key Benefits

Next.js provides powerful image optimization features that enhance performance, reduce bandwidth usage, and deliver the best possible visual experience across different devices.

- **Responsive Images:** You can define multiple sizes using the sizes attribute, and allow Next.js to serve the appropriate one based on viewport.
- **Performance Optimization:** It automatically serves compressed formats (such as WebP or AVIF) when supported, without needing extra setup.
- **Built-in CDN Support:** Images are optimized and cached through Next.js' built-in Image Optimization API, which works out of the box on Vercel, and can be configured for self-hosting.
- **Lazy Loading:** Every image is lazy-loaded by default, reducing the initial page load time.

Placeholder Support

For a smoother visual load, you can use blurred placeholders.

```
<Image
  src="/me.jpg"
  alt="My Profile"
  width={400}
  height={400}
  placeholder="blur"
  blurDataURL="/blur-placeholder.jpg"
/>
```

Remote Images

You can load external images (for example, from a CMS or CDN), but you must specify the trusted domains in **`next.config.js`**:

```
module.exports = {
  images: {
    domains: ['example.com'],
  },
};
Then in your component:
<Image
  src="https://example.com/photo.jpg"
  alt="Remote image"
  width={800}
```

```
    height={600}
  />
```

Considerations

Avoid using plain **`<img>`** tags unless you have a specific reason; these do not benefit from Next.js optimizations.

Static image imports (for example, **`import img from './img.png'`**) are also supported in Next.js 13+ with the new app directory.

Using the **`next/image`** component helps you ship faster, cleaner, and more responsive web applications with minimal setup. It is a must-use feature when building performance-oriented Next.js sites.

Properties that give you greater control over how images are rendered and optimized.

The following is a breakdown of these properties, and how they help fine-tune performance as well as visual output:

Layout (deprecated in favor of fill, fixed, intrinsic, and responsive)

Used in older versions of Next.js to control image behavior. In the newer App Router (Next.js 13+), fill is the standard approach.

Fill

Allows the image to fill its parent container, maintaining aspect ratio. You must set the parent container to **`position: relative`**.

```
<div style= {{position: 'relative', width: '100%', height:
'300px'}} >
  <Image src="/cover.jpg" alt="Cover" fill />
</div>
```

Sizes

Specifies which image size to use for different viewport widths. Helps load only what is needed.

```
<Image
  src="/hero.jpg"
  alt="Hero"
  fill
  sizes="(max-width: 768px) 100vw, 50vw"
/>
```

Priority

Preloads the image, useful for above-the-fold content like hero banners or logos.

```
<Image src="/logo.png" alt="Logo" width={200} height={100} prior-
ity />
```

Quality

Controls compression quality (default is **75**). Useful when balancing performance and visual fidelity.

```
    <Image src="/large.jpg" alt="Large" width={1200} height={800}
quality={50} />
```

Placeholder and BlurDataURL

Displays a low-res blurred version until the full image loads. Great for UX.

```
<Image
  src="/team.jpg"
  alt="Team"
  width={600}
  height={400}
  placeholder="blur"
  blurDataURL="/tiny/team-blur.jpg"
/>
```

Unoptimized

Skips all Next.js optimizations. Rarely used, typically only when external optimization is already in place.

```
<Image src="https://cdn.example.com/img.jpg" alt="CDN image"
unoptimized width={500} height={500} />
```

These options allow you to strike the right balance between image quality, speed, and UX, making `next/image` one of the most powerful features in the framework.

Code Splitting and Dynamic Imports

Code splitting and dynamic imports are optimization techniques that help improve the performance of large-scale applications by reducing the initial bundle size. In a Next.js application, these techniques are particularly valuable because they ensure that only the code necessary for a particular page or component is loaded, rather than the entire application code upfront.

Understanding Code Splitting

Code splitting refers to the process of dividing the JavaScript bundle into smaller, independently loaded chunks. Next.js implements automatic code splitting by default for each page. This means that when a user navigates to a specific route, only the JavaScript required for that page is fetched and executed. As a result, the Time to First Paint (TTFP) and Time to Interactive (TTI) are significantly reduced.

Dynamic Imports

Dynamic imports are a feature of modern JavaScript that allow modules to be loaded asynchronously at runtime. In Next.js, dynamic imports enable fine-grained control over which code is loaded and when. This is particularly useful for loading components, utilities, or third-party libraries that are not required during the initial page load.

Example:

```
import React, { useState, useEffect } from 'react';
function HomePage() {
  const [data, setData] = useState(null);
  useEffect(() => {
    import('./api').then((module) => {
      module.getData().then((response) => {
        setData(response);
      });
    });
  }, []);

  return (
    <div>
      <h1>Welcome to Next.js!</h1>
      <p>{data}</p>
    </div>
  );
}
export default HomePage;
```

In this example, the **`api`** module is only loaded when the **`Homepage`** component is mounted. This ensures that the module is not a part of the initial JavaScript bundle, leading to faster load times and better performance.

Dynamic imports can also be used in conjunction with Redact's lazy loading to load components asynchronously. This approach is ideal for non-critical UI components that can be rendered after the main content.

Thus, by applying code splitting and dynamic imports effectively, developers can create high-performing applications with lower initial load times, and smoother user experience.

Catching and Improving Data Fetching

Caching is a fundamental strategy for improving data fetching performance and user experience in Next.js applications. It reduces redundant network requests, improves load times, and enhances perceived responsiveness.

Client-Side Caching

Client-side caching can be implemented using libraries such as SWR (Stale-While-Revalidate) or React Query, which handle local caching, data synchronization, and automatic updates.

Example Using SWR:

```
import useSWR from 'swr';
function UserProfile() {
  const { data, error } = useSWR('/api/user', fetcher);
  if (error) return <div>Error loading user data</div>;
  if (!data) return <div>Loading...</div>;
  return (
    <div>
      <h1>Welcome, {data.name}!</h1>
      <p>Email: {data.email}</p>
    </div>
  );
}
```

SWR automatically caches the data fetched from **`/api/user`**, making subsequent renders faster and more efficient.

Server-Side Caching

Next.js allows caching on the server side using **`getStaticProps`** and **`getServerSideProps`**. You can configure these methods to revalidate data periodically, reducing load on external APIs or databases.

Example Using `getStaticProps` with Revalidation:

```
export async function getStaticProps() {
  const data = await fetchUserFromAPI();
  return {
    props: {
```

```
      data,
    },
    revalidate: 60, // Revalidate at most once every 60 seconds
  };
}
```

This example fetches user data at build time, and sets it to **revalidate** periodically, ensuring that the content remains fresh without fetching on every request.

External Caching

You can also integrate external caching strategies such as:

- **CDN caching:** For static assets and pre-rendered pages.
- **Edge caching:** For delivering content closer to the user.
- **Proxy caching:** For API responses at intermediary layers.

Together, these caching mechanisms reduce server load, and improve the overall application performance.

Caching Strategies with ISR (Incremental Static Regeneration)

Incremental Static Regeneration (ISR) is a powerful feature in Next.js that enables static generation of pages at runtime, allowing developers to combine the performance benefits of static sites with the flexibility of the dynamic data.

With ISR, you can statically generate pages on-demand, and update them in the background without rebuilding the entire site. This approach provides a caching mechanism where pages are served instantly, and updated only when needed.

Core Concepts of ISR Caching

Caching strategies in ISR help Next.js deliver fast, scalable, and up-to-date content by combining static generation with smart background regeneration.

- **Static Generation with Revalidation**

  When using **getStaticProps**, you can specify a **revalidate** interval (in seconds). This tells Next.js how often to regenerate the static HTML page in the background.

  ```
  export async function getStaticProps() {
    const data = await fetchDataFromAPI();
    return {
      props: {
  ```

```
        data,
      },
      revalidate: 60, // Regenerate the page every 60 seconds
    };
  }
```

On the first request, the page is statically generated and cached.

For subsequent requests within 60 seconds, the cached version is served.

After 60 seconds, the next request will trigger a background regeneration, while still serving the stale page until the new version is ready.

- **Caching Benefits of ISR**

  ISR provides an efficient caching strategy with the following advantages:

  - **Improved Performance:** Pages are served statically from cache (CDN or edge), minimizing latency.
  - **Reduced Server Load:** Data fetching and HTML generation occur only at defined intervals.
  - **Fresh Content:** Revalidation ensures that users get up-to-date content without frequent rebuilds or server rendering.
  - **Scalability:** Supports large-scale applications by avoiding server bottlenecks.

Caching Strategies with ISR (Incremental Static Regeneration) in Next.js v15

Incremental Static Regeneration (ISR) is a powerful feature in Next.js that enables static generation of pages at runtime, allowing developers to combine the performance benefits of static sites with the flexibility of the dynamic data.

With ISR, you can statically generate pages on-demand, and update them in the background without rebuilding the entire site. This approach provides a caching mechanism where pages are served instantly, and updated only when needed.

Best Practices for Caching with ISR

To ensure optimal performance and predictable content updates, it is important to follow the best practices when configuring ISR caching in Next.js.

- **Choose sensible revalidation times:**
  - Frequently updated data: **`revalidate: 10`** or **`revalidate: 60`**
  - Infrequently updated data: **`revalidate: 300`** or longer

- **Use fallback modes:**
  - `fallback: 'blocking'`: Waits for the page to generate before serving.
  - `fallback: true`: Serves a loading state, while generating.
  - `fallback: false`: Only pre-defined paths are allowed.
- **Combine with Edge Caching:**
  - Serve ISR-generated pages through CDNs such as Vercel Edge Network for global performance.
  - CDN will cache the page, and invalidate it automatically after revalidation.
- **Handle stale data gracefully:**
  - While the page is being regenerated, the stale content is served. Ensure that the UI states account for this behavior, if critical.

Example: Blog Page with ISR

```
export async function getStaticProps() {
  const posts = await getAllBlogPosts();

  return {
    props: { posts },
    revalidate: 120, // Revalidate every 2 minutes
  };
}
```

This page will be regenerated at the most once every 2 minutes, ensuring that readers get relatively fresh content without taxing server resources.

To understand where Incremental Static Regeneration fits in the Next.js data fetching model, it is essential to compare it with the two traditional strategies–Server-Side Rendering (SSR) and Static Site Generation (SSG).

Feature	ISR (Incremental Static Regeneration)	SSR (Server-Side Rendering)	SSG (Static Site Generation)
Performance	Very High (cached)	Moderate (runs on every request)	Very High (pre-built at build time)
Data Freshness	Configurable with revalidate	Always fresh	Only updated on full rebuild
Scalability	Excellent	Moderate	Excellent
CDN Cache ability	Yes	No	Yes
Use Case	Frequently read, occasionally updated	Personalized or real-time	Rarely changing content

Table 9.1: *ISR vs* SSR *and* SSG

Using Lighthouse to Measure Performance

Lighthouse is an open-source, automated tool developed by Google that audits the performance, accessibility, SEO, best practices, and Progressive Web App (PWA) capabilities of web applications. It is one of the most widely used tools for analyzing Next.js applications to identify bottlenecks and opportunities for optimization.

Lighthouse can be run in several ways:

- Directly in Chrome DevTools
- As a Node.js CLI tool
- Via CI/CD pipelines (for example, using GitHub Actions)
- Through PageSpeed Insight

Use Lighthouse for Next.js

Next.js focuses heavily on performance through features such as server-side rendering, static generation, image optimization, and routing. However, misconfigurations or heavy dependencies can still lead to slow page loads or poor Core Web Vitals. Lighthouse provides quantifiable metrics and actionable suggestions to address these issues.

Running Lighthouse in Chrome DevTools

- Open your Next.js application in Google Chrome.
- Press F12 to open DevTools.
- Navigate to the "`Lighthouse`" tab.
- Choose the categories you want to audit:
    - Performance
    - Accessibility
    - Best Practices
    - SEO
    - PWA (optional)

  Select the device type:

    - **Mobile:** Simulates slow network/CPU (realistic baseline).
    - **Desktop:** Fast network/CPU (less strict).
    - Click "`Analyze page load`".

Lighthouse will generate a report with scores and detailed diagnostics.

Key Performance Metrics

Lighthouse evaluates performance using **Core Web Vitals**, which are essential for user experience:

Metric	Description	Ideal Value
First Contentful Paint (FCP)	Time to render the first visible content (text/image).	< 1.8 seconds
Largest Contentful Paint (LCP)	Time to render the largest visible element (image, text block, and so on.).	< 2.5 seconds
Total Blocking Time (TBT)	Total time the main thread was blocked and unresponsive.	< 200 milliseconds
Cumulative Layout Shift (CLS)	Measures unexpected layout shifts during load.	< 0.1
Speed Index	Measures how quickly the content is visually displayed.	< 3.4 seconds
Time to Interactive (TTI)	Time when the page becomes fully interactive for users.	< 3.8 seconds

Table 9.2: *Key Performance Metrics*

These metrics are directly influenced by how code is split, how data is fetched (ISR/SSR), and how heavy your components and dependencies are.

Interpreting the Lighthouse Report

Lighthouse provides three main sections in its report:

- **Scores**

  A performance score between 0 and 100. A score above 90 is considered good.

- **Opportunities**

  Suggestions to reduce page load time. Examples:

  - Remove unused JavaScript.
  - Defer off-screen images.
  - Use a Content Delivery Network (CDN).
  - Minimize critical request chains.

- **Diagnostics**

  Technical details on what affects your page's interactivity and rendering:

- DOM size
- JavaScript execution time
- Main-thread work
- Preload key requests

Improving Next.js Performance Based on Lighthouse

Here are some common recommendations from Lighthouse, and how to address them in Next.js:

Lighthouse Suggestion	Next.js Solution
Eliminate render-blocking resources	Use `next/script` with `strategy="lazyOnload"` or before Interactive
Serve images in next-gen formats	Use `Next.js <Image />` with webp or avif formats
Reduce unused JavaScript	Use dynamic imports and tree shaking (`import()` as well as modular packages)
Minimize main-thread work	Offload heavy computation, and avoid large client-side libraries
Efficiently encode images	Optimize images during build using `next/image`
Preload key requests	Use `<link rel="preload">` via `custom _document.js` or through performance hints

Table 9.3: *Lighthouse Suggestion and Solution*

Advanced Usage: Lighthouse CI

For production environments or automated performance testing, you can use Lighthouse CI:

Install:

```
npm install -g @lhci/cli
```

Configure **`lighthouserc.js`**:

```
module.exports = {
  ci: {
    collect: {
      startServerCommand: 'npm run start',
      url: ['http://localhost:3000'],
    },
    assert: {
      assertions: {
```

```
                'performance': ['error', { minScore: 0.9 }],
              },
            },
          },
        };
```

Run:

```
lhci autorun
```

This allows you to block pull requests or deploy, if performance scores drop below thresholds.

Analyzing the Next.js Build Output

Understanding the build output in Next.js is crucial for optimizing performance, identifying inefficiencies, and managing bundle size. When you build a Next.js application using the next build command, the framework compiles and bundles the project, generating detailed output that helps diagnose performance-related issues.

This section explores how to interpret the build output, what each part means, and how to act on the insights provided.

Running the Build

To build a production-ready version of your Next.js application, run:

```
npm run build
```

or

```
yarn build
```

This triggers the following processes:

- Compiling server-side and client-side JavaScript.
- Optimizing images and static assets.
- Generating HTML for statically rendered pages.
- Preparing API routes for serverless deployment (if applicable).

Sample Build Output Breakdown

In a simplified example of the build output, you might see:

```
Route (pages)                              Size      First Load JS
┌ ● /                                      3.45 kB         87.9 kB
├   /_app                                  0 B             83.2 kB
├ ○ /about                                 2.15 kB         85.3 kB
├ ● /blog/[slug]                           4.12 kB         90.1 kB
├ ○ /contact                               1.95 kB         85.1 kB
+ First Load JS shared by all             83.2 kB
  ├ chunks/framework.abc123.js            45.6 kB
  ├ chunks/main.def456.js                 30.2 kB
  ├ chunks/pages/_app.ghi789.js           7.4 kB
  └ etc...
```

Figure 9.1: *Sample Build Output Breakdown*

Key Symbols in Build Output

Next.js provides symbolic indicators and performance metrics in the build output to help developers understand how each page is rendered and how efficiently it performs.

Symbol	Meaning
●	This page was statically generated using getStaticProps or ISR.
○	This page uses static optimization without data fetching.
λ	This page is server-rendered using getServerSideProps.
∞	Dynamic route without fallback (will be server-rendered on demand).

Table 9.4: *Build Output Status Symbols*

Key Metrics Explained

To ensure optimal performance and predictable content updates, it's important to follow best practices when configuring ISR caching in Next.js.

- **Size**

  The size of the JavaScript required to render this page in the browser. Lower is better.

- **First Load JS**

  Total JavaScript loaded when a user first visits the page. It includes:

  - Page-specific JavaScript
  - Shared framework and dependencies
  - Any layout-level code (for example, `_app.js`, `_document.js`)

- **Shared Chunks**

  Chunks such as **framework.js**, **main.js**, and **_app.js** are shared across all pages, and bundled separately for caching and reusability.

- **Static vs Server Rendering**

  Understanding which pages are statically generated (•, ○) and which use server-side rendering (λ) helps identify:

  - Which pages are cacheable and fast (static)
  - Which pages may be slower but dynamic (server-rendered)

Using next build with --profile

For more detailed profiling information, use:

```
NEXT_PRIVATE_DEBUG_PROFILE=1 next build
```

This generates profiling data that can be used with tools such as React DevTools or flame graphs to pinpoint rendering bottlenecks.

Bundle Analyzer (Optional Tool)

To get a visual breakdown of your bundle, install and configure the **@next/bundle-analyzer** plugin:

Installation:

```
npm install @next/bundle-analyzer
```

Configuration in next.config.js:

```
const withBundleAnalyzer = require('@next/bundle-analyzer')({
  enabled: process.env.ANALYZE === 'true',
});
module.exports = withBundleAnalyzer({});
```

Run with:

```
ANALYZE=true npm run build
```

This will open a visual tree map showing which modules contribute the most to your bundle size, making it easier to optimize or replace large dependencies.

Conclusion

We explored the essential performance optimization and deployment techniques in Next.js. First, we examined code splitting and dynamic imports to segment JavaScript bundles, and deferred noncritical code, reducing initial download size and improving time to interactive. Next, we compared caching strategies–SSR, SSG, and ISR–demonstrating how revalidation intervals can keep the content fresh with minimal rebuilds. We then used Google Lighthouse to audit Core Web Vitals, interpret performance scores, and implement actionable recommendations for reducing render-blocking resources. Analyzing the next build output, and employing tools such as webpack bundle analyzer provided deep insights into chunk sizes and shared dependencies. Finally, we reviewed deployment best practices–including serverless architectures, CI/CD pipelines, security measures, and scalable infrastructure–to ensure reliability under load. Thus, by integrating these strategies, developers can deliver faster, more maintainable applications. Ongoing monitoring and iterative improvements ensure that Next.js projects continue to meet the evolving user expectations.

The next chapter covers the unit and integration tests.

Multiple Choice Questions

1. Which feature of Next.js automatically splits each page into its own JavaScript chunk?
   a. Dynamic Imports
   b. Automatic Code Splitting
   c. Tree Shaking
   d. Minification
2. Which caching strategy uses a revalidate interval in getStaticProps?
   a. Server-side Rendering (SSR)
   b. Static Site Generation (SSG)
   c. Incremental Static Regeneration (ISR)
   d. Client-side Caching
3. Which Lighthouse metric measures the time to render the largest visible element?
   a. First Contentful Paint (FCP)
   b. Time to Interactive (TTI)
   c. Total Blocking Time (TBT)
   d. Largest Contentful Paint (LCP)

4. In the Next.js build output, which symbol indicates a page using `getServerSideProps`?
   a. ●
   b. ○
   c. λ
   d. ∞
5. Which tool provides a visual tree map of your bundle to help identify large modules?
   a. Lighthouse
   b. webpack-bundle-analyzer
   c. SWR
   d. React DevTools

Answers

1. b
2. c
3. d
4. c
5. b

Chapter 10
Unit Testing and Integration Testing

Introduction

Testing is crucial for building reliable, maintainable, and scalable Next.js applications. This chapter covers the foundations of unit and integration testing in the Next.js ecosystem, helping you ensure that your code works as expected across components, pages, and APIs.

We begin by setting up **Jest** and **React Testing Library**, the most popular tools for testing React and Next.js applications. You will learn how to write unit tests for components and pages, focusing on behavior and UI rendering, rather than implementation details.

Next, we will explore mocking techniques for **API routes** and **server-side functions** such as **`getStaticProps`** and **`getServerSideProps`**, allowing you to test server-rendered content in isolation. Integration testing of full user flows, including API communication, will also be covered to ensure your app behaves correctly in real-world scenarios.

Additionally, this chapter introduces **snapshot testing** for tracking UI changes, and shares practical tips for **debugging tests** effectively. By the end of the chapter, you will have a strong testing setup tailored for Next.js projects.

Structure

In this chapter, the following topics will be covered:

- Setting Up Jest and React Testing Library in Next.js
- Testing Next.js Components and Pages
- Mocking API Routes and Server-Side Props
- Writing Integration Tests for API Routes
- Snapshot Testing and Debugging Tests

Setting Up Jest and React Testing Library

Before writing any tests, it is crucial to establish a solid foundation for your testing environment–Jest that provides the runner and assertion library, while React Testing Library offers the utilities to render components, and query the DOM in a way that resembles how users interact with your app.

Jest + React Testing Library

Jest is a comprehensive JavaScript testing framework maintained by Facebook. It provides everything you need to write and run tests, without pulling in dozens of separate tools. Here is what makes Jest stand out:

- **Fast Test Runner**
  - Jest parallelizes test execution across worker processes. Rather than running tests one after another, it batches files, and runs them in isolation, fully utilizing multicore machines to get feedback in seconds, even on large codebases.
  - Intelligent "watch mode" re-runs only the tests affected by your latest changes, speeding up the edit–test cycle.
- **Built-in Mocking**
  - You can automatically mock modules simply by calling **`jest.mock('moduleName')`**. Jest will replace your imports with lightweight auto-generated mocks.
  - For more control, you can supply your own mock implementations or spy on individual functions and timers, making it trivial to simulate network responses, timeouts, and other side effects.
- **Code Coverage Reporting**
  - With no extra configuration, Jest can collect coverage information from your source files, producing HTML, text, and LCOV reports.
  - You can enforce coverage thresholds per file or globally, ensuring that new code maintains a minimum level of test coverage.
- **Zero-Configuration Setup**
  - By default, Jest works out of the box with Babel, TypeScript (via **`ts-jest`**), and modern JavaScript syntax (ESModules, JSX).
  - It auto-discovers test files named **`*.test.js`**, **`*.spec.js`**, or **`inside __tests__ folders`**, so there is no need to update configuration every time you add a new test.

- **Snapshot Testing**
  - Jest can take a "snapshot" of a rendered component or value, and store it alongside your tests. On future runs, Jest compares the live output to the saved snapshot, flagging any unintended changes.
  - This is particularly useful for UIs–allowing you to detect visual regressions or serialization mismatches, without writing explicit assertions for every prop or markup node.
- **TypeScript Integration**
  - Out of the box, Jest can handle TypeScript via ts-jest or Babel presets. You can write tests in **`.ts/.tsx`** files with full type checking if you choose, or lean on Babel to strip types for faster transpilation.
  - Definitions for Jest globals (**`describe`**, **`it`**, **`expect`**, and so on) are available through **`@types/jest`**, so your editor will autocomplete and validate your test code.
- **Rich Plugin Ecosystem**
  - Jest supports custom reporters, test sequencers, and runners. Popular plugins include integration with testing services (for example, BrowserStack), advanced assertion libraries (for example, Jest-Extended), and performance monitoring tools.
  - User-Centric Queries
    - Queries such as **`getByRole`**, **`getByLabelText`**, and **`getByPlaceholderText`** mirror the way assistive technologies and end-users navigate content. This leads to tests that are both more resilient (less prone to break on refactors) and more meaningful (asserting what users see and do).
    - For asynchronous behavior–like waiting for data to load–you use **`findBy...`** queries or the **`waitFor`** utility, which polls the DOM until the assertion passes or times out.
  - Minimal API Surface
    - RTL exposes only the essential methods: **`render`**, **`screen`**, **`fireEvent`**, and **`userEvent`**. This limited surface area keeps test code concise and focused.
    - There is no need for deep component tree imports or framework-specific hooks; everything runs against a real DOM (via JSDOM) under the hood.
  - Encourages Good Testing Practices
    - By discouraging tests that "reach into" components (no querying internal instance methods or state), RTL nudges you toward writing

tests based on outputs and user interactions—exactly what you want for end-to-end confidence.

- You assert on visible text, accessible names, and roles, which align with Web Accessibility Guidelines (WCAG). Tests written this way often double as accessibility checks.

- Lightweight and Framework-Agnostic
  - Although designed for React, RTL is built on top of DOM Testing Library, which works with any UI framework. This means you are not locked into a React-specific testing approach, if you decide to reuse utilities elsewhere.
  - Custom Helpers and Extensions

    You can create your own query helpers or wrap **`render()`** to include context providers, theme wrappers, or Redux stores. This keeps your actual test files clean, moving boilerplate into reusable setup functions.
- Seamless Integration with Jest
  - RTL plays nicely with all of Jest's features: mocking, snapshot testing, code coverage, and custom matchers. In fact, you will often see **`expect(element).toBeInTheDocument()`** courtesy of @testing-library/jest-dom, which enriches Jest's assertions with DOM-specific checks.
- Asynchronous Testing Made Simple
  - React apps frequently fetch data or perform transitions after user actions. RTL's async utilities (**`findBy`**, **`waitFor`**, **`waitForElementToBeRemoved`**) wrap Jest's timers and promises so that you can write clean, readable tests that await real UI updates, rather than fragile **`setTimeout`** hacks.

Installing Dependencies

Install the core testing tools:

```
npm install --save-dev jest @testing-library/react @testing-library/jest-dom babel-jest
```

If you are using TypeScript, also add:

```
npm install --save-dev ts-jest @types/jest
```

Tip: *Keep your dependencies minimal, and only include helpers you actually need.*

Configuring Jest

Create a **jest.config.js** (or **jest.config.ts**) at your project root:

```
module.exports = {
  testEnvironment: "jsdom",
  setupFilesAfterEnv: ["<rootDir>/jest.setup.js"],
  moduleNameMapper: {
    // Handle CSS imports and module aliases if you use them
    "\\.(css|scss)$": "identity-obj-proxy",
    "^@/components/(.*)$": "<rootDir>/components/$1",
  },
};
```

- **testEnvironment: "jsdom"**

  Simulates a browser-like environment.

- **setupFilesAfterEnv**

  Points to a file where you will import custom matchers (for example, **@testing-library/jest-dom**).

Adding Jest DOM Matchers

In jest.setup.js:

```
import "@testing-library/jest-dom";
```

This enables expressive assertions like:

```
expect(button).toBeDisabled();
expect(link).toHaveAttribute("href", "/about");
```

Organizing Your Tests

- Place tests alongside components (for example, **MyComponent.test.jsx**) or in a top-level **/tests** folder.
- Name files with **.test.js** or **.spec.js** so that Jest auto-detects them.

Writing Your First Test

Focus on what the user sees or does:

```
import { render, screen } from "@testing-library/react";
import HomePage from "@/pages/index";
test("renders the main heading", () => {
  render(<HomePage />);
```

```
    expect(screen.getByRole("heading", { level: 1 }))
      .toHaveTextContent("Welcome to My Next.js App");
});
```

render(): Mounts your component into the virtual DOM.

screen: Provides queries scoped to the document.

Mocking Next.js Features

Next.js pages often use the **next/router** or **next/link**. You can mock them globally:

```
// jest.setup.js
jest.mock("next/router", () => ({
  useRouter() {
    return { route: "/", push: jest.fn() };
  },
}));
```

This prevents errors when tests import Next.js-specific modules.

Running Tests and Watching for Changes

Add scripts to package.json:

```
{
  "scripts": {
    "test": "jest",
    "test:watch": "jest --watch"
  }
}
```

- Run **npm run test** for a one-off run.
- Run **npm run test:watch** to rerun tests on file changes.

Tips for Robust Tests

- **Prefer user-centric queries:** Use **getByRole**, **getByLabelText**, and so on, to mirror user actions.
- **Avoid testing implementation details:** Do not assert internal state; test what is rendered.
- **Keep tests fast and isolated:** Mock network requests, and avoid heavy setup in each file.
- **Use fixtures and factory functions:** Generate test data consistently.

Testing Next.js Components and Pages

Before diving into the test code, it is important to understand how Next.js structures components and pages—pages are just React components with special data-fetching methods—so your tests can treat them like ordinary components, with a bit of extra setup for things such as routing and data fetching.

- **Testing Simple Components**

  Even though Next.js pages live under /pages, most UI pieces are just React components—which you test exactly as you would in a CRA or other setup:

  - **Isolation:** Render your component in JSDOM via RTL's **`render()`**, providing any required context (theme, Redux, i18n).
  - **Queries:** Use **`screen.getByRole`**, **`getByText`**, and so on, to assert on rendered output.
  - **Events:** Simulate user interaction with **`userEvent.click`**, **`userEvent.type`**, and so on.

  Example Focus: *If you have a* ***`<Button disabled={loading}>`****, test that it is disabled during a "loading" state, and enabled otherwise, rather than peeking inside its props.*

- **Mocking Next.js Routing**

  Next.js pages often import and use the router. To prevent errors and control behavior in tests:

  ```
  Global Mock in jest.setup.js
  jest.mock('next/router', () => ({
  useRouter: () => ({ route: '/', pathname: '/', push: jest.fn() })
  }));
  ```

  Per-test Overrides: If you need the router to simulate different paths or query parameters, override useRouter return values via jest.mock at the top of your test file.

- **Testing Pages with Data-Fetching Methods**

  Pages export **`getStaticProps`**, **`getServerSideProps`**, or **`getStaticPaths`**. You should:

  - Unit-test the data-fetch functions by calling them directly, and asserting on returned props. Since they are plain functions, import them and run:

    ```
    import { getStaticProps } from '@/pages/posts/[id]';
    test('loads post data', async () => {
    const context = { params: { id: '123' } };
    ```

```
const { props } = await getStaticProps(context);
expect(props.post.id).toBe('123');
});
```

- **Component Tests:** Render the page component with the props you expect:

```
render(<PostPage post={mockPost} />);
expect(screen.getByText(mockPost.title)).toBeInTheDocument();
```

This separation keeps your data-fetch logic tested in isolation, and your UI tests focused on rendering.

- **Mocking External Services**

  When **getServerSideProps** or your components call APIs:

  - **Jest module mocks:** Mock your API client or fetch globally.
  - **MSW (Mock Service Worker):** For more realistic HTTP-level tests, run a lightweight service worker to intercept requests in tests. It lets you assert on how your code calls external services, and returns the predictable data.

- **Testing Dynamic and Nested Routes**

  For pages like **/products/[id]** or nested **/users/[userId]/settings**:

  - **Unit-test getStaticPaths:** Call it and assert that it returns the correct paths array.
  - **Simulated context:** For page rendering tests, pass props matching one of those paths.

  If you have client-side code that reads **router.query**, ensure that your mock router returns the intended **query** object.

- **Linking between Pages**

  Next.js' **<Link>** renders an anchor under the hood. To test navigation:

  Assert that the **href** attribute of the rendered **<a>** is correct:

```
const{ getByRole } = render(<MyComponent />);
expect(getByRole('link', { name: /details/i })).toHaveAttribute
('href', '/items/42');
```

  For click handling, you may spy on **router.push** via your mock to ensure clicks trigger client-side navigation.

- **Layouts and Nested Layouts**

  If you use Next.js's App Router or custom **_app.js** wrappers:

  - **Render with providers:** Create a custom **renderWithProviders** helper that wraps children in your layout or context.

 - **Smoke tests:** Verify that common layout elements (header, footer, and sidebar) render on pages.

- **Keeping Tests Maintainable**
  - **Avoid over-mocking:** Only mock what you truly need. If a component fetches data client-side, consider letting it run through MSW, instead of mocking the entire hook.
  - **DRY setup:** Move repeated mock implementations, wrappers, and fixtures into shared utilities.
  - **Snapshot sparingly:** Use snapshot tests for static markup (for example, email templates), but favor explicit queries for dynamic pages.

Thus, by treating Next.js pages as React components with separate data-fetching logic, and by mocking routing and data sources thoughtfully, you can create fast, reliable tests that cover both your UI and the glue code that makes Next.js applications shine.

Mocking API Routes and Server-side Props

To keep your tests fast, reliable, and isolated from external systems, treat Next.js API routes and data-fetching methods (**`getStaticProps/getServerSideProps`**) as plain functions—mock their inputs, and stub their outputs, instead of spinning up a real server or database.

Mocking API Routes

When testing your Next.js backend endpoints, treat each API route handler as a simple function—by supplying fake request and response objects, you can verify its logic in isolation, without launching a server or making real HTTP calls.

Steps to Mock Next.js API Routes

1. **Import the handler function**

   ```
   import handler from '@/pages/api/posts/[id]';
   ```

   Because Next.js API files export a `` `(req, res)` `` function, you can call it directly in your test, sidestepping any HTTP layer.

2. **Create minimal `` `req` `` and `` `res` `` mocks**

   ```
   function makeReq({ query = {}, body = {} } = {}) {
     return { query, body };
   }
   ```

```
function makeRes() {
  const res = {};
  res.status = jest.fn(() => res);
  res.json   = jest.fn(() => res);
  res.end    = jest.fn(() => res);
  return res;
}
```

Only include the fields and methods your handler actually uses–this keeps mocks focused and maintainable.

3. **Test the success scenario**

```
test('returns post data when ID exists', async () => {
    const req = makeReq({ query: { id: 'abc' } });
    const res = makeRes();

    await handler(req, res);

    expect(res.status).toHaveBeenCalledWith(200);
    expect(res.json).toHaveBeenCalledWith(
      expect.objectContaining({ id: 'abc', title: expect.
any(String) })
    );
  });
```

4. **Test error or edge cases**

```
test('returns 400 when ID is missing', async () => {
  const req = makeReq();              // no `query.id`
  const res = makeRes();
  await handler(req, res);
  expect(res.status).toHaveBeenCalledWith(400);
  expect(res.json).toHaveBeenCalledWith(
    expect.objectContaining({ error: expect.any(String) })
  );
});
```

Simulate invalid input or force your service layer to throw, and then assert that the handler returns the correct status code and error payload.

5. **Mocking dependencies inside the handler**

If your handler calls an external module (for example, a database client), stub it at the top of your test file:

```
jest.mock('@/lib/db', () => ({
    getPostById: jest.fn().mockResolvedValue({ id: 'abc', title:
'Mocked' }),
  }));
```

This ensures that your tests remain fast and deterministic, even if the real database is unreachable.

6. **Optional: Using MSW for HTTP-level tests**

   For integration-style tests where you want your components or pages to `` `fetch('/api/...')` `` and still hit your API logic, set up Mock Service Worker in "node" mode to intercept and respond to those fetch calls. It is more setup but gives you end-to-end confidence, without a live backend.

By mocking each API route handler as a pure function—with concise request/ response fakes and stubbed dependencies—you achieve fast, reliable tests that focus squarely on your route logic, free from networking or infrastructure concerns.

Writing Integration Tests for API Routes

Integration tests for your Next.js API routes verify the end-to-end behavior of your HTTP endpoints—routing, middleware, handlers, and any side effects—without mocking away the HTTP layer, giving you confidence that your API works as expected in real-world scenarios.

- **Choose a Test Runner and HTTP Client**

  Jest remains a great choice as the test runner.

  Use an HTTP client library such as Super test or the community tool next-test-api-route-handler to invoke your API routes as if over HTTP.

- **Bootstrapping a Test Server**

  Unlike unit tests—where you call the handler function directly—integration tests require an HTTP server instance:

  Create a minimal Next.js server

  ```
  // tests/setupApiServer.js
  import { createServer } from 'http';
  import next from 'next';
  const app = next({ dev: false });
  const handle = app.getRequestHandler();
  export async function buildServer() {
    await app.prepare();
    return createServer((req, res) => handle(req, res)).listen(0);
  }
  ```

  Capture the dynamic port

  After calling **`buildServer()`**, inspect **`server.address().port`** to know where to send requests.

- **Writing Integration Tests with Supertest**

```
import request from 'supertest';
import { buildServer } from './setupApiServer';
let server, url;
beforeAll(async () => {
  server = await buildServer();
  const { port } = server.address();
  url = `http://localhost:${port}`;
});
afterAll(() => server.close());

test('GET /api/posts returns list of posts', async () => {
  const res = await request(url).get('/api/posts');
  expect(res.status).toBe(200);
  expect(Array.isArray(res.body)).toBe(true);
  expect(res.body[0]).toHaveProperty('id');
});
```

Real HTTP flow: Routes, query parsing, middleware, and responses all run as in production.

Assertions on **`status`**, **`headers`**, and JSON: You can check **`res.headers['content-type']`**, response times, and full payload shapes.

- **Testing Error and Edge Cases**

Simulate malformed requests or service failures:

```
test('POST /api/posts without body returns 400', async () => {
  const res = await request(url).post('/api/posts');
  expect(res.status).toBe(400);
  expect(res.body).toMatchObject({ error: expect.any(String) });
});
```

If your route depends on a database or external API, consider:

- **Test database sandbox:** Spin up an in-memory database (for example, SQLite or MongoDB Memory Server) in **`beforeAll`**, seed known data, and tear it down in **`afterAll`**.
- **Service containers:** Use Docker Compose to bring up real dependencies, and then point your tests at those services.

- **Alternative: Using `next-test-api-route-handler`**

For a lighter setup, without a full HTTP server, use this helper library:

```
import { testApiHandler } from 'next-test-api-route-handler';
import handler from '@/pages/api/posts/[id]';
test('GET /api/posts/[id] returns 200', async () => {
  await testApiHandler({
```

```
      handler,
      params: { id: '123' },
      test: async ({ fetch }) => {
        const res = await fetch({ method: 'GET' });
        expect(res.status).toBe(200);
        const body = await res.json();
        expect(body.id).toBe('123');
      },
    });
  });
```

  - **No network layer:** Runs handler through Node's HTTP internals, but still includes URL parsing and Next.js request normalization.
  - **Easy parameter injection:** Pass **`params`**, **`query`**, **`headers`**, and **`body`** declaratively.
- **Best Practices**
  - Seed and reset your data store between tests to avoid cross-test pollution.
  - Use realistic request payloads to catch schema issues or validation errors early.
  - Assert on headers and status codes as well as response bodies.
  - Parallelize cautiously: If your tests share ports or databases, run them sequentially or isolate resources.
  - Combine with MSW if you need to intercept external HTTP calls made inside your API routes (for example, third-party services).

Thus, by spinning up a lightweight server or using a **`route-handler`** helper, and invoking your API endpoints over HTTP, integration tests give you end-to-end assurance–routing, middleware, handlers, and data layers, all verified in the same test.

Snapshot Testing

Jest's snapshot feature serializes a component's rendered output (usually the JSX tree) into a text file. On subsequent runs, Jest compares the live output to the saved "snapshot", and flags any differences.

Creating a Snapshot

  - Use **`expect(tree).toMatchSnapshot()`** in a test after rendering your component with React Testing Library or react-test-renderer.
  - The first time you run npm test, Jest writes a new file under **`__snapshots__`**, naming it after your test file.

Reviewing and Updating

- When something changes intentionally (for example, you tweak styles or markup), run **`jest -u`** or **`press u`** in watch mode to update snapshots.
- Always review diffs carefully: Snapshots should capture intentional UI changes, not incidental noise.

Best Practices

- **Limit scope:** Snapshots are most effective for small, self-contained components (buttons, form inputs), not entire pages.
- **Avoid snapshots of large trees:** Very large snapshots become unwieldy, and hard to review.
- **Combine with explicit assertions:** Do not rely solely on snapshots–assert on critical elements (for example, **`expect(screen.getByText("Save")).toBeInTheDocument()`**).

Debugging Failing Tests

When a test fails, quickly isolate and resolve the issue using Jest's watch mode, targeted logging, and interactive debugging tools to keep your test suite reliable and maintainable.

- **Use Jest's Watch Mode**
    - Run **`npm run test:watch`** to re-run only tests related to changed files.
    - In watch mode, you can filter by a filename, test name, or pattern, making it easier to focus on a single failure.
- **Isolate the Failure**
    - Prefix a test or suite with **`.only`** (for example, **`test.only(…)`** or **`describe.only(…)`**) to run just that block.
    - Use **`.skip`** to quickly disable unrelated tests, and reduce noise.

Inspect the Error Message

- Jest error output shows the expected vs. received values. For DOM assertions, it prints the HTML snapshot of the element–use that to see what is actually rendered.
- For snapshot mismatches, Jest presents a unified diff; you can scroll through this to understand exactly which lines changed.

Add Temporary Logging

- Insert **`console.log(prettyDOM(container))`** or **`screen.debug()`** in RTL tests to print the current DOM.

- Logging props or state inside the component (via jest mocks or by exposing values) can help trace the source of a mismatch.

Leverage a Debugger

- Run Jest in debug mode (for example, **`node --inspect-brk node_modules/.bin/jest --runInBand`**) and attach your editor's debugger.
- Set breakpoints in your test files or even inside component code to step through rendering and event handling.

Reset and Reproduce

- Ensure that your test environment is clean: use **`afterEach(() => jest.resetAllMocks())`** to clear mocks between tests.
- If a test passes locally but fails in CI, compare Node and Jest versions, environment variables, and dependencies that might differ.

Common Pitfalls

- **Asynchronous timing issues:** Always **`await findBy...`** queries or wrap assertions in **`waitFor`** when testing async behavior.
- **Missing cleanup:** Although RTL auto-cleans between tests, custom setup code (like manual DOM mounts) must be torn down.
- **Mock leaks:** A mocked module in one test can affect others if not reset–use **`jest.clearAllMocks()`** or **`jest.resetModules()`** as needed.

Hence, by combining targeted snapshot tests for stable, small components with methodical debugging techniques–watch mode filtering, focused logging, and interactive breakpoints–you will maintain a reliable suite that quickly highlights, and helps you resolve unintended regressions.

Conclusion

This chapter has guided you through establishing a robust testing workflow for Next.js applications, from configuring Jest and React Testing Library to crafting unit, integration, and snapshot tests. You learned how to treat API routes and data-fetching methods (**`getStaticProps/getServerSideProps`**) as pure functions–mocking their inputs and stubbing outputs to keep tests fast and predictable. Integration tests showed you how to spin up a lightweight server or use helpers such as MSW and Supertest to validate real HTTP flows, while snapshot testing captured component output at a glance, and debugging techniques (watch mode, targeted logging, and breakpoints) empowered you to diagnose failures swiftly. By isolating layers–unit-testing handlers and props functions separately, then rendering components with controlled props–you achieve comprehensive coverage without external dependencies. This layered approach ensures that your Next.js code remains reliable as it evolves, catches regressions early, and fosters confidence in both server-side and client-side logic.

In the next chapter, we will explore the full deployment workflow for Next.js applications–from building optimized production bundles to selecting hosting platforms such as Vercel, AWS, or Netlify.

Multiple Choice Questions

1. What Jest feature allows you to automatically re-run only the tests related to your changes?
   a. Snapshot Testing
   b. Watch Mode
   c. Mocking
   d. Code Coverage
2. Which function signature describes a Next.js API route handler?
   a. `(context) => { props }`
   b. `(req, res) => void \| Promise<void>`
   c. `(params) => { notFound }`
   d. `(router) => Component`
3. In testing getStaticProps, what return value signals a missing page?
   a. `{ props: {} }`
   b. `{ redirect: { destination } }`
   c. `{ notFound: true }`
   d. `{ error: 404 }`
4. Which tool intercepts real HTTP requests for integration tests, without a live backend?
   a. Supertest
   b. react-test-renderer
   c. Mock Service Worker (MSW)
   d. `identity-obj-proxy`

5. Which Jest matcher would you use to compare a component's rendered output to a stored file?

    a. `toBeInTheDocument()`

    b. `toHaveBeenCalled()`

    c. `toMatchSnapshot()`

    d. `toHaveAttribute()`

Answers

1. b
2. b
3. c
4. c
5. c

CHAPTER 11

Deploying Next.js Applications

Introduction

Once your Next.js application is built and tested, the final step is deployment–bringing your app to users in a fast, secure, and scalable way. This chapter walks you through the complete process of deploying Next.js applications, from preparing your build to choosing the right hosting provider.

We will begin by understanding how Next.js builds and exports applications for production using commands such as next build and next export. Then, we will explore various deployment options, including **Vercel** (the creators of Next.js), **Netlify**, and cloud platforms such as **AWS**, **Firebase**, and **DigitalOcean**.

This chapter also covers key deployment concepts such as **environment variables**, **custom server setup**, and **domain configuration**. You will learn how to enable **CDN caching**, **handle HTTPS**, and **set up CI/CD pipelines** for automated deployments.

Special attention is given to optimizing builds for production, monitoring performance post-deployment, and handling common issues. By the end, you will be ready to confidently launch and maintain your Next.js apps in a real-world environment.

Structure

In this chapter, the following topics will be covered:

- Deployment Options (Vercel, AWS, Netlify, and more)
- Optimizing Production Builds
- Setting Environment Variables Securely
- Incremental Static Regeneration in Production
- Monitoring and Debugging Deployed Applications

Deployment Options for Next.js Application

Deploying Next.js applications efficiently is vital for delivering performant, scalable, and reliable web applications. Popular deployment platforms include Vercel, AWS, Azure, Netlify, Firebase, DigitalOcean App Platform, Heroku, and Render. The following are the detailed insights and deployment steps for the top three platforms, followed by a comprehensive comparison of additional options.

- **Vercel**

  Vercel, the creator of Next.js, provides seamless integration, specifically tailored for Next.js applications, offering automated optimization and easy deployments.

  Pros:

  - Easy zero-configuration deployments
  - Native Next.js optimization
  - Automatic CDN and edge caching
  - Integrated serverless functions and preview deployments

  Cons:

  - Limited advanced infrastructure control
  - Costs can escalate quickly for heavy use

- **AWS (Amazon Web Services)**

  AWS provides extensive and customizable infrastructure, suitable for complex, large-scale Next.js applications requiring deep integration with other AWS services.

  Pros:

  - Extensive flexibility and control
  - Scalable infrastructure suitable for large applications
  - Robust security and compliance options
  - Integration with other AWS services

  Cons:

  - Higher complexity and learning curve
  - Manual configuration may require more setup time

- **Netlify**

  Netlify offers easy and fast deployments primarily known for static sites but has strong support for Next.js applications, including Server-Side Rendering (SSR).

  Pros:

  - User-friendly deployment process
  - Automatic builds and deployments
  - Integrated CDN and SSL certificates
  - Ideal for JAMstack architecture

  Cons:

  - Limited infrastructure customization
  - Pricing can become less economical for dynamic, heavily trafficked applications

- **Firebase**

  Firebase Hosting, provided by Google, supports static and dynamic content through integration with Firebase Cloud Functions.

  Pros:

  - Simple CLI-driven deployments
  - Integration with Firebase backend services
  - Efficient scaling through Google infrastructure

  Cons:

  - Limited server-side rendering capabilities
  - Dependencies on Firebase ecosystem

- **DigitalOcean App Platform**

  DigitalOcean's App Platform simplifies app deployment by automating infrastructure management, suitable for developers needing straightforward setup.

  Pros:

  - Easy-to-use, transparent pricing
  - Built-in scalability and CDN
  - Direct support for Node.js applications

Cons:

- Limited advanced configuration options
- Scalability limits compared to AWS or Vercel

- **Heroku**

  Heroku offers simple, fast Git-based deployments, ideal for prototyping and small to medium-sized applications.

  Pros:

  - Rapid, simple deployment process
  - Easy scalability options
  - Extensive add-ons for database, caching, and logging

  Cons:

  - Costs escalate significantly for larger applications
  - Limited control over server environments

- **Render**

  Render provides modern cloud infrastructure with automatic deployments from Git repositories, positioning itself as an alternative to Heroku and Vercel.

  Pros:

  - Automatic deployments and easy scalability
  - Native SSR support
  - Competitive pricing

  Cons:

  - Limited customization compared to AWS
  - Relatively newer platform with less mature ecosystem

- **Azure**

  Azure App Service provides a platform-as-a-service solution to deploy web applications easily.

  Pros:

  - Seamless integration with other Azure services
  - Excellent scalability and security features
  - Robust performance monitoring and analytics
  - Built-in CI/CD integration

Cons:

- Can be complex for beginners
- Pricing can escalate quickly with heavy traffic

Choosing the right deployment platform depends on your project's specific requirements. Consider Vercel for easy Next.js integration, AWS for extensive customization, Netlify for simplicity with JAMstack, Firebase for backend service integration, DigitalOcean for transparent pricing, Heroku for rapid prototyping, and Render for balanced cost-efficiency and simplicity.

Understanding the Deployment Process

Deployment in software development is the process of preparing and launching a software application, making it available for users. It includes activities such as compiling code, optimizing resources, configuring settings, and establishing the necessary infrastructure. The objective is to ensure that the application runs smoothly, securely, and efficiently in the intended environment.

Types of Deployment Environments

A deployment environment is the computing infrastructure where applications are deployed and accessed by the users. Some of the common deployment environments include:

Development Environment

The development environment is designed for coding, testing, and debugging by the developers. Typically localized on developers' machines, it provides the necessary tools, libraries, and databases. It serves as a workspace for refining applications before broader testing.

Testing/Staging Environment

The staging environment closely mirrors the production environment, allowing comprehensive testing. It validates the application's functionality, performance, compatibility, and security, helping to identify and resolve bugs before deployment to production.

Production Environment

This is the live, user-facing environment. It must be highly stable, secure, optimized, and scalable to handle real-world traffic. Production environments often require robust infrastructure and sophisticated configurations to ensure reliability and performance.

Deployment Platforms

Deployment platforms are specialized services or hosting providers like AWS, Azure, and so on. They simplify deployment, and provide essential infrastructure, tools, and management services.

Different Deployment Processes

Static Hosting

- Ideal for statically generated Next.js applications, without server-side rendering or API routes.

Deployment Steps:

1. Build the application: `npm run build`
2. Export static files: `npm run export`
3. Deploy files to hosting platforms such as Netlify, Vercel, or GitHub Pages.

Serverless Functions

Next.js API routes enable on-demand server-side logic, ideal for dynamic tasks.

Deployment Steps:

1. Create API routes in `` `pages/api` ``.
2. Build the application: `npm run build`
3. Deploy on platforms such as Vercel, AWS Lambda, or Azure Functions, configuring environment variables as needed.

Thus, understanding different deployment environments and processes ensures successful and efficient application delivery, tailored to your application's specific needs and targeted user base.

Optimizing Production Builds

Optimizing production builds is crucial for enhancing the performance and efficiency of your Next.js application. It involves several strategies such as:

- **Code Splitting:** Next.js automatically splits your application into smaller chunks, loading only the necessary code to improve initial load times.
- **Image Optimization:** Utilize Next.js built-in `<Image>` component, which automatically optimizes images to reduce file sizes, improve loading speeds, and enhance user experience.

- **Asset Compression:** Configure your build tools and hosting services to compress assets (such as JavaScript, CSS, and HTML) using gzip or brotli, significantly reducing the download times.
- **Caching and CDN:** Leverage Content Delivery Networks (CDNs) to cache static and dynamic assets close to your users, minimizing latency, and improving load times.
- **Lazy Loading:** Implement lazy loading for heavy components or assets to enhance initial page load performance by deferring loading until necessary.
- **Bundle Analysis:** Use tools such as Webpack Bundle Analyzer to identify large dependencies, and optimize bundle size.
- **Environment Variables:** Appropriately manage environment variables to optimize runtime behaviour, without compromising security.

Thus, by integrating these strategies, you ensure that your Next.js application remains fast, efficient, and responsive, providing a superior user experience.

Setting Environment Variables Securely

Environment variables are crucial for managing application configurations effectively during deployment. They offer a secure, flexible way to store the sensitive data such as API keys, database credentials, and other dynamic settings, without embedding them directly into your application code.

Set up environment variables effectively across different deployment scenarios such as: local, testing, and production environments.

- **Local Development Environment**

  In local development, environment variables help configure your application for testing and development on your personal machine:

  - **Step 1:** Create a `.env` file at the root of your Next.js project.
  - **Step 2:** Define variables within the `.env` file in a key-value format:

    ```
    API_KEY=12345
    DATABASE_URL=mongodb://localhost:27017/mydatabase
    ```

  - **Step 3:** Access these variables in your Next.js application using the built-in `process.env` object: `const apiKey = process.env.API_KEY`;
  - **Step 4:** Ensure `.env` is listed in your `.gitignore` file to prevent committing sensitive data to version control.

- **Test Environment**

  The test environment is used for thorough testing before production deployment:

- **Step 1:** Create a dedicated `.env.test` file to store test-specific variables.
- **Step 2:** Define the necessary test configurations:

  API_KEY=testapikey

  DATABASE_URL=mongodb://localhost:27017/testdatabase
- **Step 3:** Load these variables in your test scripts or frameworks to ensure correct test configurations.

- **Production Environment**

  Production environments require secure and efficient handling of environment variables:

  - **Step 1:** Configure environment variables directly on your hosting platform or server Using platform-specific tools (console, dashboard, CLI, and so on).
  - **Step 2:** Avoid embedding sensitive production data in your codebase or repository.
  - **Step 3:** Verify that these variables are correctly loaded by your Next.js application at runtime.

```
Passing Environment Variables During Local Execution
Windows Environment
Inline variable setup:
set API_KEY=12345 && npm run dev

Using a separate file (`env.bat`):
@echo off
set API_KEY=12345
set DATABASE_URL=mongodb://localhost:27017/mydatabase

Execute: call env.bat && npm run dev

Linux Environment
Inline variable setup: export API_KEY=12345 && npm run dev

Using a separate file (`env.sh`): export API_KEY=12345
export DATABASE_URL=mongodb://localhost:27017/mydatabase

Execute: source env.sh && npm run dev
```

GitHub Workflow for Testing, Building, and CI/CD Integration

Set up a GitHub Actions workflow to streamline testing, building, and deployment:

Step-by-Step Guide

- **Step 1:** Create a workflow YAML file (`ci-cd.yml`) within `.github/workflows` in your GitHub repository.
- **Step 2:** Define workflow triggers (for example, push to main branch or pull requests):

```
name: CI/CD Workflow
on:
  push:
    branches:
      - main
  pull_request:
    branches:
      - main
```

- **Step 3:** Configure workflow jobs:

```
jobs:
  test:
    runs-on: ubuntu-latest
    steps:
      - uses: actions/checkout@v2
      - run: npm ci
      - run: npm run test

  build:
    runs-on: ubuntu-latest
    steps:
      - uses: actions/checkout@v2
      - run: npm ci
      - run: npm run build

  deploy:
    needs: [build]
    runs-on: ubuntu-latest
    steps:
      - uses: actions/checkout@v2
      - run: npm ci
      - run: |
          # Insert deployment commands specific to your platform
here
```

- **Step 4:** Add specific commands and configurations for testing, building, and deployment, according to your project's needs.
- **Step 5:** Commit and push the workflow file (`ci-cd.yml`) to trigger automated workflow executions.

Thus, following this guide ensures that your Next.js application is robust, secure, and ready for reliable deployment across multiple environments.

Deploying Next.js Applications to Different Hosting Platforms

Deploying a Next.js application involves specific steps depending on the chosen hosting platform. This guide covers deployment on **Vercel** and **AWS Amplify**, two of the most popular choices, and provides clear instructions and examples to help you through the process.

- **Deploying Next.js Applications to Vercel**

  Vercel is the official platform for Next.js deployment, offering seamless integration and zero-configuration setup. Follow these steps:

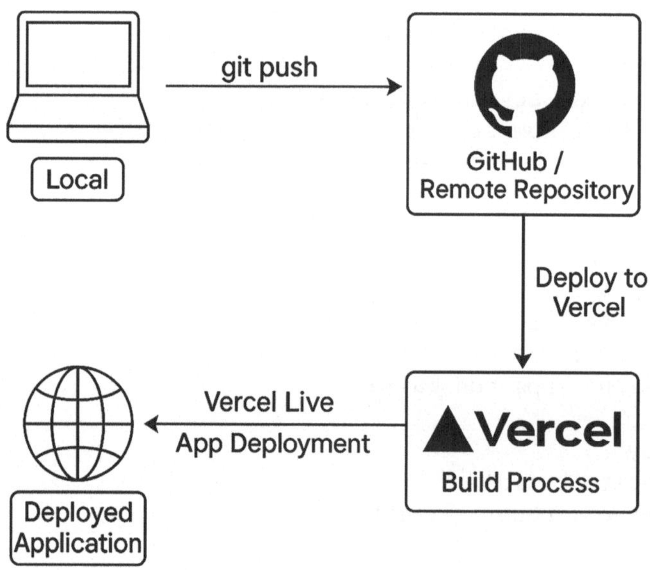

Figure 11.1: *Vercel Deployment Process*

Step 1: Install the Vercel CLI.

Ensure that Node.js and npm are installed. Then run: `npm install -g vercel`.

Step 2: Build Your Application

Navigate to your Next.js project directory and run: `npm run build`.

Step 3: Create `vercel.json` Configuration (Optional)

In the project root, create a `vercel.json` file for custom settings. Example:

```
{
  "version": 2,
  "builds": [{ "src": "next.config.js", "use": "@vercel/next" }],
  "routes": [
    { "src": "/api/(.*)", "dest": "api/$1" },
    { "src": "/blog", "dest": "/blog/index.html" },
    { "src": "/blog/(.*)", "dest": "/blog/$1.html" },
    { "src": "/(.*)", "dest": "/$1" }
  ],
  "env": {
    "API_URL": "https://api.example.com",
    "API_KEY": "@env-api-key"
  },
  "rewrites": [
    { "source": "/user/:id", "destination": "/profile?id=:id" }
  ],
  "redirects": [
    { "source": "/about", "destination": "/company/about",
"statusCode": 301 }
  ]
}
```

Key Sections:

- **`version`:** Configuration version.
- **`builds`:** Defines how to build the app.
- **`routes`, `rewrites`, `redirects`:** Manage URL handling.
- **`env`:** Securely define environment variables.

Step 4: Log into Vercel

Authenticate with: **`vercel login`**

Step 5: Deploy Your App

Run: **`vercel`**

Follow the prompts. On success, a live deployment URL will be generated.

- **Deploying Next.js Applications to AWS Amplify**

  AWS Amplify is a fully managed CI/CD and hosting service for modern web apps. Here is how to deploy your app with Amplify:

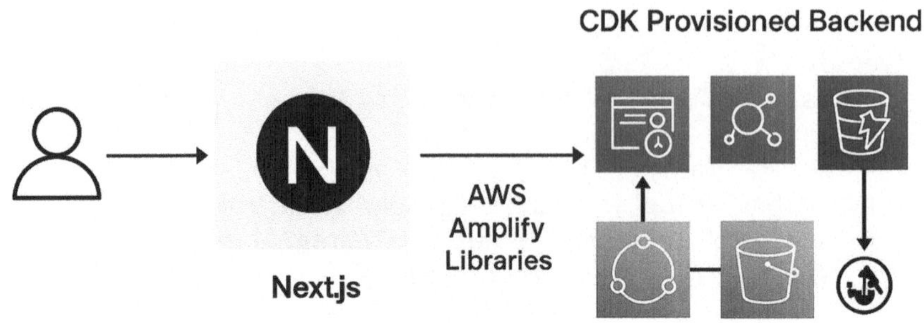

Figure 11.2: *AWS Amplify Deployment Workflow*

Step 1: Set Up an Amplify App

a. Go to the AWS Amplify console.

b. Click "**`Get Started`**" or "**`Create App`**".

c. Connect your Git repository (for example, GitHub).

d. Select a branch to deploy.

e. For build settings:

   i. Framework: **`Other`**

   ii. Build command: **`npm run build`**

   iii. Start command: **`npm run start`**

f. You can optionally configure a custom domain.

Step 2: Configure, Build and Deployment Settings

a. Navigate to your app in Amplify.

b. Under **`App settings > Build settings`**, select the branch (for example, main), and click **`Edit`**.

c. Ensure these settings:

   i. Build command: **`npm run build`**

   ii. Start command: **`npm run start`**

d. Click **`Save`** and Deploy.

Step 3: Deploy the App

Amplify will:

a. Clone your repo

b. Build your app

c. Deploy it to a live environment

Monitor progress from the Amplify dashboard.

Step 4: Access the Live App

After deployment, amplify provides a default domain. Open it in a browser to view your deployed app.

Step 5: Set Up Continuous Deployment (Optional)

a. Go to **`App settings > Branches`**.

b. Select your branch (for example, **`main`**).

c. Toggle **`Auto Deploy`** on.

d. Click **`Save`**.

Now, every push to the branch will trigger an automatic deployment.

Example: **`package.json`** Scripts

Ensure that your **`package.json`** includes:

```
{
  "scripts": {
    "build": "next build",
    "start": "next start"
  }
}
```

Push your code to GitHub, and connect your repo to Amplify.

You have now seen how to deploy Next.js applications using both Vercel and AWS Amplify. Vercel offers a zero-config and instant deployment experience, especially suited for Next.js. AWS Amplify, on the other hand, provides robust scalability, backend integrations, and CI/CD pipelines.

Incremental Static Regeneration in Production

Incremental Static Regeneration (ISR) in Next.js is a deployment strategy that combines the benefits of Static Site Generation (SSG) with the flexibility of Server-

Side Rendering (SSR). It significantly improves the deployment and user experience by enabling static content updates, without requiring a full redeployment or rebuild of the site.

Now, let us examine ISR in-depth, specifically focusing on deployment considerations, workflow, benefits, and best practices for production.

- **Understanding ISR in Deployment Terms**

  Incremental Static Regeneration allows your Next.js application to dynamically regenerate static pages after initial deployment. This means:

  - Your pages are initially statically generated at build time.
  - After deployment, Next.js can automatically regenerate individual pages in the background upon request.
  - You set an interval (`revalidate`) to define how frequently the static content should be updated, without manual redeployment.

- **ISR Works During Deployment of the Detailed Process:**

  1. Initial Deployment:

     a. Pages using ISR (`getStaticProps` with a `revalidate` property) are built into static HTML at build time.

     b. These static pages are cached at the CDN edge layer for optimal delivery speed.

  2. After Deployment (Production):

     a. When users request a page, they immediately receive the existing cached page.

     b. If the revalidation time has passed, Next.js triggers a background regeneration:

        i. It fetches the updated data from your data or source/API.

        ii. It rebuilds the static HTML and JSON for that page.

        iii. It updates the cache, so subsequent requests get the updated version.

Example Implementation (Deployment Context):

```
export async function getStaticProps() {
  const res = await fetch('https://api.example.com/posts');
  const posts = await res.json();

  return {
    props: { posts },
```

```
    revalidate: 60, // Revalidate page every 60 seconds after de-
ployment
  };
}
```

- **Deployment Platforms and ISR**

  ISR in Next.js works smoothly with popular deployment platforms:

  - **Vercel:** Natively supports ISR with CDN caching, instantly propagating regenerated pages globally.
  - **AWS Amplify/AWS S3 + CloudFront:** ISR can be used effectively, but additional configuration is needed to handle caching strategies and edge revalidation.
  - **Netlify:** Officially supports ISR with the Next.js Advanced Middleware plugin, offering similar incremental regeneration benefits.
  - **Docker/Custom deployments:** Can leverage ISR, if correctly configured with caching layers (for example, CDN, reverse proxies like Nginx or Varnish).

- **Benefits of ISR in Production Deployment**

  - **Improved Performance:** Pages load instantly from CDN cache, providing excellent user experience.
  - **Efficient Builds and Deployments:** Reduces full-site rebuilds, saving build time and resources.
  - **Scalable Dynamic Content:** Dynamically updates static content without sacrificing performance or SEO benefits.
  - **Cost-Efficient:** Reduces the computational resources required for frequent rebuilds or full SSR.
  - **SEO-Friendly:** Provides static HTML pages beneficial for indexing by search engines.

- **Best Practices for Using ISR in Production**

  When using ISR in a production environment, consider the following best practices:

  - Set Appropriate Revalidation Times:
    - Balance freshness of content vs. load on backend APIs.
    - For rapidly changing content (for example, news), set shorter intervals (for example, 10–60 seconds).
    - For less dynamic content (blogs, documentation, and so on), longer intervals (for example, 1 hour to 1 day) may be appropriate.

- Error Handling:
  - Always handle potential data fetching errors in `getStaticProps`.
  - Provide fallback data or error messaging to avoid disruptions in user experience.
- Monitoring and Observability:
  - Monitor the regeneration performance, caching hits, and potential latency using tools such as New Relic, Datadog, or built-in Vercel analytics.
  - Regularly check server-side logs and CDN analytics for ISR-related events.
- Caching and CDN Considerations:
  - Ensure proper CDN cache-control headers.
  - Confirm that the CDN correctly respects Next.js cache invalidation strategies to avoid stale data delivery.

- **Troubleshooting Common ISR Deployment Issues**
  - Stale Content Issues:
    - Check CDN caching policies and `revalidate` settings.
    - Verify API responses and caching headers.
  - Increased Server Load:
    - Adjust regeneration intervals.
    - Employ rate-limiting or CDN-level caching to prevent overwhelming the backend.
  - Pages Not Regenerating:
    - Confirm environment variables and configurations in deployment environments.
    - Verify Next.js version compatibility on your deployment platform.
- **Example ISR Deployment Workflow**
  - A typical ISR-based deployment workflow looks like:

    `Development → Build → Deploy → Serve Static → Background Revalidation → Update Cache → Serve Updated Content`
  - Initially, Next.js generates static HTML pages during the build step.
  - Upon deployment, static pages are served from a CDN.
  - As time progresses, pages regenerate individually based on user requests, and your defined revalidation interval.

- Updated pages automatically replace the outdated cache entries, ensuring that visitors receive the freshest content.

Monitoring and Debugging Deployed Applications

Monitoring and debugging are critical components of managing a deployed Next.js application, particularly in production environments where stability and performance directly affect user experience. Next.js, a leading React framework, offers robust integration with modern platforms such as Vercel and AWS, enabling developers to monitor, troubleshoot, and optimize their applications effectively.

Monitoring Deployed Applications

Monitoring is pivotal for maintaining application health, availability, and performance. It helps identify issues early, and provides insights for proactive optimization. The following are key monitoring techniques for deployed Next.js applications:

- **Logging:** Implement comprehensive logging to capture the key application events, errors, and contextual data. Libraries such as Winston or Pino are commonly used. Logs can be directed to local storage, remote servers, or third-party services such as Loggly and Papertrail.
- **Error Tracking:** Integrate tools such as Sentry or Rollbar for automated error tracking. These platforms offer real-time alerts, detailed stack traces, and context-aware insights, helping developers detect and resolve production issues efficiently.
- **Performance Monitoring:** Leverage solutions such as New Relic, Datadog, or AppDynamics to measure performance metrics such as response times, API latency, server utilization, and memory usage. These insights enable the identification of performance bottlenecks and optimization opportunities.
- **Custom Application Metrics:** Instrument custom metrics tailored to your business logic using tools such as Prometheus or StatsD. Tracking specific user interactions or service behaviors allows for better understanding of usage patterns and data-driven decision-making.

Debugging Deployed Applications

Debugging in production environments requires a strategic approach to identify and resolve complex issues, without disrupting the user experience. Consider the following techniques:

- **Remote Debugging:** Utilize tools such as Chrome DevTools or VS Code's Remote Debugging to attach to the running applications. These tools enable live inspection of variables, stack traces, and real-time code execution analysis in production-like environments.
- **Error Analysis:** Use collected logs and error reports to analyze failure points. Patterns in stack traces, frequency of errors, and user impact help trace issues to their root cause. Services such as Sentry enhance this process with contextual tracking.
- **Load Testing:** Employ tools such as Apache JMeter or Artillery to simulate heavy traffic, and assess application behavior under stress. Load testing reveals scaling issues and infrastructure limitations before they impact the real users.
- **A/B Testing and Feature Flags:** Implement A/B testing or feature flagging to gradually roll out features, and isolate problematic changes. This helps to identify specific updates that cause regressions or performance drops, minimizing risks.
- **Code Monitoring:** Use services such as Epsagon or TrackJS to trace function-level issues in the codebase. These tools provide insights into execution flow, identify hotspots, and help refine critical parts of the application.

Using Vercel for Monitoring and Debugging

Vercel, the official deployment platform for Next.js, offers integrated features for monitoring and debugging:

- **Deployment Hooks:** Configure hooks to trigger scripts or services post-deployment for notifications, analytics, or health checks.
- **Environment Variables:** Manage environment-specific configurations for logging, monitoring, and third-party integrations.
- **Built-in Analytics:** Monitor request counts, latency, and bandwidth usage directly from the Vercel dashboard to track real-time application performance.

Using AWS for Monitoring and Debugging

Amazon Web Services (AWS) provides comprehensive solutions for monitoring and debugging Next.js applications, particularly in serverless or containerized environments:

- **CloudWatch:** Aggregates logs, sets alarms, and tracks metrics. You can stream Next.js logs into CloudWatch Logs, and visualize key performance indicators.

- **AWS X-Ray:** Enables distributed tracing for debugging performance issues across microservices and APIs. Visual trace maps help pinpoint slow components.
- **Lambda Layers:** For serverless Next.js apps, use Lambda Layers to include logging and monitoring libraries that capture runtime insights.
- **CloudFormation:** Define infrastructure as code to provision logging, metrics, alarms, and monitoring resources as part of your automated deployment pipeline.

Thus, to ensure optimal reliability, performance, and user satisfaction, continuous monitoring and efficient debugging are essential for deployed Next.js applications. By combining built-in Next.js capabilities with powerful tools from platforms such as Vercel and AWS, developers can maintain visibility into their applications and swiftly respond to any production issues. Hence, embracing these best practices results in robust, scalable, and well-maintained applications ready for real-world usage.

Conclusion

Successfully deploying and managing a Next.js application in production requires a combination of strategic decisions, tooling, and performance optimization. In this chapter, you explored popular deployment platforms such as Vercel, AWS, and Netlify, each offering distinct advantages depending on your infrastructure needs. We also discussed techniques for optimizing production builds to improve speed and efficiency, and how to securely manage environment variables to protect the sensitive configuration data.

Incremental Static Regeneration (ISR) was covered in-depth as a hybrid approach to static and dynamic content, along with methods for post-deployment monitoring and logging to ensure uptime and reliability. Together, these practices lay a robust foundation for building resilient, performant, and scalable web applications.

In the next chapter, we will explore advanced features in Next.js such as middleware, server customization and much more.

Multiple Choice Questions

1. Which platform is the native deployment provider for Next.js?
    a. Netlify
    b. Heroku
    c. Vercel
    d. AWS Lambda

2. What is the primary benefit of Incremental Static Regeneration (ISR)?
   a. Avoids caching
   b. Regenerates all pages on every request
   c. Updates static content without a full rebuild
   d. Requires no CDN integration
3. How are environment variables typically stored securely in production?
   a. In JavaScript files
   b. Using `.env` files uploaded to GitHub
   c. Through the deployment platform's secret manager
   d. Hardcoded into the codebase
4. What AWS service is used to collect logs, and set alarms for a Next.js app?
   a. S3
   b. CloudWatch
   c. RDS
   d. Lambda
5. Which tool helps trace and debug performance issues in distributed Next.js systems?
   a. Sentry
   b. Loggly
   c. AWS X-Ray
   d. ESLint

Answers

1. c
2. c
3. c
4. b
5. c

CHAPTER 12
Advanced Features in Next.js

Introduction

Next.js 15 introduces a suite of advanced features that empower developers to build more dynamic, scalable, and globally optimized applications. This chapter dives into the deeper capabilities of the framework, focusing on enhancements that go beyond the basics.

We begin with an in-depth look at Middleware in Next.js 15, exploring advanced use cases such as authentication, A/B testing, and on-the-fly redirects–all executed at the edge for better performance. You will also learn how to customize the webpack configuration to fine-tune your build process, and integrate custom plugins or loaders.

Next, we explore the advanced dynamic routing patterns, including optional catch-all routes and nested layouts, enabling more flexible and powerful navigation structures. The chapter also covers built-in support for localization and internationalization (i18n), making it easy to create multilingual applications.

Finally, we examine the Edge Runtime, which enables ultra-fast request processing closer to the user. By the end, you will be well-equipped to harness the full potential of Next.js 15 for modern, high-performance applications.

Structure

In this chapter, the following topics will be covered:

- Middleware in Next.js 15: Advanced Usage
- Customizing the Webpack Configuration
- Advanced Dynamic Routing Patterns
- Localization and Internationalization (i18n)
- Using Edge Runtime for Faster Processing

Middleware in Next.js 15: Advanced Usage

Middleware in Next.js 15 enables developers to run logic before a request is completed. It sits in the request lifecycle, and can decide whether to continue the request, redirect it, rewrite the path, or modify headers. This ability to intercept and transform requests before reaching a route makes middleware a powerful tool for building secure, performant, and personalized applications.

Unlike traditional API middleware, Next.js middleware runs on the Edge Runtime. This means it is executed closer to the user, resulting in low-latency operations and faster response times. It is commonly used for tasks such as authentication, localization, header injection, and custom rewrites or redirects.

- **Defining Middleware**

  Middleware is defined in a file named `**middleware.ts**` or `**middleware.js**` placed at the root of the project or inside the `**app/**` directory, if you are using the App Router.

  ```
  // middleware.ts
  import { NextResponse } from 'next/server';
  import type { NextRequest } from 'next/server';

  export function middleware(request: NextRequest) {
    console.log('Request for:', request.nextUrl.pathname);
    return NextResponse.next(); // Allow the request to continue
  }
  ```

  This is the simplest form of middleware: It logs the requested path, and allows the request to proceed.

- **Authentication and Route Protection**

  A common use case for middleware is protecting pages from unauthorized access. Middleware can inspect cookies or headers to check if a user is authenticated and redirect them, if they are not.

  ```
  export function middleware(request: NextRequest) {
    const token = request.cookies.get('auth_token')?.value;
    if (!token && request.nextUrl.pathname.startsWith
  ('/dashboard')) {
      return NextResponse.redirect(new URL('/login', request.url));
    }
    return NextResponse.next();
  }
  ```

In this example:

- The user is trying to access a protected route like `/dashboard`.
- If the `auth_token` cookie is missing, they are redirected to `/login`.
- This ensures only logged-in users can reach sensitive routes.

- **Locale-Based Redirection**

  Another common use case is internationalization. Middleware can automatically redirect users to their language-specific site based on their browser's preferred language.

```
export function middleware(request: NextRequest) {
  const locale = request.headers.get('accept-language')?.
split(',')[0];
  if (request.nextUrl.pathname === '/') {
    return NextResponse.redirect(new URL(`/${locale}`, request.
url));
  }
  return NextResponse.next();
}
```

  The homepage `/` is redirected to a localized version such as `/en`, `/fr`, etc., based on the `Accept-Language` header.

- **Rewriting URLs Internally**

  Middleware can rewrite URLs without changing the browser address bar. This is helpful when you want to serve updated content from a different path but maintain old URLs.

```
export function middleware(request: NextRequest) {
  if (request.nextUrl.pathname === '/pricing') {
    return NextResponse.rewrite(new URL('/new-pricing', request.
url));
  }
  return NextResponse.next();
}
```

  In this case, a request to `/pricing` serves content from `/new-pricing`, but the user still sees `/pricing` in their address bar.

- **Adding Custom Headers**

  Middleware can modify the response headers before the request reaches its final destination.

```
export function middleware(request: NextRequest) {
  const response = NextResponse.next();
  response.headers.set('X-Custom-Header', 'EdgeMiddleware');
```

```
  return response;
}
```

This approach is often used to inject custom headers for debugging, analytics, or security purposes.

- **Route Matching with Matcher**

  To limit middleware to specific routes, Next.js allows you to define a `matcher` configuration.

```
export const config = {
  matcher: ['/dashboard/:path', '/profile'],
};
```

  With this setup, the middleware runs only for requests starting with `/dashboard/` or exactly `/profile`, helping reduce overhead, and making your logic more focused.

- **Edge Runtime Considerations**

  - Since middleware runs in the Edge Runtime, it does not support Node.js core modules such as `fs`, `process`, or `crypto`. Your logic must use Web APIs, and remain lightweight and fast, as it is executed on every request for the matched routes.
  - Avoid heavy computations or blocking operations in middleware, and always return a response (`NextResponse.next()`, `NextResponse.redirect()`, or `NextResponse.rewrite()`).

  Thus, Middleware in Next.js 15 is a powerful tool for intercepting and modifying requests at runtime, directly within your application code. From authentication and redirects to localization and route rewriting, middleware allows developers to enforce logic consistently and efficiently across their app.

By learning to structure middleware properly, control its scope with matchers, and optimize it for the Edge Runtime, even beginner developers can implement enterprise-grade features with minimal setup. As applications scale, middleware becomes a central part for maintaining clean, secure, and user-friendly experiences.

Customizing the Webpack Configuration in Next.js

Next.js is a powerful React framework that simplifies full-stack development, offering out-of-the-box performance optimization, routing, and server-side rendering. A key part of its build system is Webpack, a module bundler that processes and compiles all the codes and assets in your application. While Next.js handles most of the configuration for you, there are scenarios where you might need more control over how the application is built. This is where customizing the Webpack configuration becomes relevant.

For many developers—especially those coming from client-side React projects—Webpack can seem complex and intimidating. Fortunately, Next.js abstracts away most of that complexity, while still offering a simple mechanism to extend or override its internal Webpack setup when necessary. Understanding how to do this safely and effectively allows developers to support advanced functionality, without compromising the stability of their project.

Understanding Webpack's Role in Next.js

Before diving into custom configurations, it is helpful to understand what Webpack does in a Next.js project:

- It bundles JavaScript and TypeScript files into optimized chunks.
- It processes and compiles assets such as images, CSS, SCSS, SVGs, and fonts.
- It supports code splitting, enabling faster page loads by sending only the required code for a page.
- It handles tree shaking, which eliminates unused code to reduce bundle size.
- It provides the foundation for hot reloading, environment variables, and file watching during development.

All of this is configured automatically by Next.js, but when your use case goes beyond the default behavior—for example, adding a custom loader for Markdown files, injecting compile-time variables, or replacing a specific plugin—you can modify the Webpack configuration through a standard API.

Customize the Webpack Configuration

All customizations are made through the **next.config.js** file. This file sits at the root of your project, and exports a configuration object. Within this object, you can define a **webpack** function to access and modify the internal Webpack setup.

```
// next.config.js
module.exports = {
  webpack: (config, { buildId, dev, isServer, defaultLoaders,
webpack }) => {
    // Modify the config here
    return config;
  },
};
```

This function receives two arguments:

- **config:** The current Webpack configuration object.
- **context:** An object containing information about the build environment (for example, **isServer**, **dev**, **webpack**).

Therefore, modifications must always return the updated **config** object for the build to continue.

Adding Custom File Loaders

One of the most common reasons to customize Webpack is to support additional file types that are not handled by default. For example, suppose you want to import **.md** files directly into your components and parse them as raw text.

```
module.exports = {
  webpack: (config) => {
    config.module.rules.push({
      test: /\.md$/,
      use: 'raw-loader',
    });
    return config;
  },
};
```

This adds a rule that tells Webpack to use **raw-loader** for **.md** files. After this, you can do:

```
import doc from './README.md';
console.log(doc); // Raw markdown string
```

Similarly, you can support **.csv**, **.yaml**, **.graphql**, or any custom format by using appropriate loaders.

Adding SVG Support with SVGR

SVG files are often used for icons and illustrations. By default, Next.js treats SVGs as static assets, but you can customize Webpack to import them as React components using the **@svgr/webpack** loader.

```
module.exports = {
  webpack: (config) => {
    config.module.rules.push({
      test: /\.svg$/,
      issuer: /\.[jt]sx?$/,
      use: ['@svgr/webpack'],
    });
```

```
    return config;
  },
};
```

This allows you to write:

```
import Logo from './logo.svg';
<Logo width={100} height={100} />
```

This is extremely useful in design systems and component libraries where SVGs are treated as first-class UI elements.

Using Webpack Plugins

Webpack plugins provide more complex transformations and optimizations during the build. For example, you can inject custom environment variables using **DefinePlugin**:

```
const webpack = require('webpack');
module.exports = {
  webpack: (config) => {
    config.plugins.push(
      new webpack.DefinePlugin({
        'process.env.MY_CUSTOM_VAR': JSON.stringify('This is
custom'),
      })
    );
    return config;
  },
};
```

This value is embedded at build time, and can be used anywhere in your code as:

```
console.log(process.env.MY_CUSTOM_VAR);
```

You can also integrate plugins for bundle analysis, performance reporting, compression, or progressive web app support.

Customizing Aliases

Webpack supports path aliases to simplify imports. Instead of writing **../../../components/Button**, you can define an alias like **@components**.

```
const path = require('path');
module.exports = {
  webpack: (config) => {
    config.resolve.alias['@components'] = path.resolve(__dirname,
'components');
    return config;
```

```
  },
};
```

Now, you can import components using:

```
import Button from '@components/Button';
```

This improves code readability and helps manage large codebases.

Overriding Optimization Settings

While not commonly needed for small projects, advanced teams might want to fine-tune how Webpack optimizes the bundle. For example, you can disable code splitting or customize how vendor files are grouped:

```
module.exports = {
  webpack: (config) => {
    config.optimization.splitChunks = {
      cacheGroups: {
        vendor: {
          test: /[\\/]node_modules[\\/]/,
          name: 'vendors',
          chunks: 'all',
        },
      },
    };
    return config;
  },
};
```

Use this only when you have a strong reason, such as improving load performance in controlled environments.

Important Considerations

Customizing Webpack should be done thoughtfully. While Next.js provides the flexibility, there are risks involved such as:

- Overriding too many settings can make upgrades harder.
- Poorly configured rules or plugins may introduce bugs or increase bundle size.
- Using unsupported Node.js modules in client-side builds will break in production.

To maintain performance and compatibility:

- Stick to modular and minimal changes.
- Test both server and client environments.

- Use environment flags (**`dev`**, **`isServer`**) to scope your logic.

Customizing the Webpack configuration in Next.js empowers developers to handle non-standard file formats, enable additional optimizations, and extend the build pipeline to support new workflows. Thus, whether it is adding SVG support, injecting environment variables, or introducing new plugins, the **`webpack`** key in **`next.config.js`** gives you precise control over how your application is compiled and bundled.

By understanding Webpack's role in the Next.js ecosystem, and applying thoughtful modifications, developers can support advanced use cases, while still benefiting from the simplicity and performance of Next.js's default setup. This balance between flexibility and convention is what makes Next.js a standout framework for modern web development.

Advanced Dynamic Routing Patterns

Dynamic routing in Next.js offers much more than just mapping URL segments to page files. As your application scales, organizing and managing routes–especially complex ones–becomes crucial. Advanced dynamic routing patterns provide the flexibility to handle everything from deeply nested content structures to optional parameters and custom layouts, all while keeping the codebase maintainable.

In this section, we will explore advanced concepts and best practices related to dynamic routing in Next.js:

- **Catch-All Routes (`[...slug].js`)**

  Catch-all routes let you match multiple segments with a single file. This is particularly useful for blogs, product categories, or documentation pages with a deep hierarchy.

  Example:

  ```
  // pages/docs/[...slug].tsx
  import { useRouter } from 'next/router';
  export default function DocsPage() {
    const router = useRouter();
    const { slug } = router.query;

    return <div>Route: {JSON.stringify(slug)}</div>;
  }
  Visiting /docs/nextjs/routing will result in slug = ['nextjs',
  'routing'].
  ```

- **Optional Catch-All Routes (`[[...slug]].js`)**

  Optional catch-all routes behave like regular catch-all routes but also match the root path when no segment is provided.

Use Case: A search page or category index page where parameters are optional.

```
// pages/search/[[...filters]].tsx
export default function SearchPage({ params }) {
  return <div>Filters: {JSON.stringify(params.filters || [])}</
div>;
}
```

- **Nested Dynamic Routes**

  You can create dynamic routes at any folder level, enabling deeply nested paths such as **`/users/[userId]/posts/[postId]`**.

  Folder Structure:

  ```
  pages/
  └── users/
      └── [userId]/
          └── posts/
              └── [postId].tsx
  ```

  This leads to intuitive and scalable route definitions where each dynamic part is clearly scoped.

- **Combining Static and Dynamic Segments**

  Next.js allows a mix of static and dynamic segments, enabling more descriptive URL structures.

  For example:

  ```
  /products/electronics/[productId]
  /products/furniture/[productId]
  You can organize this as:
  pages/products/
  ├── electronics/
  │   └── [productId].tsx
  ├── furniture/
  │   └── [productId].tsx
  ```

- **Custom 404 Handling in Dynamic Routes**

  When using dynamic or catch-all routes, make sure to handle not-found cases manually, especially for slugs that do not resolve to real content.

  In `getStaticProps`:

  ```
  if (!data) {
    return {
      notFound: true,
    };
  }
  ```

This tells Next.js to render the default 404 page for unmatched slugs, improving UX and SEO.

- **Programmatic Navigation with Dynamic Parameters**

  Use **next/router** for programmatic navigation between dynamic routes.

```
import { useRouter } from 'next/router';
router.push({
  pathname: '/products/[category]/[id]',
  query: { category: 'electronics', id: '123' }
});
```

  This helps in building navigation components such as menus or custom buttons.

- **Using Middleware for Dynamic Routing Logic**

  With Next.js Middleware, you can dynamically rewrite routes, enforce authentication, or redirect users based on route parameters—before a page even loads.

```
// middleware.ts
export function middleware(req) {
  const url = req.nextUrl;
  if (url.pathname.startsWith('/admin') && !isAuthenticated(req))
{
    url.pathname = '/login';
    return NextResponse.redirect(url);
  }
  return NextResponse.next();
}
```

- **Shared Layouts in Dynamic Routes**

  For deeply nested dynamic routes, you may want a shared layout (like user dashboards). This can be handled using the **app/** directory with nested layouts or with **_app.tsx** in traditional structure.

Advanced dynamic routing in Next.js allows developers to build highly scalable, SEO-friendly, and deeply nested route structures with minimal configuration. Thus, whether you are working on a multi-level blog, e-commerce platform, or complex dashboard, mastering these patterns ensures both maintainability and flexibility in your codebase.

Localization and Internationalization (i18n)

In today's global digital landscape, web applications often need to serve users from different linguistic and cultural backgrounds. To meet this demand, applications must be designed with internationalization (i18n) and localization in mind. Next.js, starting from version 10, provides built-in support for i18n, simplifying the development of multilingual applications.

Internationalization

Internationalization, commonly abbreviated as i18n, is the process of designing and structuring your application, so that it can be easily adapted to different languages and regions. This preparation involves:

- Avoiding hard-coded strings
- Designing layouts flexible enough for different languages
- Making date, time, currency, and number formats configurable
- Preparing for text expansion or direction changes (for example, left-to-right vs right-to-left, and so on)

Internationalization is a developmental step that sets the stage for localization.

Localization

Localization is the process of adapting an internationalized application for a specific language or region. It includes:

- Translating UI text and messages
- Formatting dates and times according to regional standards
- Switching currencies, units, and number formats
- Displaying content that is culturally relevant or legal in a particular region

In fact, Localization ensures that users have a natural and familiar experience, regardless of their location.

Next.js i18n Configuration

Next.js supports i18n through its configuration file. You define your supported languages (locales) and a default locale in **next.config.js**.

```
module.exports = {
  i18n: {
    locales: ['en', 'fr', 'es'],
    defaultLocale: 'en',
  },
};
```

- **locales:** An array of supported language codes.
- **defaultLocale:** The fallback language, if the user's preferred locale is not available.

This configuration automatically enables locale-prefixed routes such as **/fr**, **/es**, **/en**, and so on.

Locale-Based Routing

Once i18n is enabled, Next.js automatically rewrites URLs based on the user's selected or detected locale:

- **/about** → English version
- **/fr/about** → French version
- **/es/about** → Spanish version

This helps serve region-specific content, without additional client-side logic.

Automatic Locale Detection

By default, Next.js uses the browser's **Accept-Language** header to determine a visitor's preferred language. This allows the application to redirect users to the most appropriate localized version of the page. If needed, this behavior can be turned off:

```
i18n: {
  locales: ['en', 'fr', 'es'],
  defaultLocale: 'en',
  localeDetection: false,
}
```

Translation Management

To display the localized content, most applications maintain translation files. These are typically JSON files organized by locale and namespace:

Example Structure:

```
locales/
├── en/
│   └── common.json
├── fr/
│   └── common.json
├── es/
│   └── common.json
```

```
common.json (English):
```

```
{
  "welcome": "Welcome",
  "logout": "Log out"
}

common.json (French):
{
  "welcome": "Bienvenue",
  "logout": "Se déconnecter"
}
```

These files can be imported and used with translation libraries like:

- `next-translate`
- `react-i18next`
- `next-intl`

These libraries offer hooks or components to render translations dynamically based on the current locale.

Localized Static and Server-Side Rendering

You can access the current locale in data fetching methods such as **`getStaticProps`** or **`getServerSideProps`**:

```
export async function getStaticProps({ locale }) {
  const messages = await import(`../locales/${locale}/common.
json`);
  return {
    props: {
      messages: messages.default,
    },
  };
}
```

This allows your pages to load the content appropriate to the user's language during build time or request time.

Formatting Dates, Numbers, and Currencies

Next.js does not provide formatting utilities out of the box, but JavaScript's native Intl API supports robust locale-based formatting:

Example:

```
const price = new Intl.NumberFormat('fr-FR', {
  style: 'currency',
  currency: 'EUR',
```

```
}).format(1234.56);
// Output: "1 234,56 €"
```

This helps to maintain consistency and professionalism in your UI when displaying region-specific data.

SEO Considerations for Localized Routes

Localized websites must follow the best practices to remain search engine friendly such as:

- Include **`<link rel="alternate" hreflang="...">`** tags for different language versions.
- Set proper **`lang`** attributes in the HTML document.
- Ensure that the localized routes are properly indexed with unique metadata (title, description, and so on.)

Thus, Next.js automatically sets route structures that help with locale-based indexing, but adding meta tags and hreflang is your responsibility.

Next.js makes it practical and efficient to build multilingual applications. Its built-in i18n support handles the following:

- Locale-aware routing
- Automatic language detection
- Configuration via **`next.config.js`**

Hence, by combining these with proper localization libraries and formatting tools, developers can build scalable and culturally adaptable applications that are accessible to a global audience.

Using Edge Runtime for Faster Processing

The Edge Runtime in Next.js is a specialized execution environment designed to run server-side code closer to the user's geographic location. It enables developers to build faster, more scalable applications by reducing latency and improving responsiveness through distributed computation. Instead of relying solely on centralized server regions, the Edge Runtime leverages the global network of edge locations (often provided by platforms such as Vercel's Edge Network or Cloudflare Workers).

Edge Runtime

The Edge Runtime is a lightweight, sandboxed JavaScript environment optimized for performance at the network edge. Unlike traditional Node.js environments, the Edge Runtime:

- Is designed to be cold-start-free
- Has a restricted API surface
- Runs with Web APIs instead of Node.js APIs
- Has better concurrency and lower latency
- Executes in a streaming and distributed fashion

This runtime is ideal for short-lived functions, such as authentication, redirects, headers manipulation, feature toggling, or A/B testing logic.

Benefits of Using Edge Runtime

- **Lower Latency:** By executing code closer to the user, responses are delivered faster. This is especially beneficial for users geographically distant from the origin server.
- **No Cold Starts:** Edge Functions are typically executed instantly, without waiting for a server to warm up, ensuring snappy interactions even for the first request.
- **High Scalability:** Edge functions scale automatically across global edge locations, handling spikes in traffic, without requiring infrastructure configuration.
- **Improved User Experience:** Use cases such as localization, authentication gates, or geolocation-aware content can be performed before rendering, leading to faster and more personalized pages.

Use Cases Ideal for Edge Runtime

- Authentication and session verification
- Middleware logic (for example, redirects, headers, and so on)
- Feature flag evaluation
- Geolocation-based content
- Bot detection and rate limiting
- Dynamic personalization or A/B testing

Use Edge Runtime

- **Middleware**

  The most common way to utilize the Edge Runtime in Next.js is via Middleware. Middleware runs before a request is completed, and can modify the response, redirect users, or add headers.

Create a **_middleware.js** or **middleware.ts** file at the root or within a directory:

```
// middleware.ts
import { NextResponse } from 'next/server';
import type { NextRequest } from 'next/server';
export function middleware(request: NextRequest) {
  const country = request.geo?.country || 'US';
  if (country !== 'US') {
    return NextResponse.redirect(new URL('/intl', request.url));
  }
  return NextResponse.next();
}
```

This logic runs at the edge before your page loads, enabling you to customize the experience instantly.

- **Edge API Routes**

  You can define API routes that use the Edge Runtime instead of the Node.js runtime:

```
// pages/api/edge-function.ts
export const config = {
  runtime: 'edge',
};
export default async function handler(request: Request) {
  return new Response('This is an Edge API route');
}
```

  These are lightweight, and suitable for use cases like content gating, token validation, or fast backendless APIs.

Limitations of the Edge Runtime

While the Edge Runtime offers speed and distribution, it comes with a limited execution environment:

- No access to Node.js APIs (for example, **fs**, **net**, **child_process**, and so on).
- No long-running computations.
- Limited package support (only Web-compatible packages work).
- Restricted fetch behavior and execution time (5s–30s depending on the platform).

This makes it best suited for fast, lightweight tasks, not complex server-side rendering or heavy backend logic.

Conclusion

Throughout this chapter, we have methodically examined Next.js's more sophisticated capabilities, beginning with the implementation of middleware in Next.js 15 to intercept and transform requests at the edge. We then demonstrated how to extend and customize the webpack configuration to optimize build performance and accommodate unique project requirements. Our discussion of advanced dynamic routing patterns illustrated techniques for managing flexible URL structures, including optional and catch-all segments. We also explored localization and internationalization (i18n) strategies for delivering seamless multilingual experiences and reviewed best practices for detecting and serving locale-specific content. Lastly, we investigated the Edge Runtime's potential to reduce latency by executing code geographically closer to end users. By mastering these advanced topics, you are now equipped to design and deploy robust, high-performance applications capable of scaling to a global audience.

In the next chapter, we will apply these concepts to real-world project scenarios, demonstrating practical solutions and patterns that address common development challenges.

Multiple Choice Questions

1. Which Next.js feature allows you to run code, before a request is completed, at the edge?
   a. `getServerSideProps`
   b. Middleware
   c. API Routes
   d. Static Generation
2. How can you modify the default webpack configuration in a Next.js project?
   a. By editing `next.config.js`
   b. By installing a separate `webpack.config.js` at project root
   c. By using `babel.config.json`
   d. By setting environment variables only
3. Which routing pattern would you use to capture all nested paths under `/blog` (for example, `/blog/2025/05/16`)?
   a. `/blog/[...slug]`
   b. `/blog/[slug]`

   c. `/blog/[year]/[month]/[day]`

   d. `/blog/*`

4. Which Next.js feature provides built-in support for multiple languages and locale detection?

   a. **`next-i18next`** plugin only

   b. Static Generation

   c. Internationalization (i18n) in **`next.config.js`**

   d. API Routes

5. What advantage does the Edge Runtime offer in Next.js?

   a. Automatic code minification

   b. Running server code in the browser

   c. Reduced latency by executing code closer to end users

   d. Built-in database connections

Answers

1. b
2. a
3. a
4. c
5. c

CHAPTER 13
Real-World Projects with Next.js

Introduction

Building real-world projects is the best way to solidify your understanding of Next.js, and apply its features in practical scenarios. This chapter focuses on hands-on examples that simulate real business needs, helping you bridge the gap between learning and production-level development.

You will explore how to structure full-stack applications using Next.js, from setting up pages and routing to integrating APIs, databases, and authentication systems. Each project will highlight different core and advanced features of Next.js, such as **Server-Side Rendering (SSR)**, **API routes**, **middleware**, **Edge functions**, and **dynamic routing**.

We will walk through building apps such as a **blog platform with Markdown support**, an **e-commerce storefront**, a **dashboard with role-based access control**, and a **real-time chat application**. These examples demonstrate how to manage state, connect with third-party services, optimize performance, and deploy at scale.

Thus, by working on these projects, you will gain the confidence and experience needed to build robust, scalable web applications using Next.js in real-world environments.

Structure

In this chapter, the following topics will be covered:

- E-Commerce Platform
- Dynamic Product Pages with getStaticPaths
- API Route Integration for Cart Functionality
- Authentication with NextAuth.js
- Blog with CMS Integration

- Static Generation with Content from a CMS (for example, Sanity or Contentful)
- Preview Mode Implementation
- Admin Dashboard
- Role-Based Routing and Authentication
- Real-Time Data Updates with SWR and WebSocket

In this chapter, you will build a unified car-commerce and editorial blog platform using Next.js. By leveraging file-based routing, serverless API routes, and built-in authentication, you can deliver fast, SEO-friendly product pages, a fully featured cart, secure sign-in flows, and a headless-CMS-powered blog—all from one codebase.

E-Commerce Platform

The **E-Commerce Platform** is the heart of our application's commerce experience. It lets visitors browse vehicle models, add them to a shopping cart, and check out securely, without leaving your Next.js project. Under the hood, it combines three main capabilities—pre-rendered product pages, a serverless cart API, and built-in authentication—so you get performance, simplicity, and security in one package.

When deciding how to build the e-commerce platform for this project, we weighed up a set of essential factors, each one shaping why Next.js and its built-in capabilities became our foundation:

- **Performance and User Experience:** Pre-rendering pages (via `getStaticProps` and `getStaticPaths`) means every product detail loads instantly, without waiting for server responses. Fast pages keep shoppers engaged, and reduce bounce rates.
- **SEO and Discoverability:** Search engines favor fully rendered HTML. By statically generating product and blog pages, we ensure that crawlers see the complete content, boosting rankings for model names, specs, and editorial posts.
- **Developer Productivity:** A single framework that handles routing, data fetching, API endpoints, and authentication lets your team stay focused on features, instead of boilerplate. The file-based conventions in `pages/` and `pages/api/` remove configuration overhead.
- **Scalability and Deployability:** Static assets can live on a global CDN edge, serving millions of reads with minimal cost. Serverless API routes auto-scale with demand—cart operations and auth flows grow seamlessly as traffic spikes.

- **Maintainability and Code Organization:** Co-locating pages and their related API logic in one repository that keeps the mental model simple. Naming conventions in Next.js ensure that every file has a clear purpose and path, reducing context-switching.
- **Integration Flexibility:** Whether sourcing product data from a local JSON, a headless CMS, or a traditional database, Next.js data-fetching methods adapt easily. Likewise, API routes can call payment gateways or third-party services, without leaving the project.
- **Security and Session Management:** NextAuth.js provides battle-tested session handling, token storage, and CSRF protection right out of the box. Serverless functions run in a V8 sandbox, isolating cart and auth logic from your front end.
- **Time to Market and Cost:** By avoiding separate back-end servers and heavy DevOps, you can launch faster with lower hosting bills. Static sites and serverless functions are often covered under generous free tiers at major providers.
- **User-Centric Features:** Built-in image optimization, Incremental Static Regeneration (ISR), and client-side data fetching strike a balance between static speed and up-to-the-minute freshness–key for price updates or limited-time offers.

Thus, by evaluating these factors, performance, SEO, productivity, scalability, maintainability, integration, security, cost, and user needs, we arrived at a serverless, file-based architecture that delivers enterprise-grade e-commerce capabilities with minimal complexity.

The following is an **architecture layout** to complement the factors that drove our E-Commerce Platform design. This file- and folder-based structure shows where each concern lives and how data flows through the system:

```
src/
├─ app/
│  ├─ layout.js              # Root layout (header, footer, global providers)
│  ├─ page.js                # Home route (links to cars listing, blog listing)
│  ├─ cars/
│  │  ├─ layout.js           # Cars section layout (optional sidebar or nav)
│  │  ├─ page.js             # /cars page listing all models (uses fetch in server component)
│  │  └─ [slug]/
│  │     └─ page.js          # /cars/[slug] dynamic product pages (generateStaticParams, fetch)
│  ├─ cart/
│  │  └─ page.js             # /cart overview page (client component fetches /api/cart)
│  ├─ checkout/
│  │  └─ page.js             # /checkout protected page (uses getServerSession in server component)
│  ├─ blog/
│  │  ├─ layout.js           # Blog section layout (optional)
│  │  ├─ page.js             # /blog listing page (fetch posts)
│  │  └─ [slug]/
│  │     └─ page.js          # /blog/[slug] static post pages (generateStaticParams, fetch + revalidate)
│  └─ api/
│     ├─ cart/
│     │  └─ route.js          # /api/cart (POST/DELETE handlers, cookies/session)
│     └─ auth/
│        └─ [...nextauth]/
│           └─ route.js       # /api/auth/[...nextauth] (NextAuth handlers)
│
├─ components/
│  ├─ Header.js              # Navigation, sign-in/out UI
│  ├─ Footer.js              # Site footer
│  ├─ ProductCard.js         # Server/client component for car previews
│  ├─ CartItem.js            # Client component for cart line items
│  └─ BlogCard.js            # Preview component for blog posts
│
├─ lib/
│  ├─ dataClient.js          # Fetch helper for car data (JSON, DB, CMS)
│  ├─ cmsClient.js           # Sanity/Contentful client helpers
│  └─ authOptions.js         # NextAuth configuration (providers, callbacks)
│
├─ styles/                   # Global CSS or Tailwind config
│
└─ public/                   # Static assets (logos, default images)
```

Figure 13.1: *File-Based Architecture Layout*

Data Flows through This Layout:

- **Build Time**
  - Next.js reads **`pages/cars/[slug].js`** and **`pages/blog/[slug].js`**.
  - **`getStaticPaths`** collects slugs from **`lib/dataClient.js`** or **`lib/cmsClient.js`**.
  - **`getStaticProps`** fetches full records (car specs or post content) via the same clients.
  - Static HTML and JSON are generated and deployed to a CDN.
- **Runtime (Client → Serverless)**
  - "**`Add to Cart`**" in **`components/ProductCard.js calls fetch('/api/cart'), hitting pages/api/cart.js`**.
  - Cart data is persisted via HTTP-only cookies or a lightweight session store.
- **Authentication**
  - Layout.js exposes "**`Sign In`**"/"**`Sign Out`**" using **`NextAuth's signIn()`** and **`signOut()`**.
  - Protected pages (checkout.js) use **`getSession()`** in **`getServerSideProps`** to ensure that only signed-in users can access them.

- **Incremental Updates**
  - Blog post pages use revalidate in **`getStaticProps`** to enable ISR, so that new posts appear without a full rebuild.

This structure orchestrates your build-time static generation and runtime serverless endpoints to deliver a cohesive, high-performance e-commerce experience.

Dynamic Product Pages with `generateStaticParams`

Pre-rendering each car's detail page ahead of time ensures that shoppers see fully rendered HTML immediately, without any client-side loading delays. Here is how the architecture and content flow come together in your Next.js 15+ App Router setup:

Architecture Layout

```
src/
└── app/
  └── cars/
    ├── layout.js       # Optional shared layout for all car pages
    └── [slug]/
      └── page.js       # Dynamic product page component
```

`[slug]/page.js`

- Exports a **`generateStaticParams()`** function that returns an array of **`{ slug }`** objects.
- Fetches detailed car data in a server component using the **`params.slug`**.
- Renders a React component displaying the car's name, image gallery, specifications table, and purchases CTA.

- **Gathering Slugs at Build Time**
  - **`generateStaticParams()`** runs once when you build your app.
  - It calls a data-fetching helper (for example, **`lib/dataClient.getAllCarSlugs()`**) to retrieve every car identifier.
  - Returns:

```
export async function generateStaticParams() {
  const slugs = await getAllCarSlugs(); //
['tesla-model-3', 'bmw-x5', …]
  return slugs.map(slug => ({ slug }));
}
```

- **Fetching Car Details**
  - For each slug, Next.js invokes the server component in `page.js` with `params.slug`.
  - Within the component, you call `await getCarBySlug(params.slug)` to load name, specs (range, price, features), and images.
- **Rendering the Page**

  The server component returns JSX that structures content into:

  - **Hero Section:** Car name, hero image, starting price.
  - **Gallery:** A responsive image carousel showing exterior and interior shots.
  - **Specifications:** A table of key details (range, top speed, 0–60 mph).
  - **Purchase Section:** "`Add to Cart`" button wired to your cart API.

  Example Snippet:

```
export default async function CarPage({ params }) {
    const car = await getCarBySlug(params.slug);
    return (
      <div>
        <h1>{car.name}</h1>
        <Image src={car.images[0]} alt={car.name} width={800}
height={450} />
        <table>
          <tbody>
            <tr><th>Range</th><td>{car.specs.range} miles</
td></tr>
            <tr><th>Top Speed</th><td>{car.specs.topSpeed}
mph</td></tr>
            <!-- more specs -->
          </tbody>
        </table>
        <AddToCartButton productId={car.id} />
      </div>
    );
}
```

- **Outcome and Benefits**
  - **Build-Time Generation:** Pages like `/cars/tesla-model-3` are generated once and served as static assets.
  - **Performance:** No server-rendered round-trips on page load–instant paint and interactive UI.
  - **SEO:** Crawlers see complete content in the HTML, improving discoverability for every model.

- **Maintainability:** All logic for routing, data fetching, and rendering lives in one well-organized folder structure under `src/app/cars`.

With this setup, your dynamic product pages achieve the maximum speed, reliability, and ease of development—letting you focus on enriching content and user experience, rather than boilerplate routing or performance tuning.

Serverless Cart API Integration

Managing the shopping cart via Next.js API routes keeps your e-commerce logic co-located with your front end, scales automatically, and removes the need for a separate backend service. Here is how the architecture and request flow work in your Next.js 15+ App Router setup:

Architecture Layout

```
src/
└── app/
   └── api/
      └── cart/
         └── route.js        # Handles POST (add/update) and DELETE (remove) cart
   operations
```

`route.js`

- Exports HTTP method handlers (`export async function POST(request)` and `export async function DELETE(request)`).
- Reads and writes the user's cart via secure cookies or a session store.
- Returns the updated cart state as JSON.

Request and Data Flow:

- **Client Triggers Cart Update**

  A React component (example `AddToCartButton`) calls:

```
await fetch('/api/cart', {
  method: 'POST',
  headers: { 'Content-Type': 'application/json' },
  body: JSON.stringify({ productId: 'bmw-x5', quantity: 2 })
});
```

  For removals, it sends:

```
await fetch('/api/cart', {
    method: 'DELETE',
    headers: { 'Content-Type': 'application/json' },
    body: JSON.stringify({ productId: 'bmw-x5' })
  });
```

- **Serverless Handler Processes Request**
    - `POST` handler in `route.js` parses the request JSON:

```
export async function POST(request) {
  const { productId, quantity } = await request.json();
  let cart = await getCartFromCookie(request);
  cart = updateCart(cart, productId, quantity);
  return setCartCookie(new Response(JSON.stringify
(cart)), cart);
}
```

    - `DELETE` handler parses the request JSON, removes the item, and sets the cookie similarly.
- **Cart Persistence**
    - **Cookie-Based:** `getCartFromCookie` reads a signed, HTTP-only cookie containing the current cart.
    - **Session Store:** Alternatively, you could look up a session ID in a Redis or database store.
    - **Response:** `setCartCookie` attaches a `Set-Cookie` header to the response, persisting the updated cart for the user.
- **Client Receives the Updated Cart**
    - The JSON response contains the full cart object (array of items, quantities, and totals).
    - The React component updates the local state or a global store (Context, Zustand, and so on) to reflect the new cart contents instantly.

Benefits

- **Unified Codebase:** Cart logic lives alongside your page and component code–no separate repo or server to maintain.
- **Automatic Scaling:** Serverless functions scale up and down with traffic, so spikes in "Add to Cart" requests do not require extra DevOps.
- **Low Latency:** Cloud functions close to users, and lightweight JSON payloads ensure snappy interactions.
- **Security:** HTTP-only, signed cookies (or secure session stores) protect the cart data from client-side tampering.
- **Developer Efficiency:** Using familiar `fetch` calls and collocated handlers minimizes context switching, and speeds up feature development.

Thus, by leveraging Next.js API routes for your cart, you maintain a streamlined architecture that emphasizes simplicity, performance, and security–the key factors in a successful e-commerce platform.

Authentication with NextAuth.js

Integrating NextAuth.js provides secure, standards-based authentication, without a separate auth server. The following is the architecture and request flow for using NextAuth in your Next.js 15+ App Router setup:

Architecture Layout

```
src/
├── app/
│   └── api/
│       └── auth/
│           └── [...nextauth]/
│               └── route.js        # NextAuth route handler for all auth endpoints
├── lib/
│   └── authOptions.js        # NextAuth configuration (providers, callbacks)
└── components/
    └── Header.js          # Uses signIn/signOut and useSession hooks
```

- **`route.js`**
  - Exports the **`NextAuth`** Handler:

```
import NextAuth from "next-auth";
import authOptions from "@/lib/authOptions";
export { authOptions as GET, authOptions as POST } from
"next-auth/next";
export default NextAuth(authOptions);
```

- **`authOptions.js`**
  - Defines providers (Google, GitHub, Email), session strategy, and callbacks.
- **`Header.js`**
  - Renders "Sign In"/"Sign Out" buttons using **`NextAuth's`** **`signIn()`** and **`signOut()`**.
  - Uses **`useSession()`** to display user info or protect UI elements.

Request and Data Flow

- **User Initiates Sign-In**
  - A client component button calls:

```
import { signIn } from "next-auth/react";
// …
<button onClick={() => signIn("google")}>Sign In with
Google</button>
```

  - This triggers a redirect to the provider's OAuth consent screen.

- **OAuth Callback Handling**
  - After consent, the provider redirects back to `/api/auth/[...nextauth]/callback/google`.
  - NextAuth's route.js parses the callback, exchanges codes for tokens, and invokes any configured callbacks (for example, to persist a user in your database).
- **Session Creation**
  - NextAuth issues an encrypted, HTTP-only cookie named `next-auth.session-token`.
  - The user is redirected back to the page they attempted to access or a default URL.
- **Accessing Session on Client**

  In any React component, you call:

```
import { useSession } from "next-auth/react";
  const { data: session, status } = useSession();
```

`status` indicates "authenticated" or "unauthenticated," and `session.user` contains the profile info.

- **Protecting Server-Side Routes**

  In a server component or `page.js`, you import:

```
import { getServerSession } from "next-auth/next";
import authOptions from "@/lib/authOptions";
export async function getServerSideProps(context) {
  const session = await getServerSession(context.req,
context.res, authOptions);
  if (!session) {
    return { redirect: { destination: "/api/auth/signin",
permanent: false } };
  }
  return { props: { session } };
}
```

This ensures only signed-in users can reach pages like `/checkout`.

Benefits

- **Zero Boilerplate:** NextAuth handles OAuth flows, token storage, and session cookies automatically.
- **Security:** Sessions use encrypted, HTTP-only cookies by default, protecting against XSS.
- **Flexibility:** Supports multiple providers and custom credential strategies.

- **Co-Located Code:** All auth logic lives under `src/app/api/auth`, keeping your codebase organized and maintainable.
- **Consistent UX:** Client and server can both access the session data–enabling personalized UI and protected routes seamlessly.

Thus, by leveraging NextAuth.js in your App Router setup, you gain robust and flexible authentication integrated directly into your Next.js project, minimizing setup time, while maximizing security and developer ergonomics.

Blog with CMS Integration

Integrating a headless CMS lets your marketing team author content independently, while Next.js statically generates fast, SEO-friendly blog pages. The architecture and data flow work in a Next.js 15+ App Router setup:

Architecture Layout

```
src/
└ app/
  └ blog/
    └ layout.js       Optional shared layout for all blog pages
    └ page.js         /blog listing page (fetch all posts)
    └ [slug]/
      └ page.js       /blog/[slug] dynamic post pages
```

- `blog/page.js`
  - A server component that calls a CMS client (for example, Sanity or Contentful) to fetch all posts' titles, excerpts, dates, and slugs.
  - Renders a list of preview cards linking to each `/blog/[slug]` page.
- `[slug]/page.js`
  - Exports `generateStaticParams()` to return all post slugs at build time.
  - Fetches full post content–title, body (rich text or MDX), images, metadata–in the server component.
  - Sets a `revalidate` value to enable Incremental Static Regeneration (ISR).

Request and Data Flow

- **Listing Posts**
  - **When:** At build time or on every request if you choose server-side rendering for the listing.
  - `blog/page.js` calls `getAllPosts()` from `lib/cmsClient.js`.
  - Renders previews (title, date, and excerpt) with links to each detail page.

- **Generating Detail Pages**
  - **Build Time:** `generateStaticParams()` in `blog/[slug]/page.js` fetches `getAllPostSlugs()`.
  - Returns an array such as `[ { slug: 'how-to-maintain-your-car' }, … ]`.
- **Fetching Post Content**
  - For each slug, Next.js invokes the server component in `page.js` with `params.slug`.
  - Calls `getPostBySlug(params.slug)` to retrieve full post data:
  - Title and publication date.
  - Rich text body (rendered via Portable Text or MDX).
  - Featured images and author metadata.
- **Incremental Static Regeneration (ISR)**
  - In `page.js`, export a `revalidate` value (for example, `export const revalidate = 60`).
  - After the initial build, any request older than 60 seconds triggers a background rebuild of that page—new CMS content appears, without a full redeploy.

Benefits

- **Empowered Content Team:** Editors work in Sanity or Contentful dashboards, with no developer involvement for each new post.
- **Static Speed + Freshness:** Pre-rendered pages load instantly, while ISR ensures that updates go live within your chosen interval.
- **SEO Optimization:** Fully rendered HTML, semantic markup, and meta tags improve search rankings for your articles.
- **Modular Architecture:** Co-locating blog logic under `src/app/blog` keeps the content concerns separate from commerce features.
- **Maintainability:** CMS client code lives in `lib/cmsClient.js`, making it easy to switch providers or adjust queries, without touching the UI components.

Therefore, by leveraging Next.js's App Router with `generateStaticParams`, server components, and ISR, you create a robust blog platform where the content is both performant and easily updated—complementing your e-commerce features in one cohesive codebase.

Static Generation with Content from a CMS

Pre-rendering blog posts at build time lets you serve the fully formed HTML to readers and search engines, while a headless CMS gives editors a familiar interface for creating content. Here is how it fits into your App Router architecture and the flow of data:

Architecture Layout

```
src/
└─ app/
   └─ blog/
      ├─ layout.js          Shared layout for blog (header, footer, sidebar)
      ├─ page.js            Blog index (lists all posts)
      └─ [slug]/
         └─ page.js         Blog post page (dynamic route)
```

- **`blog/[slug]/page.js`**
  - Exports **`generateStaticParams()`** to provide all post slugs at build time.
  - Fetches full post data–title, date, body, and images–from the CMS in a server component.
  - Defines a **`revalidate`** interval for Incremental Static Regeneration.

Content Flow

- **Collecting Slugs at Build Time**
  - **Responsible:** Next.js build process
  - **Function:** **`generateStaticParams()`** calls CMS helper (for example, **`getAllPostSlugs()`** from **`lib/cmsClient.js`**)
  - **Location:** **`src/app/blog/[slug]/page.js`**
  - **Timing:** Once, during the build
  - **Purpose:** To identify which pages to generate ahead of deployment

Sample Code:

```
export async function generateStaticParams() {
  const slugs = await getAllPostSlugs(); // ['intro-to-evs',
'maintenance-tips', …]
  return slugs.map(slug => ({ slug }));
}
```

- **Fetching Post Content**
  - **Responsible:** Server component for each slug
  - **Function:** Calls **`getPostBySlug(params.slug)`** to retrieve:

  - Title and publication date
  - Rich text body (via Portable Text or MDX)
  - Featured images and author info
  - **Location:** Inside the default export of page.js
  - **Timing:** During build for each slug, and on-demand if ISR triggers
  - **Purpose:** To embed all content in the static HTML

Sample Code:

```
export default async function PostPage({ params }) {
  const post = await getPostBySlug(params.slug);
  return (
    <article>
      <h1>{post.title}</h1>
      <time>{post.date}</time>
      <div>{renderPortableText(post.body)}</div>
    </article>
  );
}
```

- **Incremental Static Regeneration (ISR)**
  - **Responsible:** Next.js server
  - **Function:** The revalidate export (for example, 60 seconds) instructs Next.js to refresh stale pages in the background
  - **Location:** At the top of page.js
    - **`export const revalidate = 60;`**
  - **Timing:** On the first request after the revalidation interval has elapsed
  - **Purpose:** To keep content fresh, without a full site rebuild
- **Outcome and Advantages**
  - **Build-Time Speed:** All posts are pre-rendered into HTML, delivering instant page loads.
  - **Editor Autonomy:** Non-developer writers manage content in the CMS; no code redeploys for new posts.
  - **SEO Benefits:** Search engines crawl complete, semantic HTML with metadata.
  - **Freshness via ISR:** Updates in the CMS appear on the live site automatically, once the revalidate window passes.

Thus, by combining `**generateStaticParams**`, server components, and ISR in your App Router under `**src/app/blog**`, you create a blog that is both lightning-fast, and easy to maintain–perfectly complementing your e-commerce features.

Preview Mode Implementation

Preview Mode lets editors see draft content from the CMS on your live site–without rebuilding–by toggling a special cookie, and routing data-fetching calls through the CMS's preview API. It fits into your App Router layout, and the flow of a preview request:

Architecture Layout

```
src/
└ app/
  ├ api/
  │ ├ preview/
  │ │  └ route.js       # Enables preview mode (sets draftMode cookie)
  │ └ exit-preview/
  │    └ route.js       # Disables preview mode (clears cookie)
  └ blog/
    └ [slug]/
       └ page.js        # Uses draftMode() to detect preview and fetch
drafts
```

- **`app/api/preview/route.js`**: Exports a **`GET`** handler that calls **`import { draftMode } from "next/headers"`** to turn on preview mode, then redirects to the requested URL.
- **`app/api/exit-preview/route.js`**: Exports a **`GET`** handler that calls **`import { clearDraftMode } from "next/headers"`** to turn off preview mode, and then redirects back.
- **`app/blog/[slug]/page.js`**: Imports **`draftMode`** and passes a flag into your CMS client, and so it fetches draft content when the preview is active.

Request and Data Flow

- **Entering Preview**
  - **Trigger:** Editor clicks "Preview" in the CMS, calling the **/api/preview?slug=... endpoint**
  - **Process:** Preview route's GET handler enables draft mode, and redirects to the blog post

    ```
    import { draftMode } from "next/headers";
    export async function GET(request) {
      draftMode().enable();
      const { searchParams } = new URL(request.url);
      const slug = searchParams.get("slug") || "";
      return NextResponse.redirect(`/blog/${slug}`);
    }
    ```
  - **Purpose:** Sets a secure, signed cookie instructing Next.js data fetching to retrieve the draft content.

- **Fetching Draft Content**
  - **Location:** At the top of the server component in page.js

    ```
    import { draftMode } from "next/headers";
    export default async function PostPage({ params }) {
      const isPreview = draftMode().isEnabled;
      const post = await getPostBySlug(params.slug, { draft:
    isPreview });
      // ...
    }
    ```

  - **Function: `getPostBySlug`** checks the draft flag and uses the CMS preview API (for example, Sanity's previewClient) if true.
  - **Timing:** On every request to a **`[slug]`** page, while the preview mode is active.
  - **Purpose:** Allows editors to view unpublished changes live; regular visitors see published content.
- **Exiting Preview**
  - **Trigger:** Editor navigates to **`/api/exit-preview`**.
  - **Process:** Exit route's GET handler clears draft mode, and redirects to the blog home.

    ```
    import { clearDraftMode } from "next/headers";
    export async function GET() {
      clearDraftMode();
      return NextResponse.redirect("/blog");
    }
    ```

  - **Purpose:** Removes the preview cookie, so that the subsequent requests fetch only the published content.

Benefits

- **Instant Feedback:** Editors can verify the formatting, layout, and images in-context, without waiting for a rebuild.
- **Seamless Workflow:** CMS "Preview" buttons link directly to your preview API, making the content QA intuitive.
- **Code Simplicity:** Leveraging Next.js's `` `draftMode()` `` and route handlers keeps preview logic minimal and co-located.
- **Security:** Preview cookies are signed and scoped, preventing unauthorized draft access.

Thus, by wiring up these two API routes and checking `` `draftMode()` `` in your dynamic page's data-fetching, you give your editorial team a powerful, real-time preview experience, while keeping the published pages fast and static.

Admin Dashboard

The Admin Dashboard sits under `src/app/admin`, and provides privileged interfaces for site administrators. It combines role-based access control using NextAuth and Next.js Middleware with real-time data fetching via SWR and WebSockets.

Architecture Layout

```
src/
├─ app/
│  ├─ admin/
│  │  ├─ layout.js       # Admin layout (sidebar, nav, guards)
│  │  ├─ page.js         # /admin overview (server component)
│  │  └─ users/
│  │     └─ page.js        # /admin/users (list and manage users)
│  └─ api/
│     ├─ ws/
│     │  └─ route.js       # WebSocket upgrade handler
│     └─ admin/
│        └─ data.js        # REST endpoints for admin data (CRUD)
├─ lib/
│  └─ authOptions.js      # NextAuth with role callbacks
├─ middleware.ts          # Protects /admin routes based on session role
└─ components/
   ├─ AdminNav.js         # Navigation links for admin
   └─ RealTimeTable.js      # Client component using SWR + WebSocket
```

Role-Based Routing and Authentication

Only authenticated users with an "admin" role may access any `/admin` routes. We enforce this with NextAuth session callbacks, Next.js Middleware, and protected server components.

- **NextAuth Configuration**
  - In **`lib/authOptions.js`**, include a session callback to attach **`user.role`** to the session object (for example, admin, editor, and viewer).
  - Ensure that your user database or identity provider records roles.

```
callbacks: {
  async session({ session, token }) {
    session.user.role = token.role;
    return session;
  }
}
```

- **Middleware Protection**
    - Create **`middleware.ts`** at the project root to intercept requests to **`/admin`**, and check the session role:

```
import { withAuth } from "next-auth/middleware";
export default withAuth({
  callbacks: {
    authorized({ token }) {
      return token?.role === "admin";
    }
  }
});
```

    - export **`const config = { matcher: ["/admin/:path"] }`**;
        - **Execution:** Next.js runs this on every request under **`/admin`**.
        - **Effect:** Redirects users without admin role to **`/api/auth/signin`**.
        - **Purpose:** Ensures only admins access the admin dashboard.
- Server Components for Admin Pages
    - In **`src/app/admin/page.js`** and subpages, assume only admins reach the code.
    - Use **`getServerSession(authOptions)`** in server components to retrieve session details, if needed.

Real-Time Data Updates with SWR and WebSocket

Display live metrics (for example, new sign-ups, order status, and so on) by fetching initial data with SWR, and subscribing to backend events over WebSocket for instant updates.

- **WebSocket API Route**
    - In **`src/app/api/ws/route.js`**, handle HTTP **`GET`** upgrades to WebSocket:

```
import { NextResponse } from "next/server";
export async function GET(request) {
  if (!request.headers.get("upgrade")?.includes("websocket")) {
    return NextResponse.next();
  }
  const [client, server] = Object.values(new WebSocketPair());
  await handleWebSocket(server); // your logic to broadcast
events
  return new Response(null, { status: 101, webSocket: client });
}
```

- **Location:** **`app/api/ws`**
- **Trigger:** On client WebSocket connection to **`/api/ws`**
- **Purpose:** Enables server to push live events to connected dashboards

- **SWR Hook for Initial Data Fetch**
  - In **`RealTimeTable.js`**, use SWR to load the initial data snapshot:

```
import useSWR from "swr";
const fetcher = url => fetch(url).then(res => res.json());
export default function RealTimeTable() {
  const { data, error } = useSWR("/api/admin/data", fetcher);
  // ...
}
```

- **WebSocket Subscription for Live Updates**
  - After SWR loads initial data, open a WebSocket connection, and update the state on incoming messages:

```
import { useEffect, useState } from "react";
export function useRealTime(initial) {
  const [items, setItems] = useState(initial);
  useEffect(() => {
    const ws = new WebSocket(`${location.origin.replace
(/^http/, "ws")}/api/ws`);
    ws.onmessage = e => {
      const update = JSON.parse(e.data);
      setItems(prev => applyUpdate(prev, update));
    };
    return () => ws.close();
  }, []);

  return items;
}
```

  - **Role:** Client component
  - **Function:** Merges live events (for example, new user sign-up, order status changes, and so on) into the displayed data.
  - **Purpose:** Provides admins with real-time insights, without manual refresh.

- **Combining SWR and WebSocket in Admin Page**
  - In **`src/app/admin/users/page.js`** (or any admin subpage):

```
import RealTimeTable from "@/components/RealTimeTable";
import useSWR from "swr";
const fetcher = url => fetch(url).then(res => res.json());
export default function UsersPage() {
  const { data } = useSWR("/api/admin/users", fetcher);
```

```
    const users = useRealTime(data);
    return <RealTimeTable data={users} />;
  }
```

Benefits

- **Security:** Middleware and NextAuth ensure that only admins access sensitive interfaces.
- **Developer Clarity:** Co-located routes, middleware, and components keep the admin code organized.
- **Responsiveness:** SWR provides caching and revalidation; WebSockets push updates as they happen.
- **User Experience:** Admins see the live data (for example, new registrations, order changes, and so on) without refreshing the page.

This combination gives you a robust, secure, and real-time admin interface fully within the Next.js ecosystem.

Conclusion

This project showcased a comprehensive Next.js application covering the key modern web development features. We built an E-Commerce platform with dynamic product pages using getStaticPaths and integrated API routes to handle cart functionality seamlessly. User authentication was implemented securely using NextAuth.js. The blog section demonstrated static generation powered by a CMS like Sanity or Contentful, including a preview mode for content editors to review the unpublished changes. The admin dashboard introduced role-based routing and authentication, ensuring that only authorized users could access the sensitive areas. Real-time data updates were enabled using SWR and WebSocket, enhancing the user experience with live information. All source code and detailed implementations are available in the accompanying GitHub repository for reference and further learning.

In the next chapter, *Preparing for Front-End Development Jobs*, we will focus on practical skills, interview strategies, and building a strong portfolio to help you land your first role in front-end development.

Multiple Choice Questions

1. Which Next.js method is used to generate dynamic product pages at build time?
   a. `getServerSideProps`
   b. `getStaticProps`
   c. `getStaticPaths`
   d. `useEffect`

2. What is the main purpose of NextAuth.js in a Next.js application?
   a. Data fetching from CMS
   b. User authentication and session management
   c. Styling components
   d. Handling API routes
3. Which CMS integration feature allows previewing unpublished content in Next.js?
   a. Static generation
   b. Incremental Static Regeneration
   c. Preview mode
   d. Server-Side Rendering
4. Which technology combination is commonly used to enable real-time data updates in the admin dashboard?
   a. Redux and REST API
   b. SWR and WebSocket
   c. GraphQL and Axios
   d. React Query and Fetch API
5. Role-based routing in Next.js is primarily used to:
   a. Improve SEO performance
   b. Control access to routes based on user roles
   c. Manage global state
   d. Optimize page load speed

Answers

1. c
2. b
3. c
4. b
5. b

CHAPTER 14
Preparing for Front-End Development Jobs

Introduction

Mastering front-end development with Next.js opens doors to a wide range of job opportunities in modern web development. This chapter provides a focused guide for showcasing Next.js skills, and becoming job-ready in the competitive front-end space.

Start by refining core web development knowledge—HTML5, CSS3, JavaScript (ES6+), and React—while leveraging the advanced features of Next.js such as routing, server-side rendering, and API integration. Learn how to **highlight Next.js expertise on your resume**, incorporating impactful project summaries and relevant technical contributions.

Build a professional **portfolio with real-world Next.js projects** that demonstrate problem-solving, performance optimization, and scalable design. Practice **commonly asked Next.js interview topics**, covering dynamic routing, SSR/SSG, data fetching, and middleware usage. Strengthen technical proficiency with **hands-on coding challenges** that simulate real interview tasks.

This chapter offers actionable insights to help build confidence, structure preparation, and present skills effectively—ensuring a strong impression during interviews and technical assessments in front-end roles focused on modern web technologies.

Structure

In this chapter, the following topics will be covered:

- Highlighting Next.js Expertise in Resumes
- Building a Portfolio with Next.js Projects

- Common Interview Questions Related to Next.js
- Hands-On Coding Challenges

Highlighting Next.js Expertise in Resumes: A Detailed Guide

Next.js has become one of the most popular React frameworks for building performant, SEO-friendly web applications. If you want to stand out as a Next.js developer in your resume, it is crucial to communicate your skills and experience clearly and strategically.

Understand What Recruiters Look for in Next.js Expertise

Recruiters and hiring managers typically look for:

- Strong foundation in React.js, since Next.js is built on top of React.
- Experience with Server-Side Rendering (SSR), Static Site Generation (SSG), and Incremental Static Regeneration (ISR), which are key Next.js features.
- Knowledge of API routes and backend integration within Next.js.
- Proficiency with routing, dynamic routes, and file-system based routing.
- Familiarity with performance optimization techniques supported by Next.js.
- Experience with deployment and scaling of Next.js applications.
- Integration with modern web technologies and tools such as GraphQL, TypeScript, CSS-in-JS, and Headless CMS.
- Version control, CI/CD pipelines, and cloud platforms (for example, Vercel, AWS).

Best Practices for Showcasing Next.js Skills in Your Resume

- **Include Next.js in Your Technical Skills Section**

  Make sure Next.js is clearly listed under technical skills or frameworks. For example:

  - **Technical Skills:** React.js, Next.js, Node.js, TypeScript, GraphQL, Vercel, REST APIs, and Tailwind CSS.

  This ensures recruiters scanning resumes quickly spot your Next.js expertise.

- **Detail Next.js Projects in Your Experience Section**

  Describe your professional experience by highlighting Next.js-specific accomplishments and responsibilities.

Example:

Frontend Developer

Company Name | Duration

- Developed and maintained high-performance, SEO-optimized web applications using Next.js with React.
- Implemented Server-Side Rendering (SSR) and Static Site Generation (SSG) to improve page load times by 40%.
- Built dynamic routes and API routes to enable seamless user interactions and data fetching.
- Integrated Next.js with GraphQL backend to create efficient and scalable data querying layers.
- Deployed applications using Vercel, automating CI/CD pipelines for smooth releases.

- **Highlight Specific Next.js Features You Master**

  Recruiters appreciate specifics, so mention your hands-on experience with Next.js features such as:

  - **`getStaticProps`** and **`getServerSideProps`** for data fetching.
  - API routes for backend functionality.
  - Incremental Static Regeneration (ISR) to update static content without redeployment.
  - Image optimization with `` `next/image` ``.
  - Custom `` `_app.js` `` and `` `_document.js` `` modifications.
  - Middleware for authentication and redirects.

  Example Phrasing:

  "Utilized Next.js getStaticProps and ISR to build fast-loading e-commerce pages that update daily without downtime."

- **Demonstrate Your Understanding of Performance and SEO**

  Next.js is prized for improving SEO and performance. Highlight your knowledge:

  - Improved SEO by using Next.js Head Component for meta tags and structured data.
  - Reduced Time to First Byte (TTFB) through SSR and optimized caching.
  - Employed Next.js Image component to serve optimized images, and reduce page weight.

Example:

"Enhanced SEO and accessibility by implementing dynamic meta tags via Next.js Head, resulting in 25% increase in organic traffic."

- **Mention Collaboration and Toolchain**

  Include your experience collaborating with backend teams, designers, and DevOps for Next.js projects.

  - Used TypeScript for type safety in Next.js projects.
  - Employed Tailwind CSS for rapid UI development.
  - Coordinated deployments on Vercel, configured environment variables, and managed staging/production environments.
  - Integrated testing frameworks such as Jest and React Testing Library to ensure app stability.

Sample Resume Snippet Showcasing Next.js Expertise

John Doe

Frontend Engineer

Email: john.doe@example.com | LinkedIn: linkedin.com/in/johndoe | GitHub: github.com/johndoe

Technical Skills:

React.js, Next.js, TypeScript, GraphQL, Node.js, REST APIs, Vercel, Tailwind CSS, Jest

Professional Experience

Frontend Developer

ABC Technologies | Jan 2023 – Present

- Built and maintained a multi-regional Next.js e-commerce platform serving 1M+ monthly users.
- Leveraged Next.js SSG and ISR to deliver fast, SEO-friendly pages updated daily, without downtime.
- Developed custom API routes in Next.js to support user authentication and real-time product data fetching.
- Improved page load time by 35% using Next.js Image optimization and SSR techniques.
- Collaborated with backend engineers to integrate GraphQL API endpoints, ensuring efficient data retrieval.

- Managed deployments and environment configurations on Vercel, implementing CI/CD pipelines.

Bonus Tips

- Link to your Next.js projects or portfolio in the resume.
- Mention certifications or courses related to React and Next.js.
- Use metrics and outcomes to show the impact of your Next.js work.
- Tailor your resume keywords for Applicant Tracking Systems (ATS) by including "Next.js" frequently but naturally.

Thus, to effectively highlight Next.js expertise in a resume, job seekers should:

- Explicitly list Next.js in skills.
- Provide detailed, outcome-focused descriptions of projects using Next.js.
- Showcase mastery of Next.js-specific features.
- Emphasize SEO, performance optimization, and deployment experience.
- Include relevant toolchains and collaborative experiences.
- Support claims with metrics, and links to codes or demos.

This approach will maximize visibility to recruiters, and demonstrate the candidate's true proficiency with Next.js.

Building a Next.js Portfolio: A Guide to Freshers and Experienced Candidates

In today's competitive job market, having a strong portfolio of projects is crucial, especially for developers specializing in Next.js. A well-crafted portfolio demonstrates your practical skills, problem-solving abilities, and understanding of modern web development, beyond just listing technologies in your resume.

- **Demonstrates real-world experience:** Employers want to see what you can build, not just what you know theoretically.
- **Showcases Next.js expertise:** It highlights your ability to use Next.js features such as SSR, SSG, API routes, routing, and optimization.
- **Builds credibility:** A portfolio with working projects builds trust with recruiters and clients.
- **Supports interview discussions:** Projects give concrete examples to discuss during technical interviews.
- **Improves learning:** Building projects helps deepen your understanding, and keeps your skills sharp.

Choose a Good Hosting Platform

Deploy your projects on platforms such as Vercel (creator of Next.js), Netlify, or GitHub Pages for easy sharing and accessibility.

- Vercel offers seamless Next.js integration with zero-config deployment.
- Link your portfolio site and individual project demos in your resume and LinkedIn.

Include a Portfolio Website Built with Next.js

Your portfolio website itself can be a Next.js project showcasing:

Your bio, skills, and contact information.

A project gallery with links to demos and source code.

- Blog or articles demonstrating your understanding of Next.js concepts.
- Responsive design and SEO best practices using Next.js features.

Select Projects That Showcase Core Next.js Concepts

Your portfolio projects should collectively demonstrate:

- **Server-Side Rendering (SSR):** Build a blog or e-commerce homepage that fetches data on each request.
- **Static Site Generation (SSG):** Create a documentation site or portfolio landing page with pre-rendered pages.
- **Incremental Static Regeneration (ISR):** A product catalog or news site that updates content, without redeployment.
- **API Routes:** Implement backend functionality like user authentication or contact forms.
- **Dynamic Routing:** Showcase a blog or marketplace with dynamic URLs for posts or products.
- **Image Optimization:** Use `next/image` for optimized images in portfolio or gallery projects.
- **Middleware:** Add authentication guards or redirects on protected pages.

Project Ideas for Freshers

For freshers, focus on projects that highlight your learning and ability to work with Next.js fundamentals:

- **Personal Portfolio Website (built with Next.js, deployed on Vercel):** Includes SSR homepage, SSG blog posts, and contact form using API routes.

- **Blog Platform:** Uses Markdown files or headless CMS with SSG, and dynamic routing for posts.
- **Product Landing Page:** Implements static generation with optimized images and SEO metadata.
- **To-Do List App:** Uses API routes to store tasks in a simple database or local storage.

Project Ideas for Experienced Candidates

Experienced developers can create more complex projects to showcase advanced Next.js skills:

- **E-commerce Website:** Uses SSR for product pages, ISR for catalog updates, and secure API routes for checkout.
- **Dashboard with Authentication**: Middleware protects routes, integrates OAuth or JWT auth, and uses dynamic routes.
- **Multi-language Website:** Implements Next.js internationalized routing and localized content fetching.
- **Real-Time Chat Application:** Combines Next.js API routes with WebSocket or third-party services.
- **Integration with GraphQL Backend:** Uses Apollo Client or Relay with Next.js for performant data fetching.

Document Your Projects Well

Write clear README files explaining project purpose, technologies used, and setup instructions.

- Include screenshots or GIFs demonstrating the key features.
- Provide a live demo URL and GitHub repository link.
- Mention challenges faced, and how you solved them – this shows problem-solving skills.

Share Your Portfolio

Add the portfolio URL to your resume and LinkedIn profile.

- Share your projects in developer communities, GitHub, and relevant job portals.
- Regularly update your portfolio with new projects and blog posts to keep it fresh.

Building a Next.js portfolio is essential for developers at any level of experience. Freshers should focus on foundational projects demonstrating SSR, SSG, and API routes, while experienced candidates should tackle complex use cases such as e-commerce, dashboards, and real-time apps.

A well-hosted, documented, and visually appealing portfolio:

- Highlights your practical Next.js skills.
- Provides evidence of your coding and problem-solving abilities.
- It gives you an edge in interviews and job applications.

Common Interview Questions Related to Next.js

When preparing for interviews focused on front-end development or full-stack roles that involve React and Next.js, candidates are often evaluated not only on their theoretical knowledge but also on their practical understanding of the framework's core features. Interviewers typically ask a range of questions from basic concepts to advanced optimizations to gauge your proficiency with Next.js.

The following is a list of some commonly asked interview questions, along with concise explanations. These will help you anticipate the kind of topics you might be questioned, and prepare strong, clear answers.

Basic Questions and Answers

1. What is Next.js, and why would you use it over plain React?

   Answer: Next.js is a React framework that enables server-side rendering, static site generation, and automatic code splitting, which improves SEO and performance compared to plain client-side React apps.

2. Explain the difference between SSR, SSG, and CSR.

   Answer:

   - **SSR (Server-Side Rendering):** Pages are rendered on each request on the server.
   - **SSG (Static Site Generation):** Pages are pre-rendered at build time as static files.
   - **CSR (Client-Side Rendering):** Rendering happens in the browser after JavaScript loads.

3. What are `getStaticProps`, `getServerSideProps`, and `getStaticPaths`?

   Answer:

   - `getStaticProps`: Fetches data at build time for static generation.

- `getServerSideProps`: Fetches data on each request for SSR.
- `getStaticPaths`: Specifies dynamic routes to pre-render at build time.

4. How does Next.js routing work? Explain the dynamic routes.

   Answer: Next.js uses file-based routing where each file in the `pages` directory maps to a route. Dynamic routes use square brackets, for example, `[id].js`, to create routes with parameters.

5. What are API routes in Next.js? How are they different from traditional backend APIs?

   Answer: API routes are serverless functions inside the `pages/api` folder that run on-demand. They allow building backend endpoints inside a Next.js app, without a separate server.

Advanced Questions

- How does Incremental Static Regeneration (ISR) work in Next.js?

  Answer: ISR allows static pages to be updated after deployment by re-generating pages in the background at a specified interval, without needing a full rebuild.

- How can you optimize Next.js apps for performance?

  Answer: Use SSR or SSG appropriately, leverage `next/image` for image optimization, enable code-splitting, use lazy loading, and apply caching strategies.

- Explain middleware in Next.js 15+, and how it differs from API routes.

  Answer: Middleware runs before a request is completed, and can modify responses or redirect requests. It runs at the edge, and is ideal for auth or localization, whereas API routes handle business logic.

- How would you handle authentication in Next.js?

  Answer: Use JWT or OAuth tokens stored in cookies or local storage, protect pages with middleware or client-side guards, and use API routes to manage login/logout.

- What are some deployment options for Next.js apps?

  Answer: Vercel is the official platform, but Next.js apps can also be deployed on Netlify, AWS, DigitalOcean, or any platform supporting Node.js.

Hands-on Coding Challenges

These challenges test the practical knowledge of Next.js features and coding skills. Encourage readers to implement these themselves for real experience.

- **Challenge 1: Build a Static Blog with Dynamic Routing**

  In this challenge, you are tasked with creating a blog where the posts are generated statically at build time. The blog should support dynamic routes to serve individual posts using Next.js's data-fetching methods such as getStaticProps and getStaticPaths. This exercise tests your understanding of Static Site Generation (SSG), dynamic routing, and how to fetch data efficiently during the build process to generate pages ahead of time.

- **Challenge 2: Implement a Server-Side Rendered Page with Data Fetching**

  Here, the goal is to create a dashboard page that fetches user-specific data on every request, displaying a personalized welcome message. You will use **`getServerSideProps`** to achieve Server-Side Rendering (SSR), ensuring that the data is always fresh and relevant. This challenge helps you practice SSR and data fetching on each page load, critical for user-personalized applications.

- **Challenge 3: Create an API Route for Form Submission**

  This task involves building a contact form within a Next.js page, which upon submission sends the input data to a Next.js API route. The API route should validate the data, and simulate storing the message. This challenge assesses your ability to handle API routes in Next.js, manage forms in React, and implement backend logic directly within the Next.js framework.

- **Challenge 4: Optimize Images Using next/image**

  In this challenge, you will create a simple gallery page that uses the Next.js Image component to display images. The images should be optimized for different screen sizes, and loaded lazily to enhance performance. This task evaluates your skills in image optimization, creating responsive images, and using lazy loading techniques to improve user experience and page speed.

- **Challenge 5: Implement Middleware for Authentication**

  The final challenge requires writing middleware that verifies if a user is authenticated by simulating a cookie check. If the user is not authenticated, they should be redirected to the login page, when attempting to access the protected routes. This exercise tests your understanding of Next.js middleware, authentication workflows, and managing redirects as well as request handling at the edge.

Additional Tips for Interview Preparation

To prepare effectively for Next.js interviews, practice explaining the core concepts clearly and concisely. Build small projects to reinforce your knowledge, and demonstrate your skills practically. Regularly review the official Next.js documentation, and stay updated with release notes. Since Next.js is built on React, strengthen your React fundamentals as well. During coding challenges, focus on writing clean and maintainable code. Finally, be ready to discuss the trade-offs between Server-Side Rendering (SSR), Static Site Generation (SSG), and Client-Side Rendering (CSR) in real-world applications, showing your ability to choose the right approach for different scenarios.

Conclusion

This chapter covered all the essential strategies for advancing your career as a Next.js developer. We began by exploring how to effectively highlight your Next.js expertise in resumes, ensuring recruiters quickly recognize your skills. Next, we discussed building a strong portfolio with practical Next.js projects tailored for both freshers and experienced candidates, showcasing your hands-on abilities. We then reviewed common interview questions related to Next.js, helping you to prepare clear and confident answers. Finally, we delved into hands-on coding challenges designed to reinforce your understanding of the key Next.js concepts, and improve your problem-solving skills.

Thus, by combining these elements–resume optimization, portfolio development, interview readiness, and practical coding experience–you are well-equipped to stand out in the job market, and excel in technical interviews. So, embrace this comprehensive approach, and you will be ready to seize opportunities, and grow as a proficient Next.js professional.

Remember, mastery comes with continuous learning and practice, and your journey with Next.js is just the beginning.

Multiple Choice Questions

1. What is the primary purpose of `getStaticProps` in Next.js?
    a. Fetch data on every client-side request
    b. Fetch data at build time for static generation
    c. Fetch data on every server-side request
    d. Handle client-side routing

2. Which file/folder is used to define API routes in a Next.js application?
    a. `/pages/api`
    b. `/components/api`
    c. `/public/api`
    d. `/lib/api`
3. How do you create a dynamic route in Next.js?
    a. Using parentheses in file name, example, `(id).js`
    b. Using square brackets in file name, example, `[id].js`
    c. Using curly braces in file name, example, `{id}.js`
    d. Using angle brackets in file name, example, `<id>.js`
4. Which feature allows Next.js to update static pages after deployment, without a full rebuild?
    a. Server-Side Rendering (SSR)
    b. Static Site Generation (SSG)
    c. Incremental Static Regeneration (ISR)
    d. Client-Side Rendering (CSR)
5. Which component is recommended for optimized image loading in Next.js?
    a. `<img>`
    b. `<Image> from next/image`
    c. `<Picture>`
    d. `<LazyImage>`

Answers

1. b
2. a
3. b
4. c
5. b

Index

E

F

G

H

I

N

S

T

U

W